WRITER
to
WRITER

*The Republic
of Elsewhere*

For Julia Alonso Beazcochea

WRITER
to
WRITER
The Republic
of Elsewhere

Ciaran Carty

THE LILLIPUT PRESS
DUBLIN

Published in 2018 by
THE LILLIPUT PRESS
62–63 Sitric Road, Arbour Hill,
Dublin 7, Ireland
www.lilliputpress.ie

Images: John Arden, Carlos Fuentes and Derek Walcott
(Joe O'Shaughnessy); Kay Boyle and Fay Weldon (John Carlos);
J.P. Donleavy (and cover) (Suzy Freeman); Anne Enright (and cover)
(Alan Betson / *The Irish Times*); Allen Ginsberg (Brian Meade);
Seamus Heaney (and cover) (Charlie Collins); Kazuo Ishiguro (and
cover) (Jeff Cottenden / Faber & Faber); Jennifer Johnston (Jennifer
Johnston); Molly Keane (Sally Phipps, Waterford County Museum);
Michael Longley (Mal McCann / *The Irish News*); Paula Meehan
(and cover) (Dave Meehan / *The Irish Times*); V.S. Naipaul (and
cover) (Faizul Latif Chowdhury); Edna O'Brien (John Minihan /
© University College Cork); Salman Rushdie (Ed Lederman / PEN
American Center); Tom Stoppard (Matt Humphrey / Faber & Faber);
Paul Theroux (Christopher Seufert Photography); Andrei Voznesensky
(Aengus McMahon Photography).

ISBN 978 1 84351 674 3

10 9 8 7 6 5 4 3 2 1

A CIP record for this title is available from The British Library.

Set in 11 on 15 pt Caslon by Marsha Swan
Printed in Poland by Drukarnia Skleniarz

Contents

Introduction

1

Writer to Writer: The Republic of Elsewhere was inspired by an old stamp album given to me as a child. It's before me as I write, a reminder of once-powerful countries that no longer exist, and rulers and dictators who are no more. Nations are 'imagined communities', as Benedict Anderson argued in his book of the same title. The borders that define nations – or groupings of nations – are arbitrary and subject to sudden change, depending on shifting political perceptions and circumstances. One country's east is another country's west.

The rise of nationalism in the nineteenth century spawned a delusion that, as the German writer Joseph Roth wryly noted, each and 'every individual has to belong to a particular race or nation'. But humanity cannot be tidily confined within rigid categorizations. Writers, by their very nature, tend not to be of any country other than that of the imagination, a republic of elsewhere.

When the painter Georgia O'Keeffe abandoned New York for the mesa of New Mexico, she wrote to friends 'from the faraway nearby'. The poet Derek Walcott says, 'We are never where we are but somewhere else.' All art could be said to aspire to the openness of Freud's non-Jewish Jew who, when asked, 'Since you have abandoned all these common characteristics of your countrymen, what is there left to you that is Jewish?' would reply, 'A great deal, and probably its very essence.' In that same sense, art intuitively transcends its actual circumstances to reach towards a culture without boundaries, a society without divisions. *Writer to Writer: The Republic of Elsewhere* is a voyage around this inner globe in the company of strangers met by chance, invariably in a country other than their own.

Artists and writers see life differently. Through their creative vision they confront us with other worlds in a way that seems more real than if we had been there. Their fictions are another dimension of reality, a territory of the mind that overlaps and reaches beyond actual places we think we know, or may take for granted, so that we see everything afresh. Taking a cue from an earlier book, *Intimacy with Strangers: A Life of Brief Encounters*, this sequel brings together in the present tense a series of interviews caught on tape and sometimes separated by decades. It adopts the form of a flashback journey through time and place in the course of which often random meetings interweave with personal memories to form unexpected connections, a geography of the imagination.

Although the encounters are arranged as an alphabet of authors, they combine to offer an eclectic fly-on-the-wall portrait of the twentieth century and beyond through the lives of some of those whose fictions helped define it. In their otherness they are emblematic of our age.

2

Ever since *Homo sapiens* first evolved in the Olduvai Gorge in Africa there has been an urge for peoples to move on to greener pastures. It's as much a part of the human DNA as the contrary instinct to settle and form communities: a collision of ways that has energized civilization. Often driven by famine, violence or persecution, mass migrations across deserts, mountains and oceans continue to shape history.

Think for a moment of your childhood. My earliest memory is of moving to somewhere else, a car journey through the night on my mother's lap. Railway gates blocked our way. The ground shuddered and some enormous mechanical monster trundled past, hissing steam. I know now this was some-time in 1940. Our car was a black Dodge owned by Tom Reilly, a family friend who as a doctor was allowed wartime petrol. We were leaving Mount Merrion to live nearer the city so father could cycle to work each night as a sub-editor on the *Irish Press*.

The red-brick house on Sandymount Avenue with its sloping roof of black tiles became a mysterious new world to explore. One day I found the courage to crawl through the front hedge into a neighbour's garden. The children living there would soon become friends. Their father, Tom Shaw, was away in the war, a major in the British army. Their mother Babs would send us to the village on messages, rewarding us with kisses that smudged our cheeks with dark red lipstick.

The back garden had an acacia tree so tall that when we climbed to the top we could see the sea and even Killiney Hill, which we longed to explore and eventually did. Father acquired a large box radio with a dial that lit up and if you turned the knob you'd hear through the static voices in strange languages from faraway countries. He told me how the roof of his childhood home in Wexford was tarred like a ship's deck and he remembered his mother standing there watching anxiously for a glimpse of the sails of the three-mast schooner his grandfather captained. He showed me a silver watch and chain brought back as a souvenir from a voyage across the Atlantic, trading timber in Newfoundland. My dream was some day to sail the seven seas.

After the war father took me on his crossbar to the Johnston, Mooney and O'Brien bakery for the first loaf of white bread: up to then I thought all bread was black. And then there was the day Major Shaw arrived home, driving the first car seen in the neighbourhood. The father of another boy we knew around the corner came back from a Japanese prison camp, without his tongue. Father's cousin Father Kevin, a Benedictine monk who had been an army chaplain, came on a visit from England. We had other relatives in Glasgow and even as far away as San Antonio, Texas. In 1959 I too would take the boat to England.

There's nothing exceptional about any of this. Writers, like anyone else, grow up, leave home and go out into the world. They turn their experiences into fictions where readers may find echoes of their own lives, they write poems that capture moments and evoke feelings of shared humanity, of love and belonging, laughter and tears, loss and despair. Many of the writers in this book are wary about being mistaken for the characters they have imagined because to do so is to misunderstand the magic of fiction. Others confront it. E.L. Doctorow fictionalizes real-life people and incidents. Paul Theroux gives characters his own name. Michel Houellebecq goes so far as to allow his fictional self to be murdered.

There can be danger in this. In the past Ireland banned tens of thousands of books on the grounds that they were a threat to public morality because their authors had opinions or lived lives that didn't conform to Catholic beliefs. In the United States, writers were denounced on suspicion of having Communist friends or acquaintances. Literature still has the potential to become a matter of life or death. Salman Rushdie had to go into hiding under another name to escape a fatwa death threat. Pier Paolo Pasolini was murdered because he was homosexual.

More insidiously, in this time of aggressive identity politics, social media's arbitrary power to name and shame without challenge can make literary value subordinate to a writer's perceived moral acceptability as in the worst days of censorship. The remarkable hundred-year-old Diana Athill, who edited V.S. Naipaul's first novels but broke with him because she disapproved of how he treated his first wife, wrote in *The Guardian* when he died on 11 August 2018 that she never stopped admiring his literary greatness. 'You don't have to be a good person to be a good writer,' she said.

3

The migrant sense of otherness is close to the nature of creativity. No one can ever experience directly more than a tiny part of a world of over seven billion inhabitants, each an individual with hopes and dreams. Yet paradoxically, through the mythic power of films, literature and paintings, and through the eyes of others, this unvisited world can come to seem as familiar and vibrantly immediate as our own. For many people, the imagined world is as real as the actual world, perhaps even more real. As Ishmael says in *Moby-Dick*, 'it is down not on any map, true places never are.'

In the 2001 film *The Royal Tenenbaums* writer-director Wes Anderson achieves a stylized reimagining of New York that almost resembles the actual city but clearly isn't. He simulates the strange sense of déjà vu that someone visiting New York for the first time often feels. Through fiction and films, the city has taken on a fabled parallel life in the popular imagination that is if anything more vivid and familiar than the real place. 'A mythic city embodies the idea of a city, a powerful thing indeed,' James Sanders suggests in his wonderful 2001 book, *Celluloid Skyline*. 'An idea can travel, after all, as a city cannot – radiating across land and sea into the minds of millions around the world.'

The mythic New York – or any other iconic city – is not a mirror image: it is its own reality. It is a construct of dreams and fears, a magical counterpart that comes alive on the page or in the flickering projection of celluloid on a screen. Sanders, an architect by training, had the simple but brilliant idea of venturing through that screen to inhabit the singular place on the other side. *Celluloid Skyline* is a virtual tour of New York as represented by film-makers. He explores it as one would any city, wandering through the fully rendered environments in which countless films have occurred.

Films aspire to create an illusion of real places. *The Royal Tenenbaums* – not unlike Anderson's later 2014 Oscar-nominated *The Great Budapest Hotel* – is structured like an adaptation of a novel that doesn't exist. It's broken into chapters. A narrator is the voice of the story. *The Royal Tenenbaums*, a comedy about a father who belatedly in later life tries to win back the affections of his family of failed geniuses, depicts the illusion itself. Its New York is a New York of the mind, much the way the Oscar-nominated French film *Amélie* is a reimagined Paris.

'I've always felt that the New York I was fascinated with as a child in Texas doesn't exist,' Anderson said when we first met in London in 2002. 'It exists in books and films but not in real life.' He suspects it's much the way a lot of Americans dream of an Ireland that isn't really there. 'They build up a feeling of it from books and films. They're sentimentally attracted to it.' It's no surprise John Huston's film adaptation of James Joyce's short story 'The Dead' and its sense of Dublin is one of Anderson's favourite films. 'You could easily get restricted when you're recreating such a story that people know so well, but while it's very true to the story, it has an extra layer. The way the actors move around brings in an element that is not in the story. Some of the characters that were just a little bit in the story are vividly brought to life in the film.'

A suspicion that the world as we think we know it is an invention of the mind first captivated philosopher Richard Kearney when he heard Christy Mahon exclaim, in Synge's *The Playboy of the Western World*: 'You're after making a mighty man of me by the power of a lie.' Although still a schoolboy in Cork when he read this line, it set Kearney wondering about the function of creative imagination and the ability of ideas to shape events: 'It seemed to me that the Irish, deprived of expression in other ways – political, economic, religious – had turned more to the imagination to make things happen,' he said.

We were talking in a terraced house in Donnybrook where he lived with his French wife Anne. It was 1980 and he had just returned from Paris, where he prepared his doctorate on the philosophy of the imagination with Paul Ricoeur and became a regular contributor to *Esprit*. During his time there he found that Yeats, Joyce and Beckett were becoming a rich source of new thinking. 'Philosophers like Levinas were going to *Finnegans Wake, Ulysses* and *Murphy* and seeing in them the best critique of the whole Anglo-Saxon rationalist tradition,' he said.

The emergence in the late 1970s of young Irish philosophers like Kearney, then in his twenties, and the growing preoccupation of continental philosophy with the imagination suggested that this bogey was finally about to be discarded. 'From Plato, right through scholasticism and the rationalism of the Enlightenment, there has always been a great suspicion of the imagination,' Kearney told me. 'The imagination was the "diabolical faculty" and in Plato's *Republic* the poet is exiled because he has a very strong imagination and therefore belongs to the lowest level. The whole tradition of philosophy has been to give priority to reason and to treat the creative faculty of the imagination as something quite disreputable.'

Kant first brought imagination in from the philosophical cold, opening the way for Husserl and Heidegger, and later French thinkers, to develop what we know today as existentialism. 'Existentialism put the imagination first, saying that it is the imagination that gives structure to the senses and that also gives rise to our logical categories, that they themselves are creations of the human mind,' argued Kearney. 'While in Western civilization we may have certain concepts of substance, time and space and so on, these are in fact inventions of our imaginations. Other civilizations, in China or India, may have different concepts. Logical structures are not necessarily universal but the creations of the imagination.'

From the academic haven of UCD's metaphysics department Kearney launched a wide-ranging challenge to the cultural assumptions that conditioned the politics of a divided Ireland. Through his co-editorship (with soon-to-be Benedictine abbot Mark Patrick Hederman) of the biannual cultural journal *The Crane Bag*, which was founded in 1977 and acclaimed by *Le Monde* as 'Ireland's principal cultural journal', he mooted the notion of an all-Ireland parliament of ideas, ideas too little debated, if not ignored altogether, by the Dáil and Westminster.

Putting forward the metaphor of a 'fifth province' of the mind that transcends geographic and sectarian divisions, he looked forward to a post-national pluralist society beyond the mutually exclusive extremes of unionism and republicanism. He suggested that the perimeters of tomorrow's Ireland lay within the experience of literature and the arts. With *The Irish Mind: Exploring Cultural Traditions*, which he edited in 1985, he set out to show through Berkeley, Swift, Burke and others that our intellectual history did not constitute one single monolithic or homogeneous identity, but consisted of a rich plurality of different cultural heritages.

Field Day, a grouping of writers and intellectuals drawn from both communities in the North – its directors were Seamus Heaney, Brian Friel, Tom Paulin, Stephen Rea, Seamus Deane and David Hammond – was formed in 1980 to stage Friel's play *Translations* at the Guildhall in Derry, bastion of Unionist domination in a predominantly Catholic city. It would join with *The Crane Bag* in, as Kearney had argued, 'attempting to rediscover a province of the imagination, of the intellect ... and thereby in some way fulfil the Socratic dictum that intellectuals and artists should be the gadfly of society, that they should have a certain distance whereby they can put into question the divisions and the conflicts and try to resolve them.'

As Brian Friel said in *Translations*, it is not the literal past, the 'facts' of history, that shape us, but images of the past embodied in language. *The Crane Bag* and Field Day, at a crucial stage in the transition of the island of Ireland to peace, posited the idea that in order to understand our political situation we must comprehend not just the political and socio-economic data but the images, myths and ideologies that condition that data. We must come to terms with the multiplicity of culture that is Ireland.

Mary Robinson would pick up on the *Crane Bag* concept in her inaugural speech as President of Ireland in 1990: 'The Fifth Province is not anywhere here or there, north or south, east or west. It is a place within each one of us; that place that is open to the other, that swinging door which allows us to venture out and others to venture in.' Michael D. Higgins, then a senator but later also to become President of Ireland, told me:

The academic interest in Joyce has concentrated almost entirely on his breaking the mould of language. But he broke all the moulds. His imaginative achievement lay in seeking a freedom that cut across the whole dimension of twisted religion, twisted sex, twisted literature and twisted etymology ... Any socialist manifesto that doesn't address itself to the question of consciousness is obviously doomed to failure. It's as if we're looking through a broken window. We accept a distorted view instead of getting a new glass. We live with fantasies. Democracy for most people means voting twelve to sixteen times in their lifetime. Yet this same 'democracy' accepts that it is four times more likely for a working-class person to end up in a mental asylum and that the child of middle-class parents has eight times a better chance to receive third-level education. Our experiences of democracy exclude women from many of the key roles in life. We abuse language. We're a most undemocratic country. And yet we lecture the rest of the world on the subject. If Ireland is to change it will require a quantum leap of the imagination.

Higgins accepted Gabriel García Márquez's view that the revolutionary role of the writer is simply to be a writer. 'There isn't a socialist way of riding a bicycle. The point is where you go.'

Perhaps the Russian poet Andrei Voznesensky puts it best. 'I am not a genius of politics who gives answers to political problems. I can only give the method to go deep inside events in people's everyday lives, to help them survive and find truth. Yes, poetry can change things. It changes everything because it changes people's minds.'

4

Facing a packed Salon du Livre writers' forum in Paris in 1996, Seamus Heaney quoted Joyce's *Portrait of the Artist* in which Stephen Dedalus gives his address as Class of Elements, Clongowes Wood College, Sallins, Co. Kildare, Ireland, The British Isles, Europe, the World, the Cosmos. 'I think,' Heaney said, through an interpreter, 'that poetry dwells in the parish and in the universe and it fails if it misses the universe. That can be the death of consciousness as well as the beginning of it.'

To label writers possessively as Irish writers, or Catholic writers, or gay writers, or black writers, or women writers, or Jewish writers is to precondition how they and their work are perceived. For politicians, label-ling is not just manipulative but breeds demagogues. On the eve of Ramadan in June 2016, the newly-elected mayor of London Sadiq Khan, who had defeated the Tory candidate in defiance of racist smears in the House of Commons, told *The Guardian*: 'I don't call myself a Muslim politician. I'm not a Muslim spokesman or leader, and it's important to clarify that because otherwise you're defined solely by your faith. We all have multiple identities.'

An instance of the absurdity of national and religious branding was provided by then British Education Secretary Michael Gove – subsequently a leader with Boris Johnson of the anti-immigration Brexit campaign – who decreed in 2014 that British schools had to teach 'British values', which he defined as 'democracy, the rule of law, individual liberty and mutual respect and tolerance of those with different faiths and beliefs.' The implication seemed to be that in some way these were exclusively 'British'.

To appropriate fundamental human values for political advantage is to undermine them. A challenge for art and literature in the twenty-first century is to subvert this move towards cultural exclusion by reaching out to a world that can't be pigeonholed by ideology or any cartographer or computer algorithms. If the many diverse voices in *Writer to Writer* have one thing in common it is an openness to all that is other rather than conforming to estab-lished norms. Through the sheer power of imagination they peel away layers of doublespeak and hype to reveal deeper truths that make us what we are.

Before cheap foreign travel and the advent of the internet with its social networking tweets and face-to-face Skype reunions, exile was often a life sentence, a goodbye forever. Nowadays, with migrants seldom more than a weekend away from home, it has become for some more a state of mind than a matter of forced separation from family: for political or socio-economic reasons, people may choose not to identify solely with the class or creed or nation they are born into.

Even in the case of the millions of war refugees fleeing across the Mediterranean in makeshift boats, their hazardous routes to Germany and other safe countries are often worked out online. A remarkable image by UN photographer Giles Duley shows a Syrian mother in a camp in Iraq holding a mobile on which her husband, who has reached Germany, is reassuring her and promising to find a way to bring her and their small child to safety.

The European Union is in the process of becoming a transnational super state to which most of Europe's present states are gradually ceding economic sovereignty, although this process suffered an unexpected reverse when Britain voted itself out in a referendum on 23 June 2016. With significant majorities in Scotland and Northern Ireland voting to stay in Europe, the break up of the United Kingdom itself is no longer inconceivable.

The French National Front leader Marine Le Pen proclaimed in her victory speech after the May 2014 European elections, that 'our people demand one type of politics; they want politics to be French, for the French, with the French. What is happening in France heralds what will happen in all European countries, the return of the nation.' Her opportunism was echoed by similar ultra-right populist parties in Poland, Hungary and Denmark. It fostered a regressive sense of national identity that by definition scapegoated low-skilled immigrants and other minority groups, whether Muslims or Romas or, as Arjun Appadurai argued in *Fear of Small Numbers*, 'any sort of collective stranger.'

Yet the crushing defeat of Le Pen by Emmanuel Macron in the 2017 presidential election, a victory emphasized by his imaginative gesture of stepping out in front of the Louvre to the strains of the European anthem rather than the Marseillaise, undermined Le Pen's claim to speak for France. Far-right demagogues in Denmark and Austria also suffered defeats. But flag-waving xenophobic populism remained a global threat. Donald Trump was elected US President in 2017 by promising, as did Brexiteers in England, to introduce draconian measures against migrants. During the campaign for Britain to leave the EU, this isolationism became a rabble-rousing 'Give Us Back Our Country' slogan, or, as President Trump chanted at his inauguration, raising his pudgy fist, 'America First'.

'In the absence of any serious strategy to protect democracy, the right resorts, instead, to a defence of "culture" reinvented as "tradition", elevated to "heritage" and imagined as immutable,' argued Gary Younge in *The Guardian*.

In 2012, the year President Obama, son of a Kenyan migrant, was re-elected for a second term, an exhibition called 'Migrations' opened at Tate Britain. Its theme was the way migration shaped British art. 'Like languages, diseases and the alphabet, through trade, invasion or colonization, art migrates,' the poet Ruth Padel wrote in *The Guardian*. 'Artists pulled by hunger, politics, persecution, war, or simply hope go to where the work is. Art and migration belong together.' She hoped the exhibition would 'open up all sorts of new ways of seeing art as migration, as a continual flowing in from somewhere else.'

The Pakistan-born, US-educated, British resident Mohsin Hamid, arguing the case for a world without borders, wrote in *The Guardian* in 2014: 'We are all migrants ... Without migration, the human population of these and all other islands would be zero.' The fusing of cultures invariably nurtures creativity.

When Theresa May, who became Tory prime minister after the UK voted to quit the European Union in the 2016 referendum, sneered that 'a citizen of the world is a citizen of nowhere', she was denying history. There are migrants in everyone's blood. 'At one point in time this island had no people, so everybody on this island immigrated to it,' archaeologist Ronan Swan pointed out to *Irish Times* journalist Mark Hilliard during excavations for the Luas tramway. No one can claim to be purely Irish, purely Aryan or purely anything else. My maternal grandmother was Jane Hester, my father's mother was Margaret Storey: both names are originally Cromwellian. My children's grandmother was Estefania Alonso Beazcochea. Coming from migrants makes us who we are. At the heart of the English word 'mother' is 'other'.

'I rhyme', Seamus Heaney wrote in his first collection, *Death of a Naturalist* (1966), 'to see myself, to set the darkness echoing.' *Writer to Writer: The Republic of Elsewhere* is an attempt to eavesdrop on this echoing and provide a platform for the testimony of 'migrants' who in opening eyes to other worlds may provide clearer glimpses of the actual world and give it deeper meaning.

Acknowledgments

Writer to Writer: The Republic of Elsewhere is drawn from conversations with a wide range of writers over several decades, versions of which were originally published in *The Sunday Independent* and later *The Sunday Tribune*. Sadly, many are no longer with us but they live through their words and immediacy of each shared moment. *Writer to Writer* follows a similar format to its companion volume, *Intimacy with Strangers: A Life of Brief Encounters* (Lilliput 2013), which featured John Updike, William Trevor, Harold Pinter, Amos Oz, John McGahern, Doris Lessing, Hugh Leonard, Brian Friel, Anthony Burgess, André Brink, William Boyd and Chinua Achebe.

I am indebted to all the writers who gave up their time to talk with me and also to the many people who helped in providing introductions and arranging interviews, in particular Joanna Mackle of Faber & Faber, Peggie O'Brien, Máirín de Burca, Marie Rooney, Rose Parkinson, Cormac Kinsella, Trish Long, Geraldine Cooke, Louisette Fargette, Christine Aimé, Kate Bowe, Sarah Wilby, Caroline Michel and Gerry Lundberg.

I've been lucky all my life to work for editors who gave me freedom to interview whoever interested me, wherever and whenever I wanted, especially Hector Legge who brought me back from England in 1961, Conor O'Brien who first sent me to Cannes in 1972, Vincent Browne who lured me to *The Sunday Tribune* in 1985 and Matt Cooper who gave me a new contract on the day I reached retirement age in 2002. I have been similarly lucky at Lilliput, where Antony Farrell championed me from that start and Suzy Freeman fought for this book through many hiccups while Djinn von Noorden edited it sympathetically in its multiple drafts. My gratitude, too, to all the photographers who came forward with images from the past.

Martin Amis (and Julian Barnes), 1985

Martin Amis regards having a famous writer for a father as a mixed blessing. He credits his novelist stepmother Elizabeth Jane Howard – rather than his father Kingsley Amis – with getting him going on literature by persuading him to read Pride and Prejudice *as a teenager. After her death in January 2014 he acknowledged in* The Guardian *her encouragement: 'I think there's a certain peculiarity in my case – being the son of – which if anything was a slight boost when I started out. Then the culture changes: it became a curse.' His first novel,* The Rachel Papers, *about a student's bungled relationship with an American girl, has comic echoes of the hapless college assistant whose hopes of romance keep being foiled in his father's 1954 debut* Lucky Jim. *Both novels are send-ups of youthful chutzpah and were to establish first Kingsley and then Martin as leading English satirists. Like his father, whose motto was 'if you can't annoy somebody with what you write, I think there's little point in writing', Amis, who has lived in New York since 2011 with his novelist wife Isabel Fonseca, has a talent for being provocative, not just in novels dissecting contemporary social mores, ranging from* Money *and* London Fields *to his 2014 Holocaust black farce* The Zone of Interest, *but in frequent headline-grabbing public utterances. In a documentary on Englishness screened by BBC4 in March 2014 he argued that 'there's meant to be another layer to being English. There are qualifications other than citizenship and it's to do with white skin.' Later he sneered at Jeremy Corbyn's supposed lack of education ('Two E grades at A level, that's it'). The first and only time we met was at the Shelbourne Hotel in April 1985, by coincidence a few months after talking with his long-time friend and fellow novelist, Julian Barnes.*

Martin Amis is perplexed. He lights a cigarette and sits down in a chair at a window overlooking St Stephen's Green. He has the vaguely diffident aura of someone who might have stepped out of *Brideshead Revisited*. He's trying to make sense of all the scurrilous things people have been saying about him, treating him as if he's a celebrity rather than a writer. But his new novel *The Information*, with its theme of jealousy between two English novelists in their forties, one a success, the other a failure, so eerily anticipates what has happened to him that it has to be confronted.

The furore over the way he switched his agent Pat Kavanagh, wife of Julian Barnes, for a hotshot American who got him a £500,000 deal with Harper Collins, followed by the break up of his marriage to Antonia Philips – he's now with the novelist Isabel Fonseca – and a silly tabloid saga about his £20,000 dental implant, read like an extension of his novel. 'Sometimes with startling irony,' he concedes. 'The book is about a literary enmity and the deal of the book created this literary enmity that wasn't there before. When I realized that, I was stunned by the symmetry of it all. You hope that business and personal matters are separate but of course they're not. How can they be?'

Inevitably there have been rumours that the best-selling Gwyn Barry in *The Information* is Barnes, while the resentful and unpublishable Richard Tull is Amis. After all, in the novel Barry and Tull play snooker and tennis with each other just like Barnes and Amis did.

'It was never Julian. You don't go into your study for five years to write about any real person except yourself, those bits of yourself you're trying to turn into a comedy. When Pat read the book she said it never occurred to her that it had anything to do with Julian. If there had been a resemblance, she'd have got it.'

An added irony is that Barnes has long lived a double life as a literary novelist while at the same time doubling as the crime writer Dan Kavanagh. 'My second novel *Before She Met Me* and my Kavanagh's *Fiddle City* were both slated on the same *Critics Forum* programme,' Barnes said when we met in his terraced house on Dartmouth Park Avenue just up the hill from Tufnell Park tube station. 'A bad review on radio is particularly awful. You just sit there with these guys talking to you and saying you're no good at all.' The floors are polished wood. He makes a pot of tea and pours a cup carefully so it won't drip on the antique desk. 'All writers half want to be other writers,' he says. He only became Kavanagh to avoid confusing readers. 'It wouldn't have been fair if a reader picked up one of my straight novels expecting a thriller.'

He got the name for his other literary self from his wife. 'Her grandparents were Irish via South Africa. So the cover note for the first book *Putting in the Boot* reveals that Kavanagh was born in Sligo in 1946.' Barnes too was born in 1946 but in Leicester, where his father was a teacher. 'I've never been to Sligo. I just thought it was time it had another writer apart from Yeats.' Nor has Barnes ever flown light planes on the Colombian cocaine run as the blurb for *Fiddle City* claims. 'I change the Kavanagh biography to suit each Duffy thriller. By now our twin identity has become an open secret.'

Playing around with identity is a recurring Barnes theme. His novel *Flaubert's Parrot*, shortlisted for the Booker Prize in 1984, uses fiction to get around the well-known aversion to biography of the author of *Madame Bovary* who maintained that 'giving the public details about oneself is a bourgeois temptation that I have always resisted.'

Barnes has long been drawn to the ambiguities of literary identity. Writing under different names in different styles comes easily to him. Under yet another guise he's been the much-feared restaurant critic Basil Seale. For a while, Edward Pygge in *The New Review* was Barnes too (in between being John Fuller, Clive James and Hunter Davies). Much of the fun in *Flaubert's Parrot* lies in his deft talent for pastiche. By switching around identities, Barnes keeps throwing up red herrings. With him nobody can be quite sure where fiction ends and fact begins.

Flaubert would have approved, arguing that 'the artist must manage to make posterity believe that he never existed'. It can be a dangerous game as Amis is discovering although, being the son of Kingsley Amis, and publishing his first novel *The Rachel Papers* at a precocious twenty-three, he is by now accustomed to a certain amount of begrudgery. 'I never feel happy accusing my detractors of envy, but it definitely is an English disease,' he says. 'But they can't really think that being the son of a famous writer is like taking over the family castle or marrying the boss's daughter. Perhaps they do subliminally believe that I got it at birth, that the ability to write was just injected into me by my father's genes.'

As a child, he used to think that 'divorce was a disease that one's friends' parents kept catching'. Then his mother Hilly and father divorced, his father marrying the novelist Elizabeth Jane Howard. He remains close to his father, however. 'We can talk to each other. I get on with my dad better almost than anyone I know gets on with theirs. I see him once or twice a week. He's been marvellous during all this.' He never saw his father as a literary rival. 'Nothing is more unexotic than what your father does for a living because you see him doing it every day. I never feel competitive with older writers, anyway. Candid admiration is what I give them.'

Making a £500,000 deal has meant becoming part of a celebrity machine, touring the chat shows here and in the States, just like Gwyn in *The Information*. 'I have certain uneasiness about it but I also feel this is no longer a business for shrinking violets. Perhaps it's just better to meet it head on rather than shy away from it. 'Every writer is torn this way. You don't want it, you do want it, and nowadays you have to have it. If what you're after, and I think this is what most writers are after, is more than your fair share of readers, well then you have to compete for their attention as everything else in modern life competes for attention. You find yourself obliged to become a hireling of your own work after you have finished it.'

What he can't understand is why there should be such resentment about the money he is earning. 'It turns out that no one minds someone getting a lot of money for rubbish. The only thing you can't get a lot of money for is a literary novel, thank you.'

John Arden, 1988

When English playwright John Arden died at his home in Galway in March 2012, theatre critic Michael Coveney mourned the passing of 'one of the few twentieth-century dramatists you could mention in the same breath as Shakespeare, Molière and Brecht without the parallels sounding too far-fetched.' The Irish President, Michael D Higgins, one of many friends who attended the funeral service, spoke of him as a 'dissident intelligence' whose words, like those of Blake and Shelley, 'had the authenticity of life'. Seven months later his widow Margaretta D'Arcy – a veteran of the 1980s Greenham Common anti-nuclear protests – walked onto the runway at Shannon Airport to protest against the airport's use by the US military. Nobody noticed at first, so a friend had to notify security. She was subsequently found guilty of illegal incursion and given a three-month suspended sentence. When she refused to sign a bond guaranteeing that she would no longer try to disrupt flights, she was arrested and taken to Limerick jail, where she was controversially visited by her friend, Sabina Higgins, wife of the President. The government rejected a petition by writers and artists for the release on humanitarian grounds of the 79-year-old cancer-stricken activist, who also had Parkinson's disease. D'Arcy was simply being true to values she shared with Arden throughout their life together. 'I'm quite happy to be on the losing side, and that is what really annoys my attackers,' she said when I visited her in Connemara in 1988.

The Irish are quick to complain about being stereotyped by the English. But they do the same to the English. John Arden, reared in the bosom of Yorkshire Protestantism, frequent scourge of the English theatre establishment, a self-styled radical liberal with a stubborn nature who thrives on being in awkward corners, could appreciate the irony.

'I dare say if I were a retired English colonel who comes over for the fishing I would achieve a better degree of acceptance,' he says. 'The people would at least know where they stood with me because that's not so different from the landlord class that was here before.'

It was much the same when he was jailed in India in 1970 for trying to enter Nagaland. 'An Englishman who reminded them of the Raj but no longer has power over them is more affectionately regarded than someone whose class in England they can't quite place.' As it is, he's tended to get the worst of both worlds. 'In England they say, why do you keep writing Irish stuff? Why don't you write about what really matters? And over here, people don't want to know.'

He sits on a stool in a sparsely furnished room in their telephone-free cottage at Corrandulla, the familiar curly hair of his *enfant terrible* days now white. A colour poster of Picasso's *Guernica* is pinned to the bare wall. 'It's a curious relationship with Ireland. It's not been entirely smooth at all. But I've got used to it.'

Now in 1988, he's been here long enough to see his own country in many ways as an Irish person sees it. But he cannot do the same for Ireland. 'Nor can I expect the Irish to be completely at ease with my comments on them.' He admits that it always cheers him 'to hear an Irish politician actually saying something that infuriates them in London, even though I might not agree with it.' 'There's an awful feeling you get from the British media that Irish public figures fall into two categories, those who will do as they are told by the English and those who won't. The former are referred to as moderates and the implication about the others is that they spend their evenings with the IRA planning dreadful things.'

When Arden – who was born in Barnsley, the son of a glass factory manager, and trained as an architect – first came to live with Margaretta on an island in Lough Corrib in 1966 he was widely regarded as the most challenging and original of the new playwrights revolutionizing English drama. With *Serjeant Musgrave's Dance* and *Armstrong's Last Goodnight*, in particular, he had brilliantly exploited the power of a theatre rooted in historical events to subvert the complacency of English attitudes towards themselves.

The soldiers who run amok in a strike-bound England mining town in 1860 in *Musgrave* are straight out of newspaper reports of a 1958 atrocity involving British troops, 'a sort of Bloody Sunday'. Conor Cruise O'Brien's book on Katanga similarly provided the trigger for *Armstrong*. In the play, a Scottish feudal chieftain trying to remain independent in the sixteenth century could double for a politician in one of the newly emerging African states, someone like Patrice Lumumba. The poet diplomat character negotiating with him for the king has echoes of O'Brien's involvement in the Congo on behalf of the UN. 'It isn't really about O'Brien. It's just that an idea from his book suggested the historical parallel.'

Cruise O'Brien has been something of a disappointment to Arden: 'You get the feeling he's obsessed about certain particularly unpleasant aspects of Ireland. He seems to see the IRA everywhere he goes in the world. I got the impression that when students started objecting to him in the University of Cape Town he was automatically identifying them with Sinn Féin.'

Real life can sometimes be too real to stage. A libel action in 1972 stopped production of *The Ballygombeen Bequest*, which he wrote in collaboration with Margaretta. It had been partly inspired by an eviction report. 'But one of the characters was similar enough to cause people to identify him with a real person. It was a dodgy issue. We settled out of court and we agreed to alter the play so that recognizable features of the character were removed.'

Arden has written a succession of Irish plays, the most spectacular of which was *The Non-Stop Connolly Show*, which lasted twenty-six hours when it premiered in Dublin's Liberty Hall in 1975. It was staged over fourteen days in London the following year. Arden later staged parts of it in Belfast, coincidently just before the Gibraltar shootings by the SAS of three IRA activists. 'Nobody in Belfast seemed prepared to understand Connolly. The Provos think he's too much of a socialist; the Worker's Party think he's too much of a terrorist; the SDLP don't really want that kind of thing at all; to Unionists he's just a Fenian. Yet things can't be settled in Ireland until people understand Connolly better than they do. All the questions that are still agitating everybody were raised in his lifetime.'

Even before he fell in love with Margaretta in 1955, Arden had been drawn to Ireland. He read the legends of Cuchulainn as an eight-year-old, 'a present from my Uncle Harold who'd married in Belfast and even learned to speak Irish, something I've never managed to do although I have tried.' There was already an anarchic streak in him that found an echo in Celtic mythology. 'They struck to my heart, with their unpronounceable names, their combination of battlefield butchery with hallucinatory landscapes, druid-haunted bogs, bare mountains, bottomless lakes, their alarming women.' It was quite a contrast to the rigid values of public school at Sedbergh, where he started writing historical plays. This was to be the recurring tension in all his work: the conflict of order with disorder.

His family could trace their name back to Ardens who lived in Warwickshire, one of whom, Mary, was reputedly Shakespeare's mother. 'It's a joke really, one of those family things. I don't know if there's a direct connection.' Early in the nineteenth century, another relative by marriage burned down York Minster. 'He objected to cathedrals on principle and had written pamphlets denouncing bishops and their pagan ways. He had dreams about doing the work of God.' Great-uncle Charlie, nine times mayor of Beverly, operated a Tory public house where golden sovereigns were dispensed as bribes to voters through a special hatch during elections: it led to the constituency being forbidden to have an MP for several years.

With *The Island of the Mighty*, the contradictions in Arden's background found their most explicit expression in a retelling of the Arthurian legend that foreshadowed twentieth-century post-colonialism. Too much so, apparently, for the Royal Shakespeare Company who staged it at the Aldwych Theatre in 1972. 'The play came out the opposite to what we intended.' Their wishes denied, Arden and d'Arcy went on strike, picketing their own play with the support of the Society of Irish Playwrights.

He no longer writes for the theatre. 'The concept of the play now seems less interesting than the presentation of it. The production values and even the export value are what seem to matter most. The whole basis of running the RSC and the National Theatre as a means of increasing Gross National Product has an effect on the sort of plays they can put on and the way they do them and the attitudes of management towards the author.'

Switching to fiction, his first novel, *Silence Among the Weapons*, was nominated for the 1982 Booker Prize. He was prompted to write it originally because with three sons at school he needed money. But he soon began to relish a form that unlike theatre allowed him 'to live totally within the world of my own free imagination.' With fiction and, to a lesser extent, radio drama he finds himself 'writing what I want to write most.'

With his second novel, *Books of Bale*, he found in John Bale, notorious in the sixteenth century as the author of anti-Catholic plays, a figure who in many ironic ways parallels his own career. 'He was marginal in the history of English theatre because he came between the full-blown medieval morality plays and the secular plays of the Elizabethan period. Nobody does his plays now because they are so dreadfully detailed on aspects of Protestant theology, which nobody is interested in except maybe Ian Paisley, and I don't think he'd like the plays, either.'

As Bishop of Ossory, Bale staged one of his plays in the streets of Kilkenny in an attempt to bring the Reformation to Ireland. 'He was the first divine who came here determined to change the religion. Whereas others were inclined to accommodate themselves to Protestantism in a hedging sort of way so that it didn't look too serious and didn't upset the Irish too much, he tackled it head on.'

With the ensuing riots Bale was brought hastily back to England. Queen Elizabeth I eventually brought in a law banning controversial plays which continued into the twentieth century. 'There was no scope in English theatre for strong controversy right through until the Lord Chamberlain abolished it.' Arden brings Bale and his times wonderfully alive with a kaleidoscopic approach that draws on his widow's dreams and his daughter's reminiscences as well as letters and other viewpoints to present a multi-faceted *Citizen Kane*-style portrait in which the final layer of meaning lies not in the sixteenth century but in Arden's own twentieth century.

For Arden there has never been any such thing as true history. Autobiography and history inevitably merge. 'It's not so much a question of what actually took place as what I grew up believing took place.'

Margaret Atwood, 1989

A few weeks before Donald Trump was declared winner of the 2016 American presidential election, Margaret Atwood received the Pinter Prize from English PEN. As with Harold Pinter before her, the 79-year-old Canadian author has never hesitated to speak out against bigotry and intolerance. Readers of her 1985 dystopian satire The Handmaid's Tale *have been quick to find eerie parallels between the novel's imagined theocratic America called Gilead, where women were treated as childbearing chattels, and the advent of Trump with his bully-boy misogyny and promises to ban Muslims from America and deport millions of what he termed as illegal 'aliens'. 'The book is more relevant now than when it was written,' Atwood says. So much so that in 2017 it became Amazon's number one bestseller, while an advert for a ten-part TV adaptation, screened during a commercial break at the Super Bowl, was watched by 111 million people. The adaptation went on to sweep the Emmy Awards. Its sardonic depiction of Canada as a place of sanctuary to which Americans flee could yet become reality, as it did for Atwood's French Huguenot and English Puritan forebears. 'If you can get across the border, you're going to have a better chance of not getting slaughtered.' She was no less acerbic when we first met in London in 1989 .*

Women historically have been too often treated as little more than breeding machines. Churches routinely blessed this supposedly God-given role. Society applied reassuring euphemisms, such as maternal instinct or romance. Set in the near future, Margaret Atwood's novel *The Handmaid's Tale* (1985) subverts such pretences. With most women infertile as a result of the cumulative effect of pollution and nuclear contamination, reproductive functions have been nationalized by a right-wing fundamentalist American government that grabbed power after an assassination. ('They blamed it on the Islamic fanatics at the time,' says the narrator.) Women still capable of childbearing are deemed 'handmaids' and harvested for the exclusive use of the ruling male elite.

'I'm always amazed at the idea that all change is for the better,' says Atwood. 'It's particularly prevalent in the US. In Canada we're more realistic about what is possible and what isn't possible. We're educated in a different way. We're educated to be much more conscious of the rest of the world than Americans are. Being a smaller country, we can't afford not to be. We have to see ourselves in a much larger context.'

Anyone eavesdropping – it's a cold February afternoon in 1989, and we're lunching in a London hotel – might have presumed she was English, or perhaps American. Canadians are used to passing for someone else, much like the Irish. Nobody seems to notice that actually they speak English differently, they make it their own. 'There are many different English languages,' Atwood says. 'But for someone from a very large powerful country, in a way, there is no reason to pay attention to other countries. We're expected to pay attention to them.'

It's like the fly on the elephant's back. If you're beside a bigger neighbour, you have to be more observant and more aware to survive. This can be useful conditioning for a writer. But Atwood has even more reason to be observant. Her father was a botanist specializing in insects. She and her sister would miss school for months on end going with him on field trips into the northern wilderness. 'But it was never pushed on us in a heavy-handed pedagogical fashion. If the thing was there and you were interested, then you would get it explained to you. It was just a general part of life.'

While it might sound uncannily like the childhood remembered by the middle-aged painter Elaine in Atwood's novel *Cat's Eye* (1989), fiction doesn't really happen like that. 'Although *Cat's Eye* is autobiographical in its form, it is not me.' She has even inserted a disclaimer reminding readers that it's fiction. 'Because with every single one of my books there are people who imagine it is autobiographical.' After *Lady Oracle*, which featured a fat heroine, 'people wouldn't believe that I was never that size. They thought I had some magic diet secret.'

She watches you closely as she talks, head tilted to one side, scrutinizing responses. It's rather like being put under a microscope. She speaks almost without opening her mouth, her big eyes on you. 'I find myself making the same assumptions when I read other people's novels,' she admits. 'I'm as nosy as anybody else.'

She was readily persuaded to write a foreword to *The Cambridge Guide to Literature in English*, which, as its title states, rejoices in the richness and plurality of the language. 'A good deal of the colour and variety of English is being generated from those who have taken the language of the former colonizers and modelled it to their own uses.'

English hasn't just mutated geographically, but sexually as well. 'Women, who for many centuries functioned merely as objects in the grammatical scheme of things – and if they wrote, were considered remarkable, not for doing it well but for doing it at all – have begun to reclaim their mother tongue and to describe and explore their own realities with it.'

Even before feminism took off in the 1960s, Atwood had anticipated it with her first novel *The Edible Woman*, which faced the heroine with a choice between a career going nowhere and marriage as an escape. 'These were the options for a young woman, even an educated young woman, in Canada then.'

Although it appeared in 1969, *The Edible Woman* was actually written in 1965 when she was twenty-four, long before the women's movement had surfaced: her male publisher lost the manuscript and eventually published it out of embarrassment after her first published work, *The Circle Gone* (1966), a collection of poems, won the Governor-General's Prize. Atwood is not above depicting women behaving nastily. 'Why should women be better than men? Women are human too.' But this is not to say she's no longer a feminist. Western society is far from moving into the post-feminist era that some already complacently imagine to have arrived. 'It would be a mistake to assume that much has changed. Things change very gradually, if at all.'

The important thing in fiction is not the details that might be true to life but the other imagined world they help to create. Atwood's Grade 4 teacher becomes Elaine's. So does her Scottish high-school principal, who ran the school like a clan. 'Yet everyone says that was the most improbable part of my novel.' Both their fathers collected insects and Atwood, like Elaine, showed a liking for art. But she uses these personal facts to create a context in which the characters can live their own very different lives. 'It's my generation, but it's not me.'

The ambivalent period in a girl's life just before adolescence, 'when girls are playing mostly with girls and boys are playing mostly with boys', provides the core of *Cat's Eye*. Remembered from middle age not so much in flashback but rather by peeling away layers ('you don't look back along time but down through it, like water') is the sometimes disturbing relationship between shy and sensitive Elaine and the domineering, often sadistic, Cordelia. As they go through life the balance shifts: it is as if they are two sides of the one self. Toronto is the particular setting for *Cat's Eye*, as it was for her *The Edible Woman*. 'Back then it was very daring, almost subversive, to set a book in Toronto. Books had to be in London, New York or Paris, real cities, not like Toronto.' All that is changed thanks partly to Atwood's own international status as a writer. So much so that she even had to research how things looked in the 1950s.

So how will the 1980s be seen a decade from now? 'As the age of greed,' she says. Playing back the tape recording of her prediction is a reminder of how right she was then, and still is. As the global economy struggled to contain financial meltdown with misguided austerity programmes that punish the victims rather than the culprits, a documentary inspired by Atwood's 2008 book *Payback: Debt and the Shadow Side of Wealth*, screened at the 2012 Sundance Film Festival, attempted to weigh the guilt of greedy capitalists against the hyped-up demands of insatiable consumers.

It opens with Atwood clacking on her keyboard, writing the text. Her thoughts on the nature and consequences of debt are visualized in a series of case histories ranging from a blood feud over land and the plight of exploited Florida tomato farmers to the catastrophic BP oil spill in the Gulf of Mexico and the jailed press baron Conrad Black.

Afterwards, in an interview, Atwood makes a surprising admission. 'I never really believed in the idea that we were all innately selfish,' she says. 'If you read enough history, you know people throw themselves on grenades to save complete strangers. You know people run into burning buildings, or throw themselves into freezing rivers to save others because it is the right thing to do.'

Alan Ayckbourn, 1986

The bank manager frowned. 'You know, most people in your position would have traded up by now,' he said, surprised that we were still living in the same suburban semi-detached we bought for £3000 in 1962 when my salary as a Sunday Independent *sub-editor was £21 a week. To get a mortgage we had to borrow £400 for the deposit. He was even more surprised to hear we were perfectly happy where we were and had no intention of changing house. In 2017 we're still in that same house, the garden flowering with apple and pear blossoms and ripe with figs, artichokes, redcurrants and strawberries. The once sleepy village of Dundrum has grown into an urban shopping hub with cinemas, a theatre and gourmet restaurants, a paradise of consumerism. The virtue of suburban life is that everybody may know your business but nobody mentions it. Or, as Confucius used to say, How you are matters more than how you seem to be. There can be freedom in the planned conformity of estates of seemingly identical-looking houses. When the foibles of the middle classes are satirized by playwrights like Hugh Leonard, Alan Ayckbourn and Bernard Farrell, the audiences that laugh the most are the same middle classes. Much of the popularity of the classic TV comedy series* Fawlty Towers *comes from a shared inbred fear of embarrassment. John Cleese, the creator of its gaffe-prone proprietor, Basil Fawlty, once told me: 'The supreme aim in life for the average middle-class person is to be able to get safely to the grave without ever having been seriously embarrassed.' Laughter is the natural voice of social discomfort, which is why Alan Ayckbourn's jaundiced view of English middle-class family life has kept West End audiences – and TV audiences – in stitches ever since his breakthrough with* How The Other Half Loves *in 1964. He directed a revival forty years later in 2009 to celebrate his seventieth birthday, and despite a stroke continues to write plays with over seventy now to his credit. Like Harold Pinter, his great obsession is cricket and this helped break the ice when he talked with me in 1986.*

'Hadlee plays and misses just outside the off stump ...' Alan Ayckbourn has one eye on the television while we're talking. New Zealand are beginning to look like building up a first innings total that could prove decisive in the Second Test at Trent Bridge. 'The 250 comes up with a crisp stroke back past the bowler ...' Each ball is as if Ayckbourn is at the crease himself. Like all wicket-keepers, he rather fancies himself with the bat when he plays for the local club at Scarborough. 'Gower dives at second slip to cut off a certain four ...'

A passion for cricket can be misleading. Ayckbourn isn't nearly as typically English as he seems, least of all in his plays. With *Relatively Speaking* and *How the Other Half Loves* in the late 1960s he appeared to have brought English drama back from the kitchen sink of the 'angry young men' to the clever drawing-room comedies of the Noel Coward and Terence Rattigan era.

All his plays are rooted in the attitudes and behaviour of the English middle classes, which apart from the accents are probably similar to that of middle classes everywhere. Ostensibly they are comedies of suburban manners. They operate within the conventions of social rituals with which the audience is assumed to be familiar – the family weekend of *The Norman Conquests,* with the same six characters in each play but in a different part of the house, the Christmas party of *Absurd Person Singular,* the dinner party of *How The Other Half Loves,* the local committee meetings of *Ten Times Table.*

Yet beneath the laughs the recurring concern is domestic pain. Ayckbourn is in fact undermining the very values he's assumed to represent. Marriage for his characters is invariably destructive. It provides an excuse for male insensitivity towards women. Through it, people ruin each other often without even realizing what they have done. It's not for nothing that critic Michael Billington dubbed Ayckbourn the 'Scarborough Ibsen.' Ayckbourn's own parents never married and Ayckbourn, after a brief marriage, which prompted him to reflect that he and his wife never got on until their marriage was over, waited thirty years before getting divorced and marrying his lifetime partner Helen Storey. Yet because he coats his despairing themes with humour and is hugely popular with audiences he has tended to be dismissed as a lightweight, rather like Hugh Leonard. Giving people a good time in theatre is somehow suspect.

'It's a residue from Cromwell,' he says. 'There's a guilt element about being rocked with laughter, particularly when you're in company.' He's adept at employing the familiar devices and conventions of comedy as a way of surprising audiences with truths they wouldn't otherwise face.

'The human mind is like a human eye. We learn to blink and not concern ourselves with the many horrible things that are happening around us. If we sense we're being got at in a play, we quickly clam up. Although I don't want to get at people, comedy is a way to do it. I've been moved by more comedies than tragedies, Chekhov's in particular. The sadness only hits you afterwards.'

He remembers as the ultimate compliment someone admitting to him after one of his plays, 'I wouldn't have laughed if I'd known what I was laughing at.'

His sceptical view of family life is not unrelated to his own childhood experience. His mother wrote stories for women's magazines and his father was a violinist and deputy leader of the London Symphony Orchestra. Then his mother married a bank manager. On holidays he couldn't help observing that her relationship with his stepfather was far from perfect. But he's wary about making too much of this. 'The fact is that nice people don't make good theatre. The most difficult thing to write about is people who are totally happy.' His mother got him a typewriter when he was young. He'd sit at the kitchen table trying to imitate her writing stories. 'It was the natural thing to do. I suppose if she'd been a keen cook I'd probably be a chef by now.'

He went straight from public school at Haileybury, where he wrote house plays at the end of every term, to being a member of Stephen Joseph's Theatre-in-the-Round at Scarborough. When he complained that he wasn't getting good enough roles, Joseph told him, 'If you want a better part you'd better write one for yourself,' which he did with *The Square Cut* in 1959, the first of three apprentice works written as Roland Allen. 'I strongly believe that writing is a craft and that playwrights don't often write nearly enough early on.' He quickly made it to London's Arts Theatre in 1964 with *Mr Whatnot* only to be slaughtered by the critics. Three years later he became their darling with *Relatively Speaking*, a comedy of misunderstandings that earned the ultimate accolade of being considered 'enjoyable' by Noel Coward.

All his plays have been written and produced initially for Scarborough, where he combines the function of director of productions and writer-in-residence. 'It's far enough from London not to feel the pressure. You have the freedom to fail without being buried. And of course it meant all my plays are accepted. I've never had one rejected. I can write for myself and direct and cast and put a play on in a very short time, which suits my work method because I write very fast. It's a matter of days rather than weeks. It never takes more than two weeks to write a play and the entire creative process happens in six weeks.'

The fact of working in Scarborough, where the theatre is a converted Victorian schoolhouse that seats only 300, conditions everything he writes. 'They're plays that can be achieved in a tiny theatre with a small cast. I find the limits a challenge. That I can't have huge casts works commercially in my favour. Writing happens best under certain preconditions. It never helps if one is given an infinite budget and an infinite number of people.'

All his plays since the essentially straightforward *Relatively Speaking* ('You should always start with an orthodox play, learning the rules before you break them') are, as with Hugh Leonard – a great admirer of his work – experiments in the formal possibilities of theatre. Three floors of a house are flattened on a single plane in *Taking Steps*. *Bedroom Farce* has three bedrooms side by side on the stage. Two rooms are superimposed on each other in *How the Other Half Loves*. 'That happened because I was living at the time in Leeds in a council flat, which was identical to 200 other council flats. A colleague lived three or four floors down. One evening after a few drinks too many I was trying to find my way around his flat and became completely disorientated. Everything was the same as my flat and yet different.'

As well as having the two rooms occupying the same space in *How the Other Half Loves*, he makes the social status of the two couples different and plays certain scenes on different days at the same time. 'I'm intrigued by the use you can make of time on the stage and the way it can be shifted and shaped.' Worried that the audience mightn't understand, he wrote a long programme note explaining the mechanics of the action. 'I needn't have bothered. You should never underestimate an audience. Since the audience occupies the same space as the actors in Scarborough they have to cross the stage to get to their seats. At the interval I noticed that they were subconsciously using the set as the actors used it. As long as you explain the rules early in a play the audience will imagine whatever you want them to imagine.'

Recently he took two years off from Scarborough for other work, in particular writing *A Small Family Business* for the National Theatre. 'It's quite a change of pace. You have to deliver a play a year in advance so they can get the right cast.' This time the theme is dishonesty. 'It's about where you draw the line. People steal paper clips in the office without thinking about it. They cheat with their fares on the bus. So I explore a family that shifts imperceptibly from this to being involved in drugs. I suppose I'm moving into morality plays.'

Ayckbourn cocks his ear. 'Evan Gray scurries the ball for another single ...'

He's no intention of staying in London. 'But it's good to escape all the administrative chores for a while, not having to dream up a repertoire every season. It's nice to work in other people's theatres where they have all the worries. Let Peter Hall worry instead of me.' At least he now has time to watch cricket again.

'There's an appeal and Greg Thomas has Hadlee caught by Gooch in the slips for 68 ...'

Ayckbourn mouths a silent Howzat. I mime a handclap.

Beryl Bainbridge, 1994

My abiding memory of Beryl Bainbridge is of wandering through the cavernous soft-carpeted corridors of the Four Seasons Hotel in Ballsbridge trying to find somewhere she could smoke. 'My lung was checked last month so I don't have to worry,' she reassured me. I'd brought her to Dublin to judge the Hennessy Literary Awards and didn't want to mislay her. Frail and unsteady on her feet, she somehow survived another sixteen years before dying of cancer aged seventy-five in 2010. She'd been made a dame in 2000 but this didn't put a check on her dark impish humour and taste for mischief. Her chaotic life, littered with impulsive affairs, provided rich material for eighteen novels, three of which were filmed, collections of stories, plays for stage and screen and countless other articles, essays and reviews. 'I think all creativity comes from the sexual urge,' she once said.

About the most irritating mistake you can make with most novelists is to presume that their fiction comes from life. But not Beryl Bainbridge. She even takes it as a compliment. 'Obviously I base all my heroines on me,' she says. 'And I always base chaps of a certain age on my father and all the women are based on Mother or my aunts. Anybody in between is my brother. They're all dead, which is why I can do it.' Her Booker-shortlisted novel *An Awfully Big Adventure* is lifted straight from her precocious career as a sixteen-year-old assistant stage manager at Liverpool Playhouse immediately after the war. 'I got thrown out of school at fourteen for writing something indelicate. These days you'd be entered for a competition.'

Realizing she was a bit of a show off, her mother sent her to auditions for *Children's Hour* in Manchester, where she was signed up with Billie Whitelaw and Judith Chalmers. 'It sort of went from there. Those days you didn't need an Equity card.' Her father, a businessman who had lost all his money in the slump, made some calls and got her the Playhouse job, largely because it didn't pay and nobody else would take it. 'I had to sit in the prompt corner and call out lines. Then the education authorities said that a boy actor who was coming from Scotland to play in *The Son and I* was underage. I stepped in ten days before rehearsal. They took me to the barber, had all my hair shaved off and I played the boy.' Being at the Playhouse was a way of escaping her father, a melancholic man given to rowing incessantly with her mother. Afterwards he'd lock himself in the bedroom for hours. 'We'd leave his meals outside the door like a dog.' At one stage she even booked a cheap room in the Aber House Hotel, hoping to persuade her mother to leave him.

Not surprisingly, Stella in *An Awfully Big Adventure* doesn't really have any parents, much like other dangerously naive girl heroines in Bainbridge's novels, notably *The Dressmaker* and *Sweet William*, both of which (like *An Awfully Big Adventure*) were filmed. Stella was abandoned at an early age and brought up by her uncle, who runs the Aber House Hotel – places in Bainbridge's novels as well as people come from her real life. She's grown up headstrong and innocent, full of contradictions. 'She's very dangerous because she says exactly what she thinks. She causes chaos all around without knowing it.'

Stella has an ambivalent relationship with a flamboyant actor playing Captain Hook in a Christmas production of *Peter Pan*. Bainbridge less adventurously fell in love with the scene painter, Austin Davies. 'All I wanted to do was to marry and have children. I never wanted a career.' Married to Davies at twenty, she quickly had two children but was divorced within four years ('he was carrying on') and survived a bizarre attempt by her mother-in-law to shoot her (the bullet holes are still in the plaster of her Camden Town home). 'I had no money and I couldn't get a babysitter. So I started writing. But I didn't do anything about it for several years.'

While bringing her children to school she met up again with a writer friend who gave her the name of his agent. 'What I didn't know was that he was carrying on with the female part of the agency, who wrote me back a letter saying, why don't you get a job at Woolworths. That stopped me for a time.' Eventually Hutchinson's published *Another Part of the Wood* and *Weekend with Claude*, but then she got talking (again at school) with another publisher who'd read them but hadn't thought them any good. He asked if she'd anything else, so she gave him her first novel, *Harriet Said*, more rooted in her own life, which had been lying at the bottom of a drawer. He promptly published it and she's been with him ever since. She was advised to write only about what she knew. 'Don't make anything up,' her editor said. 'Tell it the way it was. Don't go off into fantasies. Just stick to a few characters and settings you know.'

This was all the licence she needed. 'I think most people write out of their experience,' she says.

> I've never seen the point of inventing anybody. Lots of writers get libel suits, but I've been lucky, perhaps because I've always told everybody. Usually people are quite flattered. But there has to be a time lapse. I've got to have known someone for years and years before I can write about them. I can't do it other-wise. The worst thing is that as you get older and you do more and more writing, you never go out any more. I never meet any normal people any more. They're all either in the business of writing or they're barmy. So I have to dredge them up from the past.

When that fails she's apt to turn to historical figures. She's reimagined young Adolf Hitler's youthful visit to Liverpool and put herself inside the mind of a TCD-educated serial killer. *The Birthday Boys*, nominated for the Whitbread Prize in 1992, tells the story of Captain Scott and his expedition to the South Pole from each character's point of view, 'imagining what they were thinking and saying. I still can't get over it. They walked 1600 miles with very poor equipment and very small rations. Their bodies were found in 1913. A year later World War One broke out and the world was never the same again. That was the end of patriotism and spying for the flag.'

All the characters in *An Awfully Big Adventure* are people she knew at the Liverpool Playhouse. 'Working there wasn't bad training for writing. Because the life was so peculiar, you got into all sorts of situations. And it made you think visually. You saw everything in pictures.' She still goes back to Liverpool. 'But there's nobody left there now. They're all dead.' Liverpool itself is in decay. That's why *An Awfully Big Adventure* is being filmed in Dublin, with the Olympia theatre doubling for the Playhouse and the Liffey as the Mersey (before being thrown into it last week, Alan Rickman, who plays the Captain Hook actor, was given a precautionary hepatitis inoculation).

Last time she was in Liverpool was for the opening of the stage version of *An Awfully Big Adventure*, which starred her actress daughter Rudy Davies. 'It was funny seeing her being me at the Playhouse.' Like Beryl, Rudy, who was in the TV series *A Sense of Guilt* and Brian Moore's *The Lonely Passion of Judith Hearne*, has since quit acting. 'She says it's crap. I think she's waiting for me to die so that she can write.'

J.G. Ballard, 1991

A sure indication of iconic status in literature is when a writer's name becomes a dictionary word, such as Shakespearean, Shavian, Joycean or Pinteresque. Look up the Collins English Dictionary *and you'll find the adjective 'Ballardian' defined as 'resembling or suggestive of the conditions described in J.G. Ballard's novels and stories, especially dystopian modernity, bleak man-made landscapes and the psychological effects of technological, social or environmental developments'. Born in 1930 in Shanghai, where his father ran a subsidiary of a Manchester textile firm, Ballard's post-apocalyptic sci-fi stories, particularly* Crash, *in which an obsession with crashed cars – personified by a character called James Ballard – highlights the propensity of contemporary society to create technology that leads to its downfall. By the time of his death from prostate cancer in 2009, Ballard was widely admired as a prophet of cyberpunk fiction and music, but his literary and popular reputation perhaps owes more to his partly autobiographical novels* Empire of the Sun *and* The Kindness of Women. *We met in October 1991.*

'Hello,' a twelve-year-old boy, the future star Christian Bale, told Ballard on the set of Steven Spielberg's film version of *Empire of the Sun*. 'I'm you.' An attractive couple in their thirties joined in. 'And we're your parents.' Having lived over thirty years in Shepperton – 'It's more a suburb of Heathrow airport than of London' – he now found himself actually inside the local film studios playing a bit part in his own life. 'I felt very much an interloper,' he says. 'Much of me ended up on the cutting floor. I'm just a blurred image.'

Ballard's life seems even to himself more like a film than something that actually happened. The memory of being caught up as a seven-year-old in the horrific bombing of Shanghai in 1937, climbing over the bodies of Chinese dead in the street, had within days become confused with images, something oddly apart from him. As the Japanese pulverized the city with heavy artillery, life went on as normal for his family in the privileged international enclave. 'Westerners in their tennis clothes watched it from the roof of office blocks as a kind of huge spectacle, like a military tattoo. It was an extraordinary insulation from reality.' Even being interned by the Japanese for three years after Pearl Harbor was something of a lark. 'I'd had a protected childhood. In the camp I met people my parents would never have allowed me to meet. I got on intimate terms with all sorts of scallywags, which was tremendously liberating. But my parents' memories were very different.'

In both *Empire of the Sun* and its sequel *The Kindness of Women*, his autobiographical childhood self, Jim, is alone in the camp, not knowing whether his parents are alive or dead. 'It was psychologically true to show myself alone. There was an estrangement between me and my parents, not consciously, just something affected by the war. I saw them tested in a way I wasn't tested. I spent a long time on my own as I grew older.' The middle-class England to which he returned as a stranger after the war hadn't yet come to grips with the world's changed realities:

> Everyone knew their place on the ladder. Looking back I realize that the middle class had really lost their confidence. They were confronted by the apocalypse of a Labour government that threatened the whole basis of their privilege. I can remember a friend of my parents who literally turned purple in the face at the thought of the National Health Service. People would sneer at the idea that a working-class woman was entitled to a washing machine to give her more leisure. It was a sort of corruption of the social order. I think England arrived in the twentieth century about fifty years late and it may never arrive in the twenty-first. We may go on living in a sort of twilight zone historically while the rest of Europe is getting on with discovering the future.

Perhaps this is why all his early novels and stories took the form of science fiction. 'One sensed different worlds on the horizon in the 1950s with the advent of supermarkets, television and high-rise living. One began to see a more open kind of social order.'

After seven years of marriage his young wife Mary died suddenly from pneumonia in 1964 while on a holiday in Spain with their three small children:

> It provided me with a renewed impetus to make sense of the arbitrary cruelty of the world. It was a spur to grapple with the fictionalizing of reality that increasingly took place in the 1970s and 1980s to the point where the polarity of our lives has been reversed. People now think fiction is real and the real is fiction. The curious sense of distancing from events I experienced in Shanghai prefigured shifts in public sensibility through images of television violence since the 1960s, this tremendous media-induced insensitivity to violence. Tragedy and suffering have been turned into public theatre.

Although *The Kindness of Women* reads like autobiography, much of it isn't. It's Ballard's way of coming to terms with the contemporary confusion of illusion and reality, the sense that life is increasingly lived as a media-conditioned sitcom. 'It's a kind of parallel world of greater intensity than the one I lived. Somerset Maugham once said that dialogue in plays is exactly what people would say in real life if they had two minutes to think about it first. My novel is like that. It's my life recast as if we all had time to reach the mythic core of our identities.'

For a writer preoccupied with darkness and destruction – in various novels he drowned Earth, burned it and turned it to crystal – Ballard incongruously lived a relatively conventional family life as a single father, taking annual holidays with his two daughters and son in Marbella every year – 'I'm always happier in the sun' – and, when they had grown up and given him two grandchildren, on the French Riviera with his partner Claire Walsh. His final autobiography, *Miracles of Life*, was published in 2007 and written with characteristic curiosity after he discovered he was suffering from advanced prostate cancer. 'There is no doubt that grandchildren take away the fear of death,' he said.

John Banville, 1986

*An interview is a conversation caught in the moment, an impression of someone as they once were. The interviewer is a listener but afterwards, in writing up the interview, becomes an accomplice in a reconstructed version of what took place, a sort of fiction or an imagining of who the subject of the interview seemed to be. John Banville has spent a lifetime delving into ambiguities that confuse the relationship between reality and fiction, even to the point of taking on a pseudonym – Benjamin Black – under which he could be free to write in the crime genre without distracting from his literary work. He has written novels that draw on real-life characters: whether a murderer (*The Book of Evidence*), a spy (*The Untouchable*) or his own childhood as a ten-year-old in* The Sea, *winner of the Booker Prize), while in his 2017 novel* Mrs Osmond – a sequel to *The Portrait of a Lady – he puts himself inside the mind of its author, Henry James. Several of his novels rely on the device of an unreliable narrator (*Athena *and* Ghosts*). In the late 1980s Banville reviewed books for me at* The Sunday Tribune. *He'd choose whatever book he wanted, and his copy was so perfect that it was never necessary to alter a word or a comma. In September 1986 we met in my small cluttered office for an interview that lasted all morning.*

Reading between the lines in fiction you can't help building up an impression of the real life that created it. Recurring references in John Banville's novels to Wexford ('The best memories I have of the place are departures from it'), the vanished world of The Big House ('the past turned into a wilderness') and Protestant Ireland ('how beautifully they bore their loss') suggest the divided tradition of an Anglo-Irish upbringing.

His ability to get inside the mind of a scientist – particularly in the novels *Doctor Copernicus*, *Kepler* and *The Newton Letter* – fill in another facet of our imagined profile of him. Then there is the obsessive preoccupation with twins. Just as Gabriel Godkin in *Birchwood* is searching for his lost twin sister, Gabriel Swann in *Mefisto* cannot escape his stillborn twin brother who hangs over his life 'not as a presence but a momentous absence'. The repeated theme seems too insistent not to have a parallel in actual experience. The sparse biographical facts repeated on the jacket of each of his novels – that he was born in Wexford in 1945 and now lives in Dublin with his American wife Janet and sons Colm and Douglas – do little to stop the speculation.

But John Banville's chuckle soon does. Early on he upturned the advice writers often give to younger writers: write about something you know. 'I always feel you should write about what you don't know,' he says. 'Find out something. You'll have terrible failures and the whole thing will have a glittering synthetic surface but sometimes maybe you'll strike gold.' Far from being a scientist, it turns out that he can 'hardly add two and two'. He worked for a couple of years as a computer operator with Aer Lingus after leaving school. 'But all I ever used to do was to press buttons and hope for the best.' Computers were a novelty in the 1970s. Dignitaries like President Childers were proudly brought in to view the processing of reservations and flights. With his army-like jacket and three days' growth of beard, Banville hardly projected the required Brave New World image. 'I'd be given the rest of the day off.' All of which came in handy for the professor in *Mefisto* who hooks into the most advanced software to establish that nothing can ever be proved.

Doctor Copernicus and *Kepler* didn't require massive research. 'I just read a few books. That's what novelists are for. For imagining things more vividly than historian can ever do.' Although the characters in the novels 'were men who transformed science, the novels themselves are not about science but are rather an attempt to explore the creative process without writing about artists':

I've always been fascinated by the relationship between the reader and the text. When you think about it, reading a novel is the most extraordinary process. We get this thing that we know is made up. We know bits of it are probably true because nobody can write completely outside their own experience. But we don't know which bits. And the bits that look truest of all are probably the ones that are completely false.

His second novel *Nightspawn* confronts this Faustian pact the reader unthinkingly enters into. 'It's about saying to the reader, look you believe all this despite the fact that I'm telling you on every page that it's all made up and it's all nonsense.'

There was nothing about the Big House in Banville's actual childhood. He grew up in Wexford town, not the Ferns area *The Newton Letter* might imply. The Big House, like science, is used in his fiction merely as a literary device. *Birchwood* was written as a parody of the Big House novel 'although with a lot of fond nods towards the form as well.'

The Big House resurfaces in *The Newton Letter* (this time as self-parody) and in *Mefisto* because 'in a way it's a huge museum of the past for us. It raises hackles, it raises expectations. No Irish person could be absolutely unmoved by it.' There is a sense in which the dilapidated Ashburn in *Mefisto*, empty and falling down, taken over by strange ragamuffin figures, is a symbol of Ireland. 'But I wouldn't have done any of that deliberately,' he says. 'Things in novels are other things and they're not at the same time.'

The school in *Mefisto* is an amalgam of the Christian Brothers and St Peter's College ('where I had an uproarious time despite disastrous exam results') and the town square of The Faythe where his family lived (as did my father's family). 'You're changing the familiar into something different, something that's strange even to yourself.' This is the nearest he's ever got to writing directly about his own background. 'Perhaps because in the early stages of writing it my mother died and my father was dying. I found that I was celebrating the past. But the amount of sentimentality and tripe that comes out when you start doing that is amazing.' His wife Janet soon brought him in line. 'It may be interesting to you but for me it's boring,' she complained. He realized it was unbalancing the novel so most of it had to go, 'like chipping away parts of yourself'. There had been no writing in the family. 'I'd put that book at the back of the fire,' his mother said of *Ulysses*. His father worked as a motor mechanic for Stafford's ('they were very paternalistic employers'). He knows nothing about his family beyond his grandparents. 'I often think the family forgot deliberately. You never know what skeletons might be rattling there.'

He's being writing since he was fifteen and some of the stories he wrote when he was seventeen were in his first book *Long Lankin*. Yet originally he'd wanted to be a painter. 'My mother suggested architecture instead so I could earn some money.' His brother Vincent is also a writer and novelist under the of name Vincent Lawrence who won an inaugural Hennessy Literary Award in 1971. Perhaps the creative urge comes from their father's father. ' He was some kind of inventor and always claimed to have invented a revolutionary new plough.' That might account for Banville's attraction to ideas. 'I've always been seduced by them. But there's a danger in that. You can't bring ideas into fiction and discuss them because the fiction damages the ideas and the ideas damage the fiction.' He realized that when he was writing *Doctor Copernicus* and *Kepler* and had to write something about science – like Kepler's idea of the Five Solids – another part of him would take over, 'a part that was a kind of journalist, because I was writing journalese, a kind of faction.'

It's an instinct he's well familiar with, having been a sub-editor on *The Irish Press*. 'For the moment this person would take over and write and while that was happening the artist had given up. No matter how subtle I got the effect and no matter how hard I worked over it, it would still not be there, it would still be something else.'

From his mother's side of the family he acquired a sense of music. 'My uncle would pick up any instrument and play it. I feel my writing has as much to do with music as anything else. I find myself singing in my head as I write. Rhythm is extremely important to me, a kind of rhythm in prose.' *Doctor Copernicus* is based on musical themes. 'There's a fugue and there's one whole section of themes and variations. But I don't know whether it's a good idea consciously to do that. It gives it a rather synthetic air.'

But there's nothing contrived about his repeated use of the idea of twins. Of course it serves as a literary device. Gabriel Swan's fascination with the way a twin can escape effortlessly into another name and self while at the same time asserting a separate identity is a powerful metaphor for the act of fiction: in telling a story the writer too has become someone else. But it goes much deeper than that, although there are no twins in his family.

'I suppose it's the divided self that everyone feels, so that when you're at a party or falling in love there's another voice inside saying, yeah, yeah, yeah.'

BANVILLE, JOHN

Double images keep creeping into his writing whether he intends them or not. 'There are things in fiction you do consciously and things you do because you couldn't help doing them. The notion of the lost self is something I can't help because I come back to it again and again.' None of his novels ever work out as he originally planned. That is part of his pleasure in writing them:

> I don't want to sound mystical but I think there is a part of the brain that has a hold of the thing in a complete form from the very beginning. There is some sort of Platonic ideal of it there. I always start a book from a shape more than anything else. Not a geometric shape but a sort of tension in the vacuum. Then it's a matter of filling in the words as closely to that form as possible. And of course you never quite get it. Paul Valéry says a work of art is never finished, just abandoned. There comes a stage when you have to stop poking at it.

Mefisto ('which was at first going to be about the careers of two twins but after two years working on it I killed off one of them') is the last in a four-novel series comprising *Doctor Copernicus*, *Kepler* and *The Newton Letter*. He conceived it in terms of the classical Greek notion of the tetralogy – three tragedies and a satire, with *The Newton Letter* as the satire ('sending myself up'). 'But a book is always the end of one phase and the beginning of another. That's why all novels fail. If you really thought it was just the end, you'd never write any more. *Mefisto* was even more so the beginning of a new phase I didn't know anything about. I could see there was quite a difference between it and the previous three. The science element was very low in importance. It's more my farewell to science.'

Like Banville, neither Copernicus nor Kepler were interested in the way things actually are. 'They were interested in the idea of things. Copernicus looked at the stars about six times in his life. Kepler had double vision: for every star he looked at he saw at least two. They weren't interested in the way things moved. They were interested in order. And that I suppose is what artists do.' He has an aversion to interviews because they create a presumption that he can give some special insight into what he writes:

> Yet even though I wrote *Mefisto* I don't really know what it's about. I don't understand it and I don't think I should try to understand it. It's like when you have one of those really powerful dreams and you get up in the morning and try to tell somebody about it. To you it's absolutely reverberating inside you. You feel it's more important than conscious life. That somehow it contains the nucleus of your whole life. You try to explain it to someone and they say,

hmm, yes, very interesting. A novel seems to be as if you had sat down and taken three or four years to explain a dream to someone in such a way that they could experience the weight or power of the dream that you had.

The professor advises Gabriel Swan in *Mefisto*, 'If you want order, invent it.' Banville has taken his own advice: through fiction he creates sense from the chaos of the real world.

Saul Bellow, 1985

As 89-year-old Saul Bellow lay on his deathbed in April 2005, he opened his eyes and asked a close friend, Jeffrey Eugenides, 'Was I a good man or was I a jerk?' It's the kind of question almost any one of his memorable fictional characters might have asked, forever arguing with an inner self about their role in life. Bellow, according to a memoir published by a son from the first of his five marriages, seemed to feel that his literary genius 'entitled him to let people down with impunity'. Maybe there is some truth in this, but it's hard to reconcile it with the Bellow who talked to me with such self-deprecating courtesy in Dublin in 1985.

'It's a pain in the neck,' Saul Bellow grumbles, referring to his Nobel Prize for Literature. 'You become an unpaid cultural functionary.'

There's hardly been a good – and maybe not so good – cause he hasn't been asked to put his name to since winning literature's most coveted award in 1976. 'It accelerates your progress towards transcendent questions. You say you have high-minded reasons for not doing what people want.'

The irony appeals to him, and he smiles. Like the characters in his fiction, he sees himself as forever falling short of all that he ought to value. 'You get fed up with playing it right, doing the prudent thing. You feel it's time to kick over the tracks. It comes out of the Bellow family history. People were always planning to do the right thing and ended up doing the contrary. It's the demon Goethe keeps talking about.' All the protagonists in his stories go through forms of this experience, epitomized by Corde in *The Dean's December*, who 'had his own most original incomprehensible way of screwing things up.'

There's too much of Bellow's own character in his fiction for him to feel comfortable as the cultural pillar of a community people now expect him to be. 'You adopt the middle-class survival habit and then find you're looking down your nose at yourself because of it. It's not that you want to avoid the middle-class habit but that as a system it doesn't have the greatest human successes.'

But having made this observation he then backs off: it smacks too much of a pat generalization. Life doesn't conform to tidy labels like that. Labels keep being mistaken for the reality they are supposed to represent. 'People tend to view life through categories too often. They think they can't do something because it's too middle class. But that's not a *real* consideration.'

Bellow had no idea of class distinctions until he got to college, something not many Americans could afford during the Depression. 'I never thought of myself as belonging to any particular class other than being a member of a Jewish family that didn't have enough money.' Both his parents came from Russia, 'just one jump ahead of the authorities everywhere'. It's been the pattern of his life. Wherever he's been, he's never quite belonged.

We're sipping afternoon tea at the Westbury Hotel off Grafton Street. His throat is dry after addressing the Irish Association of American Studies at Trinity on this brief visit to Dublin, the city of Leopold Bloom, another wandering Jew. He's careful to pour the milk first, which is unusual with Americans. 'Well, I grew up in Canada,' he reminds me. 'We were always having afternoon tea.'

He's a small smiling man in a soft brown suit, rather like a benign uncle. His hair is a distinguished silver grey. He keeps his hat near him on the glass table so he won't forget it.

'I still go back to Vermont in the summer because it's so near Canada. I like the wooded landscape and the familiar air,' he says. It's much like the village called Lachine in Quebec where he was born two years after his parents arrived penniless from St Petersburg, having left behind a life of cosmopolitan affluence. 'It was the post La Salle set out from to discover the

North-West Passage. When he came back they taunted him and said, 'This is China, La Chine, you got there.'

He loathed moving to Chicago when he was nine. 'They'd call me the Canuck. I didn't know their games.' It didn't help either being a sickly child or that his domineering father Abe was a failed bootlegger who ridiculed his aspirations to become a writer. 'I'd fallen ill in Canada. Damn near died. Peritonitis combined with pneumonia, either of them fatal by itself.' There were no antibiotics in 1923. But he got back his strength by forcing himself through a rigorous programme of exercise. 'I must have sensed it wouldn't do to be a weakling in a place like Chicago. I ran a lot. Pumped weights, got a punchbag, chinned myself, all that until I could intimidate my two big brothers.'

There'd been nothing to do in Montreal except read. 'Charitable ladies used to provide us with the funny papers, all very innocent in those days. If I mentioned the names of those heroes you wouldn't recognize them.' But Slim Jim and Boob McNutt led him to Fenimore Cooper and *The Last of the Mohicans*. 'Lots of frontier stuff. You read indiscriminately until you find your own taste. I was so easily influenced that I'd come out of Tarzan pictures swinging from a tree.'

Becoming a writer was all he ever wanted to do since then. 'Youthful arrogance convinces you that nothing's out of reach.' Not that there were many other options during the Depression, although he dutifully graduated with honours in anthropology and sociology from Northwestern University in 1937. 'There seemed no point in preparing for a career as my father wanted. I saw all the engineers and MDs on work gangs in the street.' A rebellious young Marxist eager for socialist change, he went to Mexico to meet Leon Trotsky in 1940 but arrived the day after the Soviet revolutionary was assassinated.

It took two novels to find a way of writing in which he was comfortable. He now regards *Dangling Man*, published in 1944, as an apprentice work. With *The Victim*, which followed in 1947, he became a journeyman. 'I had to pass the tests. It was really part of a college programme rather than real writing.'

The Adventures of Augie March, which won a National Book Award in 1954, was his 'first real job of writing'. His eyes light up as if reliving the experience. 'It was a most tremendous discovery. Suddenly I realized that I could do things in my own way, I'd found my voice.' American writers are voice writers as far as Bellow is concerned, as distinct from Thackeray or Trollope who wrote for the eye. 'It's not so much that it's autobiographical but that you're speaking with your own voice, a voice which is distinctly yours. Even Henry James, in the strange way of his, is a voice. It happened in England with people like Wells and Bennett, D.H. Lawrence too, sons of the lower classes who found themselves through writing.'

Which is what Bellow did: fiction has been his way of coming to terms with the reality of his circumstances. We're drawn into his stories through the persona of the narrator perceived from several shifting viewpoints. Even when he writes in the third person it feels like the first person in disguise, which goes against the grain of the popular conception of American fiction:

> American writers have a preference for unthinking characters, but this has become false. You can't pretend you're living in a world where thought doesn't exist. It's phoney to think in a closet and then hide it when you write. Some balance has to be struck between thinking and personal experience. The dilemma is how much to think, how much to explain.
>
> I don't really care much for explanations. I'd rather find the right story and let it tell itself. But it isn't always like that if you're writing about the way things actually are. Maybe the mistake is being a realist writer instead of a symbolic one.

Bellow prefers to leave himself open to experience, trusting to instinct rather than preconceived theory. 'It's alright for a writer to have a bet, not a theory,' he smiles. He might almost be Dr Tamkin, the engaging con man in *Seize the Day*, who enthuses over 'bringing people into the here and now. The real universe, that's the present moment. The past is no good to us. The future is full of anxiety. Only the present is real – the here and now. Seize the day.' But Tamkin's sucker Thomas Wilhelm, who reflects but then makes the decision he's rejected two separate times, might equally be Bellow. It's as if fiction has become a way of realizing the contradictions of his own nature: through it he makes a kind of sense of himself. 'We've all in our time struggled with this paradox,' he admits. 'I didn't expect it to be a rose garden when I started out.'

It's why he quit New York to return to Chicago in the early 1960s. Everything was becoming too clear-cut and intellectually dogmatic. 'The *Partisan Review* outfit had taken me into its bosom in the early days. They liked you better if you disputed everything they tried on. Dwight Macdonald had no use for agreement. Harold Rosenberg regarded it as a vice.' But with the New Radicalism, writers were expected to take an approved stand on everything. 'You really had to line up or be cast into the wilderness. Robert Lowell had moved in. Around him formed a gang, The New York Review of Each Other's Books. Rather like being in Oxford or Cambridge in the 1920s and 1930s when it was obligatory to be near the Party, what Wyndham Lewis termed 'the revolutionary rich':

> Our predecessors had the class struggle to contend with. What we have to contend with is the imposition of concepts, few of them having much reference to reality. And in a way the concepts are more oppressive for a writer than the class identifications of earlier periods. Concepts are the product of intellectuals and much harder to fight because you have to think everything through before you can cast them out as false. So you have to undo all the misleading pseudo-thought. And it's very tiring and weakening to have to do this.
>
> I think many writers in modern times show the wretchedness of living through received ideas and those received ideas are still too young to be identified as received ideas. First it was Marxism. Then it was psychoanalysis. Then it was existentialism. And then it was structuralism, one thing after another, all fated for obsolescence. It took such a long time to find out what a mistake that was.

In his masterpiece *Herzog* in 1954, partly a fictionalized account of the painful break up of his own brief disastrous marriage (the first of five), Bellow tried to poke fun at the preoccupation of contemporary literature with concepts at the expense of the reality they claim to represent. 'The futility of a PhD when an ordinary crisis jumps out at you,' he says with dry mirth. But few critics got the point. 'I meant to debunk the life of thought and instead of which I was identified as a great highbrow, which I wanted least.' It's yet another of the ironic misunderstandings that punctuate his life. 'Lots of people read that book as if they were taking a comprehensive examination in a year's course in humanities.'

He still lives in Chicago in a high-rise apartment overlooking Lake Michigan. 'I went back to Chicago and its innocent philistinism, away from New York and its sophisticated philistinism.' Or as Corde reflects in *The Dean's December*, 'By the time ideas reach Chicago, they're worn thin and easy to see through.' There he finds the kind of people who keep surfacing in his stories: conmen, eccentrics and fast-talking salesmen. 'Mayor Daley wasn't personally corrupt but it's a corrupt city and somehow that's more interesting to me.'

But this didn't stop him putting Chicago on trial in *The Dean's December* in 1982 for its failure to confront the issue of the black urban poor. 'Like anyone who's grown up in an American city, I feel that the most horrible human destruction is taking place and nobody's doing anything about it and they don't want even to discuss it. It's a completely taboo subject.'

Crash programmes under Reagan's 'Great Society' legislation have succeeded merely in improving the lot of better-off middle-class blacks while allowing the situation of the mass of inner-city blacks to deteriorate even more rapidly. 'There's a false philanthropy at the heart of all programmes of improvement that satisfies the consciences of right-thinking Americans without doing anything real for anybody,' says Bellow, and he mimics a typical white 'liberal': '*I* have the right sentiments. *I* instructed my congressman to vote for the right legislation. *I* signed petitions for civil rights. Nobody can lay a hand on me. *I'm* clean.' Nothing more vividly demonstrates this gap than the firebombing, by Philadelphia police earlier this year acting on orders of a black mayor, of black extremists besieged in a tenement block. 'They were a back-to-nature cult. They rejected all artificial contrivances, particularly plumbing. They did their business on the ground outside. Inside they went about naked. Their children weren't even taught how to speak. A small twelve-year-old boy who survived the massacre had never been outside except to pee or to squat. He didn't have three words of vocabulary. He was a little Kasper Hauser, a wolf child.'

Bellow sees this child as a symbol for the conditions of Afro-Americans in general in the cities. 'They really are an abandoned people. Nobody does anything for them. Gestures are made. People go through motions. It's like a powerful giant with leprosy of the toes, which he's too busy to notice.' With *The Dean's December* he attempts to subvert this complacency, the false consciousness induced by media labelling. 'The language of discourse has shut out experience altogether,' complains Corde. 'The first act of morality was to disinter reality, retrieve reality, dig it up from the trash and represent it as art would.'

This for Bellow is the function of fiction, too: to touch the reality obscured from our perception by what Orwell termed 'newspeak'. He picks up his hat. 'It should undermine the prevailing cognitions,' he says, 'because so many people are being damned by them.'

Kay Boyle, 1986

She was a romantic, my mother. She played us to sleep at night with Chopin nocturnes and Liszt waltzes. She read English at college but quit for a job in the civil service so she could have money of her own to go to Paris 'and walk along the Left Bank, where all the painters and writers were'. She came home and fell in love with a mild-mannered republican novelist whose politics were the opposite of her father's. She gave me French stamps with the image of a beautiful archetypal woman, Marianne, 'a symbol of the spirit of the French Revolution, unlike Ireland where De Valera's constitution states that a woman's place is in the kitchen'. Even in the morphine haze of her cancerous dying days, her face would light up as she remembered that time in Paris in the late 1920s when everything seemed possible.

'The myth of Paris in the twenties,' sighs novelist Kay Boyle. 'With the exchange rate you could live well on ten dollars a day. But I never saw it as a glamorous time. It's been built up. Like Camelot.' She's dressed in a smart grey suit with a high-necked fluffy white blouse. Her grey-white hair is swept back from her aquiline features. She carefully adjusts her seatbelt as I drive her to the American Express office in Dublin to collect a letter from her son. 'He writes to me wherever I go.'

It's August 1986 and she's just heard of the death from AIDS of Roy Cohn, the lawyer who was Senator Joe McCarthy's chief counsel in the witch-hunt of supposed communists in the United States in the early 1950s. 'This is really a very just act of the gods to punish him like that,' she says. All her life she has spoken out while others kept silent: she's hardly going to stop at eighty-four. To feign a forgiveness she doesn't feel would be hypocritical. One of Cohn's victims was her Austrian refugee husband who, although cleared at a loyalty security hearing, lost his US foreign service job in Germany. She too was blacklisted. 'The hearing would never have come up if it hadn't been for Cohn,' she says.

That was the start of the harassment she experienced as a result of her opinions. Under the US Freedom of Information Act she was recently able to find out that the FBI had built up a dossier of over a thousand pages on her alleged subversive activities. Typical of the fanciful charges recorded against her is that she had an affair with the poet Ezra Pound before World War One. 'To be true it would mean I was nine at the time,' she says. As a columnist friend on the *San Francisco Chronicle* joked, 'Kay Boyle always was precocious.' All that irked her about that was that she'd never been able to stand Pound, whom she first got to know in Paris in the twenties. 'He never wrote anything original. Even his *Cantos* (1919–70) were lifted from the classics.'

At nineteen, marriage to a Frenchman brought her from the American Midwest to Europe, where she became one of an extraordinary group of expatriate modernist writers that included James Joyce, Gertrude Stein, Ernest Hemingway, F. Scott Fitzgerald, Katherine Mansfield and Djuna Barnes, an era she helped immortalize in her book with Robert McAlmon, *Being Geniuses Together 1920–1930*. Not that she needed to go to Paris to be liberated. That had already been a part of the way she was brought up in St Paul, Minnesota. 'I grew up in a world where women had to work. It never occurred to me that women didn't look for their rights and eventually get their rights. Today it seems to me that the women's liberation movement is a little too belligerent.'

When she was very small she would visit her aunt at the land grant office in Washington where she had worked for thirty-five years. 'It's hard to believe that in this century there were still chunks of the American West unclaimed. She had this big map on the wall and she'd get up on a footstool to put in thumbtacks showing each claim. She showed me one that came in written on birch bark because there had been no paper available.' Her aunt would knock on doors getting signatures for equal rights for women. 'We hope very much to be able to get votes for women,' she told a minister who opened one door. 'Woman's place is in the home,' he told her sternly. 'Well, whose home would you suggest I go to?' she inquired.

Her mother was also politically committed and ran on the Farmer-Labour ticket for the Board of Education. 'She was very small and very gentle. She never argued. I always thought of her as my child. But she was very firm in her opinions.' She needed to be so when facing up to grand-father Boyle with his fiery Irish temper. 'My father had been absolutely crushed by him. I would ask my father something and he'd say wait a minute until I ask Dad. My grandmother told me that when he was four he had a terrible tantrum and she threw a bucket of water over him. She boasted that he never expressed an opinion after that. Certainly I don't remember him ever saying a single word to me.' As a child her instinct was to hold back too. 'I was afraid to learn to read and write in case I would be inadequate. So I would tell my stories and my poems to my mother and she would write them down.'

She met her French husband Richard Brault at the Ohio Mechanics Institute. 'I wanted to be an architect but couldn't do the arithmetic at all.' They were married in City Hall, which didn't go down well back in straitlaced Brittany. 'His family sent a cable saying they'd never receive me unless we were married by a Catholic priest.' They arrived in France in 1921 'committed to something called freedom'. For her this turned out to be running off with a dashing Irish-American aviator poet, Ernest Walsh. He approached her to write for an avant-garde literary magazine he was intending to edit. Joyce and Pound were to contribute too. But it was a doomed romance from the start. His lungs were ravaged by TB. Pregnant with his child, she watched him go through 'the terrible process of dying by haemorrhaging'. Their baby was registered at the Mairie de Nice as his legitimate daughter, Sharon.

Back in Paris, she had tea some months later with Gertrude Stein. 'Not that I ever really liked her. Wonderful people are few and far between.' The dancer Isadora Duncan's brother Raymond was speaking so glowingly of a commune he had set up in Neuilly that she impulsively decided to join. The whole thing soon turned out to be a huge fraud that ended with Duncan abducting two-year-old Sharon. She had to pursue him south to kidnap the child back. All of which sounds much like fiction, and that's what it became. The Bridget of her first novel *Plagued by the Nightingale* (1931) is a young American wife obliged to live in Brittany with her husband's bigoted family. She resurfaces as Hannah in a second novel *The Year Before Last* (1932), ditching her dull husband for an affair with a wild Irish poet dying of TB. She finishes up in a third novel, *My Next Bride* (1934), as prim and proper Victoria driven to an abortion in a Paris commune. Although drawing on different facets of Kay Boyle's own life, the books are written in a poetic elliptical style that avoids spelling things out. 'I think I was trying to analyse what was happening when I was writing those stories, which are a good deal autobiographical. I wanted to understand it better than I did by living it.'

Which is much the same as James Joyce was doing when he fictional-ized the Dublin he'd left behind him. Her face brightens up. 'Joyce was very simple,' she says. 'I was very fond of him, and of Nora. Of course, she was very different. She was really beautiful.' Joyce's children Giorgio and Lucia were forever complaining to Kay that their father's fame had ruined their lives. 'How would you feel if you walked up the Boulevard Montparnasse and someone stopped you and said, are you James Joyce's son?' Giorgio would demand.

It wasn't just her own life that Kay turned into fiction: all her short stories are very clearly situated in their time and place. They offer a human mirror of events. 'Defeat', which won an O. Henry Award in 1941, says more in a few pages about the fall of France to the Germans than volumes of history books. By then she was married to Josef von Frankenstein, an Austrian baron serving with the US Armed Forces:

> He made parachute jumps into occupied France. When the Germans were retreating from Italy he infiltrated behind enemy lines. Eventually he was captured. They interrogated him in English saying they knew he was American. However he made himself sound so convincing as an Austrian peasant that they decided to execute him for deserting his regiment. Luckily he managed to escape in the confusion of the last days of the war.

Yet this was the man McCarthy accused of disloyalty in 1954. By then he was a foreign service officer stationed in Bad Godesberg:

> We got a letter saying that certain charges had been brought against him. He could have a hearing or resign. It turned out that I was one of the principal charges against him. I was supposed to have had a long friendship with a woman who had been a member of the Communist Party but whom I had never even met, and whose name I can't even now remember except that she was the author of *My Sister Eileen* [Ruth McKenny].

Kay had been informed on by the subsequently discredited Boston College professor Louis Budenz who was collecting $125 for each name he came up with. 'He was scraping the bottom of the barrel when he got to me.'

As soon as the hearing opened, William Shawn, editor of *The New Yorker*, for which she had been a foreign correspondent for several years, promptly withdrew her accreditation. Although her husband was unanimously cleared ('some of the jury even wept'), McCarthy didn't let the matter drop. Cohn and his sidekick were dispatched to Germany. Her husband lost his job and wasn't reinstated for nine years when finally Ed Morrow and William Shirer took up the case. By then she had become professor of English at San Francisco University. She was in her sixties. She joined her students in protesting against the Vietnam War. She was jailed with Joan Baez for sitting down outside an army induction centre. More recently she's been involved in the anti-war movement and has her own Amnesty group:

> The funny thing is as the years pass all that McCarthy thing obsesses me more and more. Perhaps because I think it may well happen again. Americans today remind me of when Hitler was coming to power. I would ask Germans what they liked about him. Oh, they said, he loves the nation, he loves the German

people. Well, that's what Americans now say about Reagan. Yet we've got soup kitchens again. Mayor Feinstein in San Francisco has to hand over the buses at night so that homeless people can sleep in them.

At creative writing classes she keeps getting stories from her students about silly little domestic quarrels between a husband and a wife. 'Don't you realize,' she tells them, 'a writer has to be committed to something more. You have to be committed to your time. Otherwise your writing has no value. You can't write in a safe vacuum. Camus said that the writer above all has to speak for those who cannot speak for themselves.' Some of the students became annoyed, claiming that writers should just get on with writing, and that they don't need to understand what's happening. But that has never been Kay Boyle's way. The quality that has made her one of the great story writers of her time is precisely the fact that her writing is of its time and through it we can understand that time. 'Don't talk about politics,' staff cautioned Boyle before she lectured at a Californian college – apparently there was an FBI spy in the class. 'So of course that's what I did talk about,' she says. 'The children had never heard of McCarthy. Someone had to tell them.'

E.L. Doctorow, 1989

The grandson of Russian Jewish immigrants, Edgar Doctorow studied drama at Columbia University before being drafted into the US army to serve as a corporal in Germany during the Allied occupation. Returning to New York in 1955, he found a job at a film company reading scripts for westerns, an experience that inspired his 1960 debut novel, Welcome to Hard Times. *To support his three children, he worked as a paperback book editor and then editor-in-chief of The Dial Press, where he published Norman Mailer, James Baldwin and William Kennedy, eventually establishing himself as a writer with* The Book of Daniel *in 1971, quickly followed by* Ragtime. *Like Philip Roth, he continued writing into his eighties, publishing his twelfth – and, sadly last – novel* Andrew's Brain *in 2014, one of his finest works, an ongoing dialogue between a cognitive scientist and a therapist that pushes the 'unreliable narrator' genre to an exhilarating dimension in which the trauma of the sudden loss of a lover opens out into a satire on the 'government brain' of George W. Bush's administration. Andrew explains to the president that 'as complex as our brains are, the numbers of elements that make them work are finite. That means it's just a matter of time before we have a working out-of-body brain.' Maybe so, but will it ever imagine a novel as sad, funny and exhilarating as* Andrew's Brain?

It's Thursday evening, early autumn. We're in a pub just off Piccadilly called Shelley's. 'Appropriate name,' Doctorow says. But there's nothing poetic about the blaring canned Ravel's *Bolero*. He winces. Music has always mattered to him. He'd go to sleep as a child to the sound of his mother playing the piano. 'She was a wonderful pianist. She paid for her lessons by playing in silent movies houses. Although she's ninety-two now, she can still sit down and play.'

His daughter is a musician, his brother, too. 'There's this music thing that goes through the family. But it went round me. They tried to make a pianist of me but I was just awful. I'd improvise and make up my own notes. I would drive the rest of the family crazy.' The music has come out in writing instead. 'The rhythm of the line has always been important to me, the sound of the words.' *Billy Bathgate*, which portrays the infamous gangster Dutch Schultz through the experiences of a Tom Sawyer-like Bronx youth on the make who tags along, flows like a song. Much of the magic of *Ragtime*, his evocation of turn-of-century America through three families, one WASP, one Jewish, one black, comes from the syncopated rhythm of the narrative. He got the idea for *Loon Lake*, a lyrical account of the adventures of a young hobo in the 1930s, from the alliterative sound of the name. 'I just saw it on a sign. It was so musical it started me off.'

His father had a record business and sold musical instruments in Manhattan's Hippodrome Theatre building back in the days of the 78rpm shellac records. 'He really knew his music and his stock reflected this and many of the reigning artists of the day ordered their records from him.' Not that life in the Bronx was as romantic as this might imply:

> Getting through the Depression was a major triumph for him. Before going off to work he'd give my mother fifty cents for the day's groceries. But I didn't know anything about this. My mother named me Edgar after Edgar Allen Poe. I was surrounded by books, toys and music. I went to the Bronx High School for Science, where I'd no right to be. They were all smart kids. They knew they were going to win the Nobel Prize in chemistry in ten years' time and they did. So I gravitated to the school's literary magazine and became a writer. I had a very rich and privileged childhood.

Quite the opposite of Billy Bathgate, who was deserted by his slightly dotty mother and Jewish father but in Schultz found the father figure he lacked: the gang became his family. 'I got to like those guys,' Doctorow says, drawing on his pint, a combination of Guinness and light beer, a half-and-half. He's a tall gangling man in an open-necked shirt and jersey, not unlike a college lecturer, and speaks so soft you have to lean forward to hear. 'They were a very highly structured, working, functioning family,' he says. 'Once you accept the initial premise of their criminality everything worked out. They had certain values and ambitions, they had self-respect.' Take away Billy's immersion in evil and you could be reading a Horatio Alger rags-to-riches yarn. 'Billy is what every boy should be. He's bright, he works hard, he's plucky, he's a good scout.' Similarly Dutch Schultz can be seen as the archetypal capitalist: his lawlessness equates with the American drive to get ahead. 'It's rugged individualism carried to extreme.'

This warped ethos is partly what prompted Doctorow to write *Billy Bathgate*:

> I'm like the historians who when they talk about the past are really talking about the present. There has been an erosion of social spirit. Every class in society is rampantly committing crimes appropriate to its circumstances, whether inside dealers on Wall Street or kids pushing dope in schools. We're right back to the nineteenth-century idea that the poor are responsible for their poverty and deserve everything that happens to them.

He breaks off with an apologetic smile. 'This is an old Franklin Delano Roosevelt New Dealer talking.'

Seeing the past through the eyes of an impressionable youth is a recurring Doctorow device. 'You can shamelessly exploit your own naiveté and cover it. You can capture the wonder and the beauty of seeing everything for the first time. I don't write novels, I write romances.' He's drawn to popular forms because they have the advantage of familiarity. 'It's a great strength for an audience to know what they're watching. People want to see Sophocles and Euripides because they know what the story was.'

It's how his first novel *Welcome to Hard Times* came about. He had a job advising movie executives who didn't read if a screen play was a good idea or not. 'I read all those dreadful westerns and figured I could lie better about the West than they could. I got interested in the idea of writing a really disreputable genre and trying to do something serious with it, working in counterpoint to the reader's expectations.' He's never had any qualms about appropriating real-life figures like Dutch Schultz for his fiction. His *The Book of Daniel*, dealing with the McCarthy hysteria in the 1950s, features Ethel and Julius Rosenberg, while Harry Houdini, Emma Goldman, Sigmund Freud and J.P. Morgan make cameo appearances in *Ragtime*.

There's a sense in which his novels taken together add up to a fictional history of America's last hundred years. 'When people complain that something didn't happen, I tell them it happened now.' All historical figures are partly fictional anyway. 'If you read the official biography of J.P. Morgan, it's a very creative work.'

For Doctorow, there's no fiction and no history, there's only narrative. Everyone creates narratives out of their own lives and the lives of others. They make sense of themselves through fictions. Putting real people in novels is no different to using real places: they situate fiction in society.

New York, particularly the Bronx, is the place Doctorow keeps being drawn to. 'It's the territory of my imagination. I love every inch of that city, as hideous as it has become. But my next novel probably will not be set there. I think I've finally got it the way I want it to be in *World's Fair* and *Billy Bathgate*, and now I'm leaving.' He plans to go into hiding for a while in his home in the little whaling village of Sag Harbor, about a hundred miles from New York, waiting to see what might come to him. 'There's always some accident attached to the writing of a particular book. But it's hard to explain. I used to know a lot more about writing than I do now. Now I just do it.'

J.P. Donleavy, 1986

Johnny Depp claims that without J.P. Donleavy's iconic 1953 novel The Ginger Man, *which has sold over fifty million copies, there might never have been Hunter S. Thompson. Having filmed Thompson's cult classic* Fear and Loathing in Las Vegas, *Depp talked about doing the same with Donleavy's loosely auto-biographical account of a sexually marauding young American student at TCD on the loose in Dublin after the Second World War. Not much seems to have come of it, despite visits to the overgrown 180-acre estate on the shores of Lough Owel in County Westmeath where the author lived the life of country squire amid 'an enormous reservoir' of his paintings. A number of these were exhibited at the Molesworth Gallery in Dublin, and later in New York, to celebrate his eightieth birthday in 2006. Donleavy, who died eleven years later, joked, 'I'm the painter who became the writer who's been rediscovered as a painter.' The show included a portrait painted by Robert Ballagh depicting Donleavy as a country gentleman in tweed suit and waistcoat, glasses dangling round his neck, a silk handkerchief in his lapel pocket. Apart from the white hair, he looks remarkably like the younger Donleavy who burst into my small office in* The Sunday Tribune *twenty years earlier, saying he preferred to be interviewed there rather than on his estate because he was curious to see the inside of a newspaper.*

J.P. Donleavy claims that becoming a writer was easy enough – particularly in Dublin in the 1940s where you only had to say you were one to be believed – but surviving at it was something else. He's been doing so with varying degrees of success since being told by Brendan Behan, 'Sure I'm a writer and you're a writer too.'

Donleavy arrived at Trinity College from the Bronx, fresh out of the American Navy under the GI Bill, 'to take his degree in drinking and harlotry in the Dublin pubs.' Behan read and corrected the first 120 pages of his unpublished novel *The Ginger Man*, signing his name at the top of the manuscript at the point where he stopped. 'The astonishing thing about Behan was that he was so sure of himself as a writer. Things I'd crossed out, he'd write "put back in." Looking back I realize I followed quite a lot of his suggestions although I was angry about them at the time.'

Donleavy has been doing a bit of looking back. *The Ginger Man* was a fictional celebration of those rumbustious days of Americans at large in the Dublin of Anthony Cronin's *Dead as Doornails*. But now he's decided to tell it as it really was (or perhaps more accurately, seemed to be) in his memoir *Ireland in Some of Her Sins and Some of Her Graces*. It's been an act of rueful recall he embarked upon not without considerable trepidation. 'It took me two years to sign the contract.' But doing it gave him the urge to tell even more. Using the same format he's launched into a second book dealing with the long agonizing history of *The Ginger Man* and a litigation war waged over three continents.

The fact that Donleavy spends his life ensconced in a big house on an estate near Mullingar might suggest that fortune has been kind to him. But not the way he tells it. His tale of literary woe becomes a crash course in How to Survive As a Writer.

LESSON ONE: COMING TO TERMS WITH FAME
'American writers normally get thrown by fame,' he says. 'It's always something connected with money and it's always something an American writer has to fight with. But if it comes early enough in his career he may learn to handle it as a tool. It's necessary for economic survival because, let's face it, if no one knows who the hell you are you can't sell anything.'

Becoming a painter neatly solved the problem for Donleavy, not that he'd ever painted before. Impressed by the prices and delighted by the whorls of colour of a Yeats exhibition at the Victor Waddington Gallery, he rushed out to buy paints, brush and canvas. With John Ryan's help he was soon exhibiting at the Dublin Painters' Gallery. 'Semi-abstract stuff, not half bad,' he says. Paintings he didn't sell he's kept. 'There are hundreds of them and they still retain their personality.'

Writing catalogues for his exhibitions was the part he enjoyed most, so much so that he began having exhibitions so that he could write catalogues. 'I became famous as it were for the first time and got over a lot of initial obstacles that most people have to confront in their career.' Then he chuckles. 'Of course in Dublin to be famous was a matter for everyone. If three people in the same room know who you are, you're famous.'

LESSON TWO: BECOME AN EXPERT IN LITIGATION

Encouraged by Brendan Behan – 'This book is going to go around the world and beat the bejaysus out of the Bible' – Donleavy dispatched *The Ginger Man* to Maurice Girodias, whose Olympia Press in Paris got away with publishing the most outrageous porn by including serious writers like Genet, Beckett and Nabokov in its lists. Donleavy has been in dispute with Girodias ever since over rights. 'The twenty or thirty letters that passed between us constituted the agreement, since there was nothing else. It left open a large area of dispute.'

To get control back over his book Donleavy ultimately had to buy the Olympia Press for £5000 at a bankruptcy auction in Paris. 'So I ended up suing myself. I had to conduct the action in court, Olympia Press vs JP Donleavy.' He smiles with rueful satisfaction. 'I managed to settle with myself.'

With Olympia he acquired about 250 copyrights of all kinds of writers. 'They're subject to various agreements and I don't know what the position is on a lot of them. But Olympia is now regarded as one of the most famous publishing houses of all time.' It's an experience Donleavy could have done without. 'There's nothing worse for a writer than to have your work actually stopped. No author should have to go through what I've gone through. I might see it as amusing now but for years it was a nightmare.'

In the thick of litigation he became a virtual recluse. 'I know how Howard Hughes feels because I had to live the same way myself. A lot of people thought Hughes was crazy but he was just an intelligent businessman who was being used by everyone. He was compelled to live like that.'

Donleavy has ended up becoming one of the few authors to know everything about contracts and copyright. He does all his own legal work. Girodias even paid him the back-handed compliment, 'You may have doubts about Donleavy as a writer but have no doubts about him as one of the great legal geniuses of all time.'

LESSON THREE (PARTICULARLY IMPORTANT FOR A WRITER NEARING SIXTY): MAKE SURE TO KEEP FIT
'The dangerous thing about writing is that it's so sedentary,' he says. 'Having been an athlete I'm very conscious of the need to keep the body moving all day long.' Donleavy welcomes the chance to scythe thistles, cut hedgerows and build drystone walls on his estate. 'But heavy manual work isn't suffi-cient, its effect is nearly all psychological. To keep fit you have to do delib-erate exercises.' He thinks nothing of following up two hours of physical work with twenty minutes' running, or maybe a game of De Alfonce tennis, which he invented especially for exercise purposes.

'It's much more vigorous than ordinary tennis or even squash. We use a very light racket and a very light ball and we serve the ball at nearly 200 mph.

Yet it's so easy that almost anyone can play it. Some of the local lads of twelve or thirteen are practically unbeatable.'

All this activity ensures that he sleeps well at night. Indeed he enjoys bed so much he's taken to staying there for breakfast and to write. 'Sometimes I start work at 6 am using that method. The fact that the body is covered up releases it psychologically and you find you can concentrate. Once you get up and move around your attention begins to get diverted.'

He surveys my small room, the overcrowded shelves, the books and papers piled on the floor, the typewriter perched perilously on the edge of the desk. 'Maybe you should just have a bed here,' he suggests.

Ariel Dorfman, 1999

When the CIA revealed that Russia had hacked the American Democratic Party's computers and leaked thousands of Hillary Clinton emails in order to swing the presidential election in Donald Trump's favour, Ariel Dorfman experienced a dreadful sense of déjà vu. *'I have been through this before, overwhelmed by similar outrage and alarm,' he wrote in the* New York Times *on 16 December 2016. Back in 1970 in the aftermath of Salvador Allende's election as president of Chile there had been evidence that America was actively plotting his overthrow. The CIA eventually engineered a successful military coup by General Pinochet in 1973. Dorfman, who worked for Allende, narrowly escaped capture and eventually became a professor at Duke University in North Carolina. 'As an American citizen now, I am once again a victim of this sort of foreign meddling,' he wrote, calling for a thorough independent and transparent investigation 'because the legitimacy of Trump's presidency depends on it'. Dorfman, who successfully campaigned to have Pinochet arrested in the UK for war crimes, visited Belfast in 1999, where we spent some hours together.*

Turn off the Falls Road in Belfast into a maze of narrow terraced streets and it's easy to get lost. We inch slowly past a large *Gerry Adams Brings Peace* mural, trying to find a way out. Ariel Dorfman sits in the front seat, unperturbed. 'You don't know where you're going until you get lost,' he says.

Although he's never been in Belfast before tonight, it's as if he's back in the Chile he fled after the Pinochet coup in 1973 and that is now tentatively trying to return to full democracy. My worry is that we'll take a wrong turn and having eluded death in Chile, it will finally catch up on him through my fault. He seems blissfully unaware of any danger. 'It's so recognizable here,' he says. 'There are things we both know. We know about loss. We know about screwing things up. We know about doing everything for the right reasons. We know about burying the dead. We know about hating so much that we end up hating ourselves.' An armoured car is parked at a corner, its door open. Two RUC men have got out and are about to give a driver a parking ticket. 'That's what democracy brings you,' says Dorfman. 'It brings you traffic tickets.'

He's in Belfast with a Mexican artist, Alfonso López Monreal, who is print-maker in residence at the Arts Council. 'Ironically, living in Belfast has enabled me to understand Mexico better,' López Monreal tells him. 'Nearly all the work I've done here has been memories of there. One of the fascinating things about Mexico is that we have the Stone Age just around the corner from contemporary modern technological consumer society. Half an hour away from Mexico City you have communities that have never changed. Spanish colonization sought to destroy this other culture by imposing its own instead.'

The following afternoon Dorfman was in the House of Lords in London to hear the historic 1999 ruling rejecting General Pinochet's appeal against the British Government's refusal to allow him diplomatic immunity. 'The point is that no matter what the law lords say, Chile is still going to have to face its demons,' he says. 'Whether Pinochet goes on trial or returns to Chile heroically, we can't absolve ourselves from the fact that we have to deal with our demons. What I care about in the judgement is that it should be established that a chief of state is not immune from prosecution for human rights violations. That's the fundamental thing that should be done.'

Dorfman already anticipated the trial of Pinochet in his play *Death and the Maiden*, later filmed by Roman Polanski. The character of the doctor, in an unnamed Latin American country, who is abducted by a woman he tortured and made to answer for his actions, clearly stands for Pinochet and his regime. 'What I did is a prophecy of the trial. I did the trial because history wouldn't do the trial.' With a gun in her hand, the woman fails to shoot her abuser. The play ends at a concert when she and her husband catch sight of the doctor, listening to the same music. 'History imposed on me the ending where you have to co-exist with your oppressor. The torturer gets off scot-free and nothing happens to him. Which is what generally happens in history, usually dictators live to a ripe old age off everything they've stolen. This is a century of one Nuremberg but thousands of Milosevics. They corrupt the globe.'

Dorfman should have been in Santiago's Moneda Palace on 11 September 1973 when General Pinochet launched his coup against the democratically elected socialist government of President Allende. He was cultural and media adviser to Allende's chief of staff. 'I should have died and did not,' he says. A colleague with whom he'd swopped shifts died instead.

Dorfman hid in the Israeli embassy, watching on TV as soldiers threw his satirical book, *How To Read Donald Duck,* onto a bonfire, and was eventually forced into exile in Argentina where he'd been born in 1942. His parents were brought there as infants after their parents fled the Jewish pogroms in Russia. Dorfman was just over a year old when his father was denounced by the new pro-Hitler government as 'dirty dog Jew Dorfman'. Before he could be jailed he fled with his family to America where he got a job at the newly formed United Nations. Although he had diplomatic immunity, he was hounded out by McCarthy in 1953 and forced to accept an alternative posting in Chile.

It was yet another uprooting for his eleven-year-old son Ariel who had grown up wanting to be American to a point where he refused to speak Spanish even to his parents. 'Disney had adopted me and said it's all right. You can be free. You can be a pain in the ass. You can be whatever you want.' But, of course, he couldn't, much like Gabriel, the protagonist in his novel *The Nanny and the Iceberg* who 'keeps trying to escape history but finds out that, in fact, he's been determined by history way before he ever knew it.' Dorfman can't dodge fate. It's even in his names. His father called him Vladimiro after Lenin: his mother preferred Ariel, the spirit of goodness and magic from Shakespeare's *Tempest.* As a schoolboy Dorfman insisted on being Edward after a character in Twain's *The Prince and the Pauper,* reflecting his identification with American culture.

Never really belonging anywhere, he sought identity in language. He began writing seriously after a journey to Europe with his parents. On the ship they met Thomas Mann who was returning to Germany for the first time since fleeing the Nazis. He asked Mann what language he wrote in. 'German,' said Mann.

So back in Chile Dorfman finally embraced Spanish. With the future Argentinian president Arturo Frondizi and the future Guyanese president Cheddi Jagan, regular visitors at his home, he inevitably became involved in student politics, campaigning for Allende's 'gentle revolution' in the 1964 elections. A spell at the University of California in 1968 further radicalized him. On the night of the Pinochet coup an Allende minister, Fernando Flores, crossed his name off the roster of people to be called in. Years later, Dorfman asked him why. 'Well someone had to live to tell the story.' This is what Dorfman has done. 'If it isn't true, it makes sense,' he says. 'Once you have been spared, you make sense of the life that has been given to you.'

For two years after the coup, he couldn't write a word. 'I was a blank page. I couldn't tell the story. I had been spared and I was speechless. I didn't want to write propaganda. Bad literature is when you know what is good and evil ahead of time. Good literature is when you don't know and you're trying to figure it out.' Poetry liberated him. 'I began looking for the voices of the disappeared and the survivors. And their voices were somehow the ones that rescued me. I realized that the dead were depending on me to give them burial.'

Whether in his poems, or his novels or plays, Dorfman avoids preaching. Returning briefly from exile in 1991 – he now lives with his wife and children in North Carolina – he challenged the political reasoning that allowed Pinochet immunity on the grounds that not to do so would jeopardize the fragile democracy established after his surprise defeat in the 1988 election:

> When democracy just begins, you're testing waters, so you don't want to do anything to rock the boat. But what happens as the years go by is that the people in power get used to nobody rocking the boat. What politicians have done in Chile is that they've made democracy fragile by saying it's so fragile we can't touch it. Well, no. You've got to bring people into the process of defining democracy, testing it and pushing it. If you don't, it's not a true democracy.

Lawrence Durrell, 1985

As an author with a predilection of writing his novels in groups – a quintet, a quartet or just a duo – Lawrence Durrell would no doubt have appreciated the irony of ending up as a character in a major ITV miniseries in 2016. The Durrells is adapted from his youngest brother Gerald's three autobiographical books about their penniless widowed mother's chaotic attempts to rear them on the cheap in Corfu in the 1930s. The series, adapted by Simon Nye, is only loosely based on the original books: as producer Sally Woodward Sentle pointed out, 'Gerald and Lawrence Durrell didn't tell the truth either, they didn't let truth stand in the way of a good story'. The miniseries is produced by Christopher Hall, whose 85-year-old mother Leslie Caron has a cameo role. Such was its success that by the end of the year an additional six episodes were already in production and a third series was filming at the end of 2017. Throughout his career Lawrence avoided England as much as he could, going there only when his publisher absolutely insisted. Which is how we met in 1985, appropriately in a borrowed house in Islington.

Whatever about Kay Boyle's doubts, there has been probably no more exhilarating decade in the history of modern letters than Paris in the 1920s. All these years later, Woody Allen can still pack cinemas by evoking its name-dropping glamour in his 2011 time-warp comedy *Midnight in Paris*.

But maybe that's just Paris always. The Americans who gave the city its twenties glamour and jazz drifted home in the aftermath of the Wall Street Crash, but through the 1930s it continued to provide shelter to émigré writers and painters as it had always done, and still does. Henry Miller and Anaïs Nin were still there, entertaining Lawrence Durrell at the Villa Seurat where they set up a publishing company to launch his novel *The Black Book*. During the war Durrell worked as a press attaché in various British embassies, living in Greece and Egypt and Argentina before moving to the village of Sommières, between Nîmes and Montpellier in the south of France, where in a secluded house with a walled garden he dreamed up his *The Avignon Quintet* (1974–1985), just as his earlier days in Egypt inspired *The Alexandria Quartet* (1957–1960). His writing seems to come from the stimulus of being from somewhere else.

After the death of his fourth wife Ghislaine de Boysson in 1975 he stayed on in Sommières, alone. 'It's like living in an Irish village,' he says a decade later. 'You never feel lonely because everyone is on first-name terms. I've had twenty years of playing bowls with them, and going to their bullfights. I've received nothing but warmth and kindness.' He writes in a room without windows. There is no television to distract him. 'When I want that I go to Paris and leave it on all day to find out the latest *cause célèbre*, and when I've absorbed all that I go back to my village and vegetate.'

As he will after this rare visit to London that has brought us together. The door of the terraced house where he is staying in Shepherd's Bush is off the latch, a habit acquired from living in rural France. I push it open and find him standing on his head in the hallway. 'By now I'm able to stay in this yoga position for twenty minutes,' he says, lowering himself back onto his feet.

He shows me into a room strewn with books and manuscripts. He could have stayed at the Connaught as his publishers wished, but he prefers a place where he can potter about.

'When instinct hardens into dogma, it goes dead,' his alter ego Blandford says in *The Avignon Quintet*, a set of five novels about the same characters, which he has just completed with *Quinx*. 'So they kept everything fluid.' Durrell naturally agrees. 'That's where poets come in,' he says. 'They snatch at things.'

Perhaps after twelve novels, he'll go back to verse: his first poems were published by T.S. Eliot after the war. 'I've a poetry notebook full of leads.

Slogans, almost. Reading it is like travelling across London on the top of a bus. If I'm now retiring from the ring, and still have a few more years left, I might take it up again, together with painting, occupational therapy for the geriatric ward.' The strain of keeping a grip on the shimmering complexities of *The Avignon Quintet* – half the characters in the five novels exist only in the imagination of the other half – nearly proved too much for him. 'I'm running out of stamina. It was such a fright that I started drinking a bottle of whiskey a day.'

During this traumatic period his daughter Sappho-Jane committed suicide after her husband left her. 'It's been an enormous thump.' He'd lived with her almost as a recluse in Cyprus in the early 1950s, out of which came *Bitter Lemons* (1957) and inklings of *Justine*, the first of *The Alexandria Quartet* novels. 'I thought I'd become an alcoholic last year. I didn't see any way out. I began hiding bottles around the house so that I could have a sup in every room.' He was saved by a French doctor who practised acupuncture. 'She filled me full of drawing pins and I went to sleep for a quarter of an hour.'

He's been in a state of post-hypnotic suggestion ever since. 'I'm living between glasses. It hangs absolutely on a hair. When I see a glass I reach out for it but my hand stays in mid-air. I'm just playing along to see if it will continue. It may even be permanent. What a miracle to find something without chemicals.' He's lost weight and has doubled his yoga time. Even so he doubts if at seventy-three he'll undertake another novel. 'I don't think I've much more to say. I'm putting myself out to grass. You can't go on forever outstaying your welcome. I don't want to go nuts. It's such an indignity.'

To cheer him up I summon back his alter ego. 'The sperm does not age as man himself does,' Blandford assures us. 'Even an old man can be young inside.' He so obviously enjoys creating fiction that it's difficult to imagine him finally giving it up. It's the reality he knows best. Like Blandford, he has in a sense become a fiction of his fiction. 'Life is a complete lie,' he says. 'I like to throw it into doubt in the interests of good fun.' Then he smiles 'That's my Irish side, I suppose.'

His mother was from Northern Ireland, but he's vague about the details. 'She knew things she took with her because in those days we never bothered about documents. If there is a touch of Irish in me, it's whimsical to pretend it's very much.'

Being born in 1912 near the foothills of the Himalayas in India, where his father was in the colonial service, has contributed to his confusion of identity. 'I grew up more English than the English. Rather like a Sikh. I was reared on Dickens, Thackeray and Surtees. My England was the England of Ruskin and Omar Khayyam and Rupert Brooke. It was only when I got to England that I then realized my imagined England was not real.'

While waiting for a public-school place to fall vacant he went to Saviour's Grammar School in the centre of London. 'My Shakespeare was learned in the shadow of Tower Bridge.' Eventually he was taken by St Edmund's in Canterbury. 'Not one of the more prestigious public schools, but a clergy orphans' school beautifully located on a hill. It looked like a Betjeman drawing. Because it was small it wasn't snobbish. There was little bullying as far as I can remember, and hardly any homosexuality.' He quite happily allowed himself to be indoctrinated in public-school virtues. 'The stiff upper lip, and think before you speak, and always say yes but on the other hand.' He remembers the sunny Sundays, his pockets full of cherries, lying in the long grass and listening to cricket bat on ball, 'One of the most superlative musical experiences you can have in England.'

Being absolutely hopeless at mathematics, without which it was impossible then to get into Oxford or Cambridge, saved him from following his father into the colonial service. 'But not having a university degree became an enormous hindrance to me, particularly when I got work later on with the British Council. I had to keep proving I was literate and could talk BBC English.' Perhaps this is partly why he's chosen to spend so much of his life elsewhere. He's been living away from England so long now that he thinks in French when he writes. 'English gets too bulgy and self-indulgent by itself. It's so rich and so beautiful that if you're an injudicious person like me you just end up with a bubble bath. The French influence is a steadying one, a logical one. You need the two to make a good grain.' He considers himself a European rather than an English writer. 'I like to think that I was a Common Market writer who appeared before his time.'

His notorious novel *The Black Book*, published in Paris in 1937 when he was hanging around with his idol Henry Miller, is probably still before its time, although Faber have brought out what he calls a 'reverent' new edition. Rivalling in obscenity Miller's own *Tropic of Cancer*, but hailed by T.S. Eliot as 'the first piece of work by a new English writer to give me any hope for the future of prose fiction', it shocked even Durrell himself. 'I'm not really very revolutionary,' he says. 'I'm rather a funk. Using those four-lettered words that I knew were considered obscene went against the grain socially.' Without the support of Eliot and Miller, he might never have written anything else. 'But *The Black Book* really was an agony. I nearly had a breakdown. I didn't know what I was writing. But I felt I had to go on in that way and believe in it.'

He still believes in it but isn't so sure about the kind of permissive society it ushered in. 'Sex is not dying, it is coming of age with the freedom of women,' Blandford interrupts. But Durrell has his doubts about the imminent sperm bank civilization, what he calls 'the taming of the screw'. 'We're living in a period of complete disillusionment. Everything goes. It's liberating a great many people, but perhaps not entirely in desirable ways. I can't decide whether it's a good or a bad thing.' But it's not the novelist's job to offer answers:

> It would be acting in bad faith to suggest that I had any special philosophy to sell. I haven't. All a novelist can do is to pass an electric charge along the wire so that the reader gets a little shock or massage. It doesn't really matter what you say. The reader needn't believe anything that you believe in. The important thing is that you infect the readers in some way that they can identify it with their own preoccupations and their own worries. That way some sort of real exchange takes place.

Durrell likes to think that readers make up his novels as they go along, which is why they have defied filming. There are as many *Alexandria Quartet*s as there are readers. Not even co-directors George Cukor and Joseph Strick could give cinematic life to *Justine* in 1968. Dirk Bogarde plays the role of Durrell's alter ego Pursewarden, a British consular official in Alexandria who introduces a young schoolmaster, Darley (Michael York), to an Egyptian banker's wife, but she turns out to be involved in a plot to arm the Jewish underground movement in Palestine. 'It finished up like *Peyton Place* on camels,' says Durrell. 'The casting was inspired. Anouk Aimée might have been born Justine. She felt very strongly about the part and wanted to do it. But a film is an absolutely incalculable thing. So many people are meddling with it and it needs so much money to get off the ground and to keep in motion. They live on handouts and afterthoughts all the time.'

That's not a fate that's likely to befall *The Avignon Quintet*. Its characters, to quote Blandford, 'are not separate characters as they think, they are variations of themes outside themselves'. Ultimately they all merge into one character that is Durrell himself. 'I wanted to leave behind a kind of auto-biography,' he says. Not just with *The Avignon Quintet*, but with *The*

Alexandria Quartet, The Black Book, Tunc (1968) and *Nunquam* (1970). 'I hoped all my novels would melt together into what the French would call an *oeuvre*.'

The characters in the *Quintet* are partly extensions of some of those in the *Quartet*, not actually named but easily recognizable. 'I'm not a very copious novelist. I have to get by on a shoestring of characters. I just change the lighting all the time to keep them viable.' While *The Alexandria Quartet* drew on the Freudian and Einstein concept of relativity, with the four novels viewing the same characters from a different angle, *The Avignon Quintet* is inspired by the sense of oneness from oriental philosophy. 'The paradigm is still the same but the values have changed.'

He now prefers like Blandford to obey the logic of instinct, rolling with the punches. Perhaps as a child in India he was touched by emanation from Buddha. 'For old age, yoga and Buddha are not a bad mixture. That's the way I'd like to sign off. Phase myself out agreeably in the lotus position.'

Anne Enright, 2008

Anne Enright, in her introduction to The Granta Book of the Irish Short Story *(2010), which she edited, likens short stories to 'the cats of literary form: beautiful but a little too self-contained for some people's tastes'. She has shown a mastery of the short story form that puts her on a par with Frank O'Connor, Seán Ó Faoláin and William Trevor. Although I published her first story in New Irish Writing in 1989, a literary page for emerging writers I edited in* The Sunday Tribune, *we didn't meet for an interview until 2008, some months after she won the Booker Prize with her novel* The Gathering. *She returned to the* Gathering *theme of a family reunion in her widely acclaimed 2015 novel* The Green Road, *but this time in the third person, which allowed her to shift between differing points of view.*

'Let's share a thought with a heavily pregnant woman who finds herself alone in an elevator with a strange man. I always look people in the eye, you know? she's thinking. This is just the way I am.'

So here I am looking into the eyes of Anne Enright who created this fleeting moment in 'Shaft', a short story from her new collection, *Talking Pictures*. 'I use people's voices a lot in my stories,' she says, as we sip coffee in The Four Seasons. Her eyes are brown and watchful. 'But I don't necessarily agree with my characters.'

She recalls how someone stood up after she gave a reading in Trinity College and said, somewhat bemused, 'Men are not all that bad.' This was in response to her story 'Until The Girl Died', which is about an unfaithful husband caught out by his wife when his girlfriend dies in a car crash. 'The woman in the story says this and that about men,' says Enright. 'But her ideas are not mine. I don't have large ideas about men. I sort of take them on a case-by-case basis. What that story is really about is not about men but about getting old. Or actually it's about getting middle-aged. People who panic about age are usually in their forties. After fifty or sixty, you don't care. You kind of say, oh yeah I used to be old.'

Never mind that Enright's extraordinary fourth novel *The Gathering*, a surprise winner of the Booker Prize, deals with a dysfunctional Irish family torn apart by quarrels, neglect and suicide, or that *Talking Pictures* is mainly inhabited by women who are alone and unloved, survivors of a brutal marriage, suffering from anorexia or trying to kill each other. The dark adventurous ambiguity of her work eludes neat categorization. You start each sentence with the unsettling suspicion that it may be time-bombed.

While her fiction may have a reputation for being 'gloomy and obsessed with sex and death', increasing numbers of readers are looking behind these preconceptions and relishing what they find. Long admired by literary critics for her fiercely individual voice, Enright has watched sales of *The*

Gathering soar from a mere 834 copies when it was published by Jonathan Cape less than a year ago – and 3253 copies just before her Booker triumph – to over 250,000 copies by last month. She's been on *The New York Times* bestseller list for twenty-three weeks. 'I don't understand it,' she says. 'I don't have to understand it. I just enjoy it.'

With two small children, Rachel and Lorcan – she is married to actor Martin Murphy, who runs the Pavilion Theatre in Dun Laoghaire – she has no intention of being sucked into any celebrity whirl. 'I want to tell people that actually I can only do this part-time. It's much easier to write the books part-time than it is to be a Booker winner part-time. People say, oh why can't you do this and why can't you do that. I say I'm going to be picking up my kids in a couple of hours' time.

'My theory is that you can only do three things with your life – you can have a relationship, you can have kids and you can have work, but you can't have a big social life, you can forget about that. There is a whole swathe of things we quite cheerfully forgot about for the last seven years. I don't miss them, either. Only two things happen in our house, and that's work and kids. That's all. It's a very focused existence.'

Whether with her stories or her novels –*The Gathering* is her fourth – Enright challenges perceptions of what Irish fiction should be. 'I have to laugh at Irish people who think I am selling the same old image of Ireland abroad, of awful things happening. I'm not selling anything to anyone particularly. You write a book. You don't say I'm going to tell the truth about Ireland to the people of Peoria.

'People get labelled for all kinds of different reasons. I'm reading a lot of William Trevor stories at the moment and many of them are about sex – there's wife-swapping and all kinds of things like that going on – but nobody ever says William Trevor writes about sex. He's a man, so it's not in any way remarkable.'

Because Enright writes mostly in the first person through the eyes of women characters, there's a misconception that she's writing about herself. 'So people after *The Gathering* are looking at me in a slightly aghast sort of way. And I'm saying, you know, I made it up. It wasn't me. But that doesn't bother me because people who are close to me know that anyway, and I'm not so worried about other people.'

There are elements of an actor in the way a writer becomes other selves, taking on roles. 'It's like you bring some sort of emotional ghost of yourself to the work. It is that mixture of trying to keep yourself open without feeling vulnerable. You draw on life but you turn things upside down, so that someone English you know might surface as an American, or a woman as a man.

'It's an old trick from when as a student I was in Trinity Players along with all the people who became Rough Magic and Martin, who became my husband, and there'd be reams and reams of male parts in a show. So you'd rename parts and cast them with women.'

Enright published her first fiction in New Irish Writing when she was twenty-seven. 'It had been accepted for *The Faber Book of Introductions* at that stage, but it hadn't been published yet so it was my first outing in print ever. A terrible short story, I have to say, set in a court that might have been of Ivan the Terrible. I remember writing it on a clunky clickety-click typewriter my parents had given me. I had to cut and paste the paragraphs as I was rearranging them. For someone who redrafts so much, it was a very protracted process. I really needed the computer to come along.'

Both her parents were civil servants. She grew up between Templeogue and Kimmage, just where the country met the town lands. 'You'd go picking blackberries on Wellington Lane. On weekends, we'd go up the mountains. We never went into town, not until I was about ten.'

She was educated by the St Louis nuns in nearby Rathmines, but it wasn't a typical convent school. 'You always hate your school because you're supposed to but in retrospect it was a very good school,' she laughs. 'They liked a girl to have a bit of spirit. They didn't try to beat every idea out of your head to get you through the Leaving Cert. There was drama and debating and a lot of getting up on your hind legs, when I think about it. All the religion classes took the form of discussions. I wrote very bad poetry, and some monologues, which I do still in a funny way but just call it a story.

'Where I started from was that words were words. You could have fun. It wasn't about reality at all. The reality thing was incidental.'

This was particularly true of her first novel *The Wig My Father Wore* (1995) (a sort of magic-realism-with-a-Dublin-accent tale) about an RTÉ producer in love with an angel who committed suicide – that anticipated by about ten years the Celtic Tiger phenomenon of single girls with loads of money. She'd already won the Rooney prize with her debut short story collection *The Portable Virgin*, written on weekends while she was in RTÉ producing the groundbreaking satirical show *Nighthawks*. 'I always felt I was essentially a writer,' she says.

After Trinity, she'd won a scholarship to the University of East Anglia's Creative Writing Course run by Angela Carter and Malcolm Bradbury. 'I was a horrible student. I just sat there looking at Malcolm, loaded with disrespect because he wasn't my type of writer at the time. He didn't mind. He was completely ego-free and generous. Angela just ignored the work entirely. She discussed what are you going to do with your life, why are you going back to Ireland, which in the 1980s was a provincial backwater.

'These courses don't teach you anything, what they do is allow you to work. The job of the tutor is to keep you secure and to provide some kind of echo. It's the idea of getting it out anywhere rather than in your head all the time. So many people think they're writers but they're not putting the words on the page. I didn't write anything that was any good there. I was blown hither and thither by my emotions.

'I think over the years you realize that your emotions about your work don't have an awful lot to do with it. They are part of the process, obviously. But you finish the work and it's shite, and then everybody loves it. Or you think it's wonderful, and it's completely ignored. So you learn after a while that whatever you think about the work is a bit like a nervous tic or a spasm of some description, and the work doesn't care. It's just sitting there on the page. People will read it whatever way they read it. You have to let that happen.'

Enright has no urge to write for theatre, still less for cinema. The act of writing alone better suits her subversive instincts. 'It's the last resort of the individual voice,' she says. Her children once asked her about her work. 'The great thing is, you've no boss,' she told them. 'That's why I write.'

Her short stories are seldom more than a few thousand words. 'Things tend to condense,' she says. 'So the short story is a natural form for me and quite an instinctual one. The Irish short story doesn't do what it's supposed to do any more. It can do what it likes. In one, or two, or three steps, there it is. You just have to wait for the next one. They sit in the computer for a very long time, waiting.

'When I said I don't have any large ideas, if I did have a large idea it would be that large ideas are the enemy of fiction. Ideology is another way of describing the world that is more distant from lived experience. You have to keep your language close to what actually happens, so that it stays free.'

Louise Erdrich, 1995

Robbed of their lands and now mainly living in reservations, Native Americans have long struggled to find their proper place in American culture. They remain dogged by the racist stereotype of savage 'injuns' popularized by the Hollywood western. Louise Erdrich is one of a handful of their writers to have broken through into mainstream literature. Winner of the 1984 National Book Critics Circle Award with Love Medicine, *a finalist for the Pulitzer Fiction Prize in 2009 for* Plague of Doves *and winner of the 2012 National Book Award for* The Round House, *Erdrich is a leading figure in the Native American Renaissance. Her novel* Future Home of the Living God, *published in November 2017 and acclaimed by* The New York Times *for its 'shades of Atwood and Vonnegut', views a dystopian world of evolution in reverse through the diaries of a pregnant 24-year-old part-Ojibwe Indian who wonders if perhaps 'our level of intelligence could be a maladaptation, a wrong turn, an aberration'. Erdrich was married to Michael Dorris, her former tutor and a pioneer of Native American studies. They frequently collaborated on books, but divorced in 1996 when police investigated allegations that Dorris may have abused their daughters. Suffering from depression, he committed suicide the following year, aged fifty-two, telling a friend that he didn't want his family to suffer the trauma of a court trial. There was little inkling of this tragedy to come when we met in London in March 1995.*

It's hard to tell where a Louise Erdrich novel ends and a Michael Dorris novel begins. Their creative relationship is so close – quite apart from their marriage – that they draw on the same imaginative pool for characters and situations. 'Our fictional characters are like an extended family,' says Dorris.

They live with them for months before writing a word. Only then do they agree who's going to be the author. 'We do write each book separately, but only after we've talked about it thoroughly,' says Erdrich. 'It's a wonderful thing, because if we come to some block or problem, we can always go to each other and ask for a fresh point of view, a new voice.'

Dorris elaborates. 'Before a book goes out we basically concur on all parts of it, reading it out loud together, word by word. If one of us feels strongly that something should go in or come out, it always does.'

As happened when he almost finished his debut novel *A Yellow Raft in Blue Water*: after a long discussion with Erdrich he changed the main character from a boy to a girl. 'The characters write the books almost as much as we do,' he says. 'Once we figure out who these people are and we have a general framework of situations, they take over. We listen to their story. One of us might say to the other in the midst of writing, you'll never believe what so-and-so just did. And we'll then sit down and try to figure out why they did it and puzzle about what they'll do as a result of it.'

To pay the bills in the early stages of their careers they also wrote romance fiction under the name of Milou North, much of it published in the British magazine *Woman*. Philip Roth acclaimed Erdrich for her debut novel *Love Medicine* in 1985 as 'the most interesting new American novelist to have emerged in years'. Since then she has developed her concern for the devastation of the Native American way of life in *The Beet Queen*, *Tracks* and *The Bingo Palace*, the four novels interweaving to provide extraordinarily intimate and sensual insights into the plight of Chippewa Indians in North Dakota from the beginning of the century.

Dorris dedicates his books to Erdrich and she dedicates hers to him: 'To Michael, Complice in every word, essential as air' (*The Beet Queen*); 'The story comes up different every time but always begins with you' (*Tracks*). Yet despite the shared origins of their material each has emerged as a distinctive voice. In the actual writing, the same imaginary world they draw on makes other use of multiple narrators and intensity and richness of separate personal visions.

Dorris, an anthropologist who turned to fiction with the encouragement of Erdrich, approaches the situation of dispossessed Native Americans somewhat differently in *A Yellow Raft in Blue Water*, which is set on an Indian reservation in Montana and moves backwards in time through the conflicting memories of three different women: its theme is the tragedy of family members trapped in their own subjectivity.

'I'm drawn to the mode of different people telling the same story and adding their two bits,' he says. 'Everyone has their own perspective and believes it is right but the truth is some imaginary place in between all the versions of the story.'

Erdrich, who has a German-American father and French-Chippewa Indian mother, is a member of the Turtle Mountain Band of Chippewa. Dorris is all-Irish on his mother's side. 'The family name was Mannion and my grandmother came from Roscommon and Mayo at the turn of the century.' His father, a US army officer killed in a jeep accident in Germany when Dorris was two – it has been suggested it may have been suicide – was a Modoc Indian. 'We're both enrolled members of our respective tribes,' he says.

There are more than two hundred Indian reservations in America, each of which enjoys a government-to-government relationship to US state senates. 'They're legally defined domestic dependent nations, sort of like Lichtenstein in relation to Switzerland. They have their own judicial system, their own educational systems. So we're dual citizens in effect. When Louise is on her own reservation as a tribal member she is under the jurisdiction of the tribe, which is not the same as the US. There are different tax laws and all that kind of stuff. I don't think there's another political system like it in the world.

'But I don't want to paint a rosy picture. Indians are among the poorest people in America. They have the highest infant mortality. They have terrible health problems. They exist as a result of treaties. The treaties have all been kept on the Indian side but many of the promises of employment and training on the other side have not been honoured.'

Erdrich and Dorris met when she was a student at a Native American Studies Programme he started at Dartmouth College in 1972: she was eighteen, he was twenty-seven. By the time they married in 1981 he already had three adopted children. In 1971 he made legal history as a single man successfully adopting a two-year-old boy, Lakota Abel. He adopted a Sioux boy, Sava, in 1974 and in 1976 a baby girl, Madeline. 'Louise and I also have three biological children. We live in an isolated farm on seventeen acres in Cornish, New Hampshire. We don't see many people.'

His eldest son Abel was killed from injuries sustained when he was struck by a car in 1991. He had led a tortured life, suffering from a condition diagnosed in 1982 as foetal alcohol syndrome, which is caused by consumption of alcohol during pregnancy. Apparently Sava and Madeline also suffered from the same condition. To draw public attention to the illness Dorris, who himself had an alcohol problem, wrote *The Broken Cord*, a movingly anthropological detective story of his search for the cause of his son's deviant behaviour.

Both Erdrich and Dorris grew up in a tradition of oral storytelling. 'My grandfather Patrick Gourneau on my mother's side was widely known,' says Erdrich. 'He would do the rounds in his regalia. It was very much a part of my growing up. He would walk into the house and stories would flow. I salute him, and the four branches of the Ojibwa Nation, those of strength, who endure.' Her mother Rita had the same talent. 'I still hear her stories of reservation and bush life.'

Erdrich, born in Little Falls, Minnesota in 1954, the eldest of seven children, remembers her German father Ralph offering her a nickel for every story she wrote as a child. Her great gift has been an ability to transform this oral tradition into literature. Two of her sisters, Heid and Lise, received similar encouragement and also went on to become writers. Louise's great gift has been an ability to transform the oral tradition of the reservation into literature. 'The range of her sympathy is astonishing,' wrote Paul Bailey in *The Observer*. 'She shares with Faulkner the gift of transcending the mundane.'

It was as a student of Dorris that she first began to look into her ancestry and give expression to it in stories, poems and novels. 'That entire generation of storytelling could easily be transposed to Ireland and no one would notice,' Dorris says. 'I'm very much the beneficiary of it on my mother's side too. Members of my family could read the telephone directory and make a story of it. They had a belief that there was a story in everything. They'd see something and make up a story to explain it. It had to do with how they viewed the world, this idea that there's ultimately sense to it, an explanation, but it's hard to get to.'

With roots in another language, Erdrich and Dorris, like Irish writers, bring to their novels a different vocabulary, a different lilt, a different intonation, a different humour. 'A lot of people who come to English from a traditional language enrich it with unexpected tones,' says Erdrich.

John Fowles, 1985

Clearing through papers left by her husband, John Fowles, after his death in 2005 aged seventy-nine, his second wife Sarah Bowles – his first wife Elizabeth died in 1990 – found a stash of unpublished poems, some from the 1950s, the most recent written in a hospital ward in the weeks before the end of his life. Apart from a volume of poetry published at the beginning of his career as a writer, nobody had thought of him as a poet, least of all himself, although he once said he wished he could have been one. Edited by poet and novelist Adam Thorpe, these unknown poems were published in 2012. Apart from providing insight into the themes explored in his fiction, they stand in their own right as poetry. The following year the period house where Fowles lived most of his writing life in Lyme Regis in Dorset – and the setting for his best-known novel The French Lieutenant's Woman *– was bought by the English Landmark Trust to be restored as a centre for young writers attending the creative writing course at the nearby University of East Anglia. Writers often go through a period of neglect after their death but it seems Fowles, who shunned the literary world and was something of a recluse in later life, is unlikely to share this fate. Although a judge for the Booker Prize in 1968, he refused to allow his novels ever to be considered on the grounds that a well-off international best-selling writer like himself had no right to such awards. Literature like everything else was, to him, in danger of being demeaned by the* *cult of success. In a rare interview in early winter 1985 he talked to me about writing and his dissenting view of modern life.*

Being a Cistercian monk would appeal to John Fowles. The only snag is that he's an atheist. 'I can't share this enormous belief in God. I feel deprived by that.' But the whole idea of a contemplative existence, lived in close harmony with nature, appeals to him greatly. 'I find myself longing for simplicity.' This is particularly so whenever he finds himself in America. Last week he flew from Boston to La Guardia in forty minutes: getting to downtown Manhattan took another hour. 'That's madness, to travel 700 miles more quickly than a few miles in a bus.'

He sits behind a desk in a small study – it might also be a cell – that overlooks the quiet of Bedford Square in London. You sense he's still in some kind of psychological decompression chamber, readjusting to the more human English scale of things. As we talk an artist unobtrusively sketches him for *The Listener.*

'I find it alien, the atmosphere you get in very large cities,' he says. 'The stress, the clamouring for success, the artificiality, the enormous sense of wealth and of what you can buy if you have money – New York is really the most extraordinary supermarket in the world.' Far removed from the seclusion of the eighteenth-century house in Lyme Regis on the border of Devon and Dorset where he's lived with his wife since 1967. 'It's by the sea but I don't really love the sea in itself. I love everywhere there's an edge between sea and land.'

His garden is a jungle of rare shrubs and plants, some virtually extinct in England: preserving them appeals to the botanist in him. 'My uncle and cousin were good field naturalists. This is how knowledge spreads; by being handed down.' Although born in Leigh-on-Sea in 1926, the son of a tobacco importer, he was evacuated to Devon during the war: this is where his fiction has come to belong, too. 'You couldn't call it unspoilt but it's still one of the quieter parts of England. We even have a name for the tourists who bother us in the summer. They're known as 'grockles'. The word comes from the Latin for little Greeks and was Victorian slang for Irish labourers on the railways.'

Fowles has a liking for words that take on different meanings in this way. The maggot in the title of his novel *A Maggot* can be understood in the older and now obsolete sense of whim or quirk, which suggests the unorthodox narrative form chosen by him to project historical fiction through modern eyes. 'It's a kind of Irish mix of a word. I also mean it to be a maggot in the literal sense, perhaps eating out people's brains, which is another function of the novel.'

Maggot defined as the larval stage of a winged creature in turn suggests his central theme: the idea of religious awakening, nothing less than the second coming of Christ as a woman. 'A Holy Trinity that has no female component cannot be holy,' he says. But images rather than words trigger his fiction. One morning lying in bed half asleep he imagined a woman standing on the end of the quay at Lyme Regis and looking out to sea. To make sense of it he eventually wrote *The French Lieutenant's Woman*.

The recurring image that has now prompted *A Maggot* is a group of travellers riding across a skyline, without apparent motive. 'It was probably suggested to me by a Brazilian film about bandits I remember from the 1960s. But it became much more than this and wouldn't go away.' Only by writing another novel could he find out who the travellers were. 'A novel involves this same sense of going somewhere and not knowing where it is.'

Gradually pieces of the puzzle he unconsciously set himself fell into place. By chance he acquired a pencil and watercolour drawing of an unidentified young woman dated 16 July 1683. 'The long-dead girl's face gave me the idea of a prostitute becoming a saint, or rather some idea of her being able to change her life very deeply.'

This connected with what he had been reading about the Shakers, a diehard pacifist sect of communistic Protestant dissenters, whose leader Ann Lee was regarded as 'the female principle in Christ.' With her birth in 1735 *A Maggot* merges historical fiction with fact: this is the event towards which the mysterious travellers in Fowles's mind were heading.

'You don't really realize yourself what all the fragments are about,' he says. He's reminded of the caddis, the little fly the trout loves so much, which weaves its silken sheath, open at both ends, with bits of wood, stone and leaves. 'That's how a novel gets built, with fragments that stick together.' But although evoking a real place and set in a specific historical time halfway between the English and the French revolutions – 'the eighteenth century is on the borderline between the past and present' – *A Maggot* resolutely refuses to be historical. Contemporary similes deliberately jar any period feel. A rider's inscrutable gaze is likened to twin camera lenses. 'You could do a total pastiche but then you'd be into the historical novel, which I'm not interested in writing. History interests me only if it reflects on today.'

What Fowles is saying in *A Maggot* – and he even adds an explanatory epilogue to avoid being misunderstood – is that we have lost touch with an emotional enlightenment personified by the Shakers. 'It's a sermon,' he says. 'I know sermons are not allowed in the English novel but the rules of the classical novel don't bother me very much.'

As with *The Magus* and *The French Lieutenant's Woman* – a love story written from both a Victorian and a modern point of view – he's again playing games with fictional convention to open our eyes to the unfamiliar: in this case a past nobody alive today can have experienced. 'It's difficult to imagine what it would have been like for an ordinary person in the eighteenth century but I suspect the sense of self would have been far less than now. "I" didn't infiltrate everything. People wouldn't have had anything like the modern individualistic sense of this is me, I am I.'

The Shakers represent the point at which this hierarchical society first gave way to individualistic revolt. Their voice of conscience, by its very irrationality, upset the rigidity of eighteenth-century thinking: 'They were inspired by a vision similar to that which causes the moving statues in Ireland today, a vision we'd dismiss in our sniffy twentieth-century way as ignorance. But it wasn't ignorance for them. It couched something. It released something. It really did give them a new light on emotional reality.'

Which is partly why he feels an affinity with the Shakers: a novel too has this ability to touch a truth beyond reason. 'You depend on faith in a way. You're like one of those wandering preachers. You know you have this mysterious power to move people, to make them see a little differently.' Beneath his beard his face creases into a smile. 'You have to be an adolescent to write a novel. If you were fully mature I don't think you'd even attempt it. You'd be too much of a prisoner of reason.'

Ironically, he was in his twenties before he even thought of writing fiction. He'd been head boy at Bedford School and captain of the cricket team – actor John Hurt was among the smaller boys he'd been asked to chastise – before going on to read French and German at Oxford. This got him a teaching job on the Greek islands where he tried his hand at a travel book. Paul Scott, who was then an agent, turned it down. But a short semi-fictional passage appealed to him. 'I think you are a novelist,' he told Fowles.

This became evident with his debut novel *The Collector*, in which a shy young butterfly enthusiast kidnaps a beautiful girl to add to his collection. It was quickly followed by *The Magus*, set in the Greek islands where young hippies fall under the sway of a magician, and then *The French Lieutenant's Woman*. These three critically acclaimed novels established him as an international bestseller, a fame that has always made him feel distinctly uncomfortable.

Hollywood didn't help by bowdlerizing *The Magus*, which he regards as one of the worst movies of the 1960s: 'The cast of Michael Caine, Anthony Quinn, Candice Bergin and Anna Karina looked good on paper but they lacked a strong director to tell them all what to do.' *The Collector* was little better: 'It ought to have been black and white. But then William Wyler took over. Like so many great Hollywood directors he had contempt for audiences: no matter how silly their stock responses, they had to be pandered to.' Not surprisingly, he wouldn't let *The French Lieutenant's Woman* be filmed until a screenplay by Harold Pinter, with Karl Reisz directing and Meryl Streep in the pivotal role of the woman on the quayside, won him over.

With his novel *Daniel Martin* he got his own back on the studio system, castigating the crassness of a Hollywood where accountants reign and only profit matters. He feels misunderstood in America, which he likens to imperial Rome, 'and we're the poor Greeks'. It's as if they read a different language to that in which he writes: 'They hate having unexplained things or ambiguous endings. It really worries them. It may be because much of earlier American literacy was based on the Bible. The Bible was explained to them in very great detail and something in their mind now expects every book to be like the Bible, with a clear message and clear moral answer to everything.'

The artist has finished sketching him. Apprehensively she lets him see what she has done. 'Oh, good God!' he says. He compares it with a drawing of him she made several years before. Little about him has changed. He seems reassured.

Carlos Fuentes, 2000

Shortly before his death in Mexico City in 2012, Carlos Fuentes left a last message on Twitter: 'There must be something beyond slaughter and barbarism to support the existence of mankind and we must help search for it.' In his life and writing he pursued this hope, much to the irritation of the US where he was frequently refused visas. But he also stood up to Cuba over the imprisonment in 1970 of the poet Heberto Padilla, and was a critic of Hugo Chávez in Venezuela. Unlike Bob Dylan, Carlos Fuentes belongs among the many distinguished writers never to win a Nobel Prize for Literature.

Carlos Fuentes once imagined Latin-American fiction as different chapters of the one novel: a Colombian chapter written by Gabriel García Márquez, a Cuban chapter by Alejo Carpentier, an Argentine chapter by Julio Cortázar, a Peruvian chapter by Mario Vargas Llosa, and so on. Although Fuentes didn't lay claim to a Mexican chapter for himself, it would indisputably belong to him. With a challenging range of innovative books – non-fiction as well as fiction – he became synonymous with Mexican literature in the twentieth century.

'Ah yes,' he says. 'I remember I'm a writer of the *last* century. It's hard to get used to that.'

He's at a small party at the home of a friend, the Mexican ambassador to Dublin. A tall man with an old-world swagger, he exudes a sense of enjoyment and courtesy. There's music and we dance with each other's wives. Having been diagnosed technically dead for nearly an hour during a heart operation five years ago, it's as if he's treating each day as a gift, much like the character in his novel *Old Gringo* who wakes up coughing and spewing phlegm but eventually manages to mutter 'Thank you God for another day.'

This is early April in 2000. He and Silvia Lemus – they married in 1973 after the break up of his first marriage – are on a brief visit. He's giving a reading in Galway University, so we arrange to do an interview later in the week before he flies to Madrid for a posthumous exhibition at the Museo Reina Sofia of work by their 25-year-old photographer son Carlos, who died in a drowning accident last year.

And now, twelve years after we talked for a few hours by Lough Corrib, he has finally run out of the gift of another day. Spanish satellite television has announced his death, and the screen fills with tributes, and beside me is *Burnt Water* in which he has written: *To Ciaran, surrounded by the seas that unite us without burning our ships – his friend, Carlos.*

People who have never been to Mexico feel they know it intimately from reading Fuentes: its past and present and even its future are conjured up with challenging immediacy in *Aura, The Death of Artemio Cruz, A Change of Skin* and *Distant Relations*, to mention but a few of his novels. The outrageously, time-shifting, space-defying *Terra Nostra* is his *Ulysses*, the short-story collection *Burnt Water* – each story opening a door to the myriad essences of Mexico City – is his *Dubliners*. Like Joyce, he finds the extraordinary in the ordinary.

Yet for Fuentes, as much as for his readers, Mexico has always been somewhere he had to dream up, an imagined place to explore and populate with his inventions. By making sense of it he made sense of himself.

'I had no choice,' he is saying as he looks out over the lake that glistens in the morning sun, 'I was the son of a diplomat. Therefore I had to wander from country to country and adapt to new languages, new schools and new companions.'

Although born in Mexico City on 11 November 1928, he grew up far from Mexico, a Mexican boy going to school in Washington. He was popular there until the Mexican government, at the height of the Mexican Revolution, expropriated foreign-owned oil holdings in 1938. 'Reaction against Mexico was enormous. *Mexican Commies Steal Our Oil!* screamed the headlines. It hit me at school. Suddenly I was different. I was no longer one of the boys. I was an enemy agent. This heightened my sense of being a Mexican. I was in school with gringos but I was not a gringo. I was something else.'

His one real friend was a young German Jew. 'He arrived at school wearing *lederhosen*, without speaking English. He was the object of fun and cruelty, making his life misery. So we bonded together, because we were two aliens.'

Every summer Carlos's father would drive him down through the Deep South and across the border to the family coffee plantation in Veracruz. 'So I never lost touch with Mexico. I lived on my grandmother's ghost stories.'

Like 80 per cent of the Mexican population, his family was *mestizo*. His father's grandparents were from the Canary Islands, his great-grandmother lost her fingers to bandits because she wouldn't remove her rings when they held up her stagecoach. His mother's grandfather was a German socialist, Philip Boettiger Keller, who emigrated to New Orleans with his brother, out of disillusionment with Ferdinand Lassalle because he'd joined with Bismarck in the belief that by combining with the Junkers, socialists would defeat the hated bourgeoisie in the middle.

'The brother went on to Chicago, becoming wealthy, and a grandson married a daughter of Franklin Roosevelt. My grandfather went to Veracruz, where he promptly banished German. We became Mexicans who spoke Spanish. It's the one thing I hate him for. By not having German handed down to me, I lost the chance of reading in German.'

It's something the Czech writer Milan Kundera likes to tease Fuentes about. 'He'll say, "Have you read Kafka?" "Sure I have." "You think you've read Kafka. You've read him in translation. You don't read him until you read him in German."'

At fifteen, Fuentes was sent back to school in Mexico. 'It was a culture shock. Although my mother was a devout Catholic, my father was a non-believer. So I'd always been in lay schools that did not have religious demands. Now I was with the Marist priests.'

On his first day, the director of the school went up to a pulpit holding a lily. 'This,' he said, 'is a young and pure Catholic youth before he goes to a dance and kisses a girl.' He threw the lily on the floor, trampled it and then picked it up. 'This,' he said, 'is the Catholic youth after he goes to a dance and kisses a girl.' Fuentes chuckles. 'Wow, I thought, where am I?'

Not that he regrets his Catholic indoctrination. 'It gives you a whole cultural background. In Mexico, even the atheists are Catholic. They cannot avoid it. The culture is strong and profound. Who in Mexico would dare insult the Virgin of Guadalupe, or disbelieve in her? You'd be stoned to death.'

His father liked to take him to the theatre. 'One night when the lights were dimming, there was a sudden frenzied rattling of jewellery. No one bothered to look behind. "It's only Frida Kahlo arriving," my father said.'

When not daydreaming, Fuentes escaped into the make-believe of films. 'Again, it started with my father's influence, because he was a fanatical film-goer too. I think he saw a film every day. He kept a book of all the films he had ever seen. And this started in 1919. He bred into me not only a passion for films, but a memory of films that I've kept all my life.

He is a nephew of Fernando de Fuentes, a key 1940s director whose film *El compadre Mendoza*, dealing with the dilemma of a Zapatista revolutionary forced to choose between betraying his friends or saving his skin, was reworked by Fuentes in *The Death of Artemio Cruz*, one of his greatest novels. Its use of several contrasting viewpoints was inspired by *Citizen Kane*, which his father brought him to see as a young boy when it first opened in New York. He's intrigued to hear about my father's enthusiasm for *Artemio Cruz* ('a perfect novel') and how we'd speculate on how it might work as a film.

Fuentes chatted with Neil Jordan at the Mexican ambassador's party, and praised his adaptation of Graham Greene's *The End of the Affair*. 'Greene would have loved it,' he told Jordan. He wished he'd been so fortunate when his novel *Old Gringo* was filmed. 'Gregory Peck gave a great performance as the US journalist Ambrose Bierce covering the Mexican Revolution, but they cut most of it out.'

This fascination with cinema feeds into his fiction. The idea of a ghost temptress in his novel *Aura* derives from the Mizoguchi film *Ugetsu*. His novella *Holy Place* draws on the life of the actress Maria Félix, a regular in his uncle's films. 'She was an independent woman in a country where women over the centuries were destined to become nuns or whores.' His brief two-month relationship with actress Jean Seberg inspired his novel *Diana: the Goddess Who Hunts Alone*. In the 1960s he became even more directly involved in Mexican cinema, writing several film scripts with Gabriel García Márquez.

Recurring through his stories is a sense of the past alive in the present, something inherent in cinema's manipulation of time and space. Chronological time is abolished in *Terra Nostra*, an epic that makes fun of the idea of progress and dynasties. 'Some historians thought I was an ignoramus because I made Philip II of Spain the son of his grandmother Joanna the Mad and married him to Elizabeth of England,' he says, adding:

> Cinema has taught us to look in a different way. There is a whole renewal of the vision of the world that comes from science, from Einstein and Niels Bohr, a way of looking at time and space, which was reflected also in film, painting, poetry, the novel and architecture. It was the whole revolution of modernity that began in the early 1900s and ended with that century.
>
> The vanguard seems to be over now. It became probably too allied to the idea of progress and did not realize that art is not progress. All art happens in the present. Rembrandt is the present. Cervantes is the present. They're not in the past. The next reader of a book is also the first reader of a book. And the reader always knows more than the writer because the reader is the future.

When Luis Buñuel was filming *Nazarin* just outside Mexico City, Fuentes got to know him through his first wife Rita Macedo who had a starring role:

> We became close friends and I'd go there on Fridays and spend from four to seven with him, just talking. He talked about his friendship with Lorca and with Dali and the whole Generation of 27 that transformed Spanish poetry. He talked of surrealism and Paris in the 1930s, and his fights with director Abel Gance. I really got an extraordinary impression of the art of the twentieth century through the experience of Buñuel, the living experience.

Fuentes belongs to a generation of Latin American writers who felt obliged to use their literary stature to take on a political role wherever possible. 'There was a conviction that writers were there to give a voice to those who lacked a voice. The role was imposed on the writer because of the weakness of civil societies in Latin America. When you lived under a dictatorship where everything was banned, it was incumbent on the writer to speak.'

When Luis Escheverría came to power in Mexico, Fuentes felt that a new climate of democratization was coming about and accepted the post of ambassador to France. He resigned in 1977 when the former president Gustavo Díaz Ordaz, responsible for the massacre of several hundred students in Mexico City in 1968, was appointed ambassador to Spain. Because of his left-wing politics he often, like Graham Greene, had difficulties gaining entry to the US. As he observed in *Tiempo Mexicano*: 'The United States is very good at understanding itself, and very bad at understanding others.'

Although fluent all his life in English and French, Fuentes writes in Spanish. 'It just doesn't come to me in English,' he says. 'I don't make love in English. I don't dream in English.' He breaks into a morose chuckle. 'Maybe the nightmares are in English,' he allows.

David Gascoyne, 1985

Surrealism was coined as a word by the poet Apollinaire in 1917 and turned into a movement by the writer André Breton in a manifesto written in 1924, but its most lasting influence has been in painting and cinema rather than literature. The concept of pure automatism uncontrolled by any conscious aesthetic or moral consideration has greater affinity to the physical act of putting paint on canvas or editing celluloid images than to writing sustained works of fiction or verse. There's little in literature to match the surrealist paintings of Picasso, Dali, De Chirico, Ernst and Delvaux, or the films of Buñuel, although Graham Greene claimed that his novel The Honorary Consul *came to him in a dream. As an aspiring twenty-year-old poet, David Gascoyne found himself under the sway of Breton in Paris in the 1930s and for a while it literally drove him mad. Somehow he survived to share his story with me in Dublin in 1985. He died in 2001.*

'This is a lovely poem,' Judy Lewis remembers saying after she read a David Gascoyne poem, 'September Sun', to inmates at a psychiatric hospital on the Isle of Wight. 'I'd go there every week to try to cheer them up,' she says.

One of the inmates, a tall, sad man who always sat in silence, said quietly: 'Well, I wrote that.'

She humoured him. 'Of course you did, dear.' She later discovered he was telling the truth. David Gascoyne had been incarcerated in the hospital in a state of acute depression after the death of his parents.

She began bringing him home at weekends. 'My marriage had broken up. We were both miserable. Gradually we fell in love.' They married. 'I expected him to be a total invalid because he told me he would never recover. But now suddenly he has taken off. It's as if he's reborn. I can hardly keep up with him. He's giving readings all over Europe and writing with marvellous fluency in both English and French.'

We're taking afternoon tea in the Mount Herbert Hotel in Ballsbridge, early in 1985. Gascoyne is on his first visit to Ireland, giving readings in Galway and Cork. He wanted to come years ago but English poet Kathleen Raine dissuaded him. 'You can't go there with your ideas of black Catholicism,' she warned. 'But I'm neither Catholic nor Protestant,' he says. 'If I belong anywhere it is to the invisible church.'

Journals he kept while living in Paris in the 1930s in the heyday of surrealism, recently republished with an introduction by Lawrence Durrell, have become something a literary event in France. He'd first gone there in 1933 to celebrate his seventeenth birthday with the royalties from his first and only novel, *Opening Day*. 'A kind of stream of consciousness effort about a day in the life of an adolescent,' he says. 'Myself, of course.'

He learned French reading Baudelaire and Rimbaud with the help of a dictionary. With Cyril Connolly as a friend he soon gained acceptance with André Breton and Paul Éluard as a precocious member of the Surrealist movement. Max Ernst drew a cover for his *Short Survey of Surrealism* (1935), a book he rushed out to spread to Britain the gospel of an unconscious reality that lurks behind appearances. 'Intransigence was the key word of the surrealists,' he says. 'They were latter-day Jacobins, like Saint-Just and Robespierre. Breton had a dictatorial nature. He couldn't tolerate people with personalities as strong as his own.'

No deviation from the faith was tolerated. One poet was excommunicated for writing a potboiler. Another was taken to brothels in an attempt to exorcise his homosexuality. 'Breton didn't want people to associate surrealism with that sort of thing. He couldn't bear Cocteau.'

Gascoyne is often erroneously regarded purely as a surrealist poet because of these early experiences. 'I've had the label hung around my neck. Yet I only wrote that kind of poetry for about three years.' He distanced himself from 'automatic writing' – or navel-gazing, as he called it – in an article in Geoffrey Grigson's *New Verse*.

'I became aware that I had British roots and that there was a British tradition that was apart from the fantastic and the expressionism of subjectivity, although of course English Romanticism is very close to surrealism, both in its philosophy and in its interest in dreams and the unconscious. Coleridge and *Kubla Khan* are perfects examples of this.' Style and technique began to take over his poetry, the challenge of form. 'Everyone should know that poetry is not made of ideas but of words. It is a putting together of themes rather than ideas.'

He helped stage the International Surrealist Exhibition in London in 1936. Oswald Mosley had taken to the streets with his blackshirts. Joining the Communist Party seemed the only way to counter incipient fascism. 'Friends teased me into becoming a member. They accused me of being too much in the clouds, only interested in defending the rights of subjectivity.' Like other poets, among them the doomed John Cornford, he was drawn to the Civil War in Spain, working a while in the Catalan Propaganda Ministry with Roland Penrose and Fenner Brockway. 'We felt we had to do something to stop the drift to fascism.' But the communists wanted to control everyone and everything:

> They detested the anarchists and the Trotskyites and the various other left groups even more than they detested Franco. That was the beginning of my disillusionment with communism as a solution to the disintegration of capitalist society.
>
> The tragedy and horror of ideology in the modern world is this awful mania for labelling. Everyone has to be either black or white, communist or fascist. But the individual human being is far more complex than that.

Back in Paris he lived out the 1930s in a garret over a flat where e.e. cummings lived. Sylvia Beach's bookshop was across the street. 'But I wasn't allowed to meet James Joyce because I was too young and inexperienced.' He became friends with Samuel Beckett through a son-in-law of Matisse.

Existential philosophy 'as opposed to the existentialism of Sartre' caught his imagination, particularly the ideas of the Russian philosopher Lev Shestov, one of whose books he still carries around. He fishes in his holdall to show me, and reads, 'Philosophers know so much about what is superfluous and have forgotten or never known what is important.' He feels some of his own poetry has suffered from being too much under the influence of philosophy, 'although the kind of philosophy I was interested in was a relentless attack on cerebral thinking and the domination of reason'.

Despair over Chamberlain's sell-out to Hitler in Munich brought on the first of the severe depressions that were to plague his life. He entered into analysis with the wife of his poet friend Pierre Jean Jouve who had trained with Freud, out of which came if not relief at least a poem, 'a stream of images, which I noted down after a session with her, not a surrealist poem although the images came from the unconscious'. Poems have a tendency to come to him ready-made like that: 'When I was going crazy in one of my bouts of madness in 1964, a poem suddenly surged into consciousness in simple quatrain form, a very mysterious poem, rather like Blake. I thought there was going to be more of it, but there wasn't. So I called it 'Unfinished Poem from Elsewhere'.

Judy interrupts. 'When we first met he used to talk in the night,' she says. 'Sometimes the most beautiful lyrical lines would come out in his sleep.' Then she laughs. 'But you don't do that anymore, darling.'

He was rejected as unfit for service when World War Two broke out. 'I wasn't a pacifist. I wanted to share the experience of my generation.' So he became an actor with ENSA instead, performing for troops throughout Britain.

In between appearing with John Greenwood and playing in *Twelfth Night* opposite Wendy Hiller, Gascoyne published *Poems 1937–1942* with illustrations by Graham Sutherland. Another collection, *A Vagrant & Other Poems*, appeared after the war. By then the tone had become very disil-lusioned. He toured the US with W.S. Graham and Kathleen Raine and struggled to write *Night Thoughts* (1955). 'I more or less dried up. I got guilty because I couldn't write and couldn't write because I was guilty.'

He lives with Judy in the Isle of Wight house his parents moved to after his father retired as a manager with Midland Bank. 'I acquired a ready-made family when we married – Judy has seven grandchildren.' He disciplines himself to read aloud every day in French. Many of his poems are written in French. His *Collected Verse Translations* was published by Oxford University Press in 1970, but he's not convinced that poetry can be translated. 'The word *poésie* is not a translation of poetry and vice versa.' He quotes Robert Frost's chilling put-down, 'Poetry is that which is lost in translation,' only to qualify it: 'The perfect translation doesn't exist but I think people should make the effort. Otherwise those who haven't languages remain ignorant of what poets are trying to do in other languages. Poetry, like music, is an international feeling of solidarity.'

Allen Ginsberg, 1993

Allen Ginsberg, guru of the alternative culture that gave the world hippies, wrote his last poem 'Things I'll Not Do (Nostalgias)' in the week before his death on 5 April 1997, aged seventy, and then worked through his address book, calling nearly everyone he knew. When asked how he'd like to be remembered, he replied: 'As someone in the tradition of the old-time American transcendentalist individualism … just carrying it into the twentieth century.'

It's not just that Allen Ginsberg has no regrets for the 1960s. He rejoices in its legacy. 'The sixties now in 1993 seems a golden age to younger people, because they've been sold the myth that they can't have the same kind of light and hope for the future that people from the 1940s to the 1960s worked with,' says the 67-year-old poet.

He's arrived late from Warsaw for a reading with John Calder at the Cheltenham Literary Festival, grey-bearded with white shirt unbuttoned and goggle-sized spectacles perched on his long nose beneath a shining bald head. Then it's on to Dublin for another reading at Liberty Hall, his first visit to Ireland.

The lure is an Irish tweed suit, which will be his fee. 'Not that I needed much inducement,' he says. 'I have some friends there. Marianne Faithfull has a little house outside Dublin. And Yeats is one of my favourite poets. I have yards of Yeats in my head from when I was seventeen and had his *Collected Poems* by my bedside.' He rarely buys a new suit. 'I generally get my clothes from the Salvation Army. I've a nice blue silk suit with me that I got for ten bucks in Iowa City, in a Goodwill store, I think.'

Ginsberg's first epic poem, *Howl*, seized by US customs and subject of an obscenity trial, electrified America in 1956. Writers and critics testified on his behalf and it was declared legal by a San Francisco court in 1967. Ginsberg sardonically lists the verdict in his CV among his literary awards. Along with the writings of his friends Jack Kerouac and William Burroughs, it proclaimed the arrival of the beat generation.

Much of *Howl* was composed during a peyote vision, while *Kaddish*, a moving eulogy to his dead mother, Naomi, was written in one long weekend of amphetamine ingestion, plus a bit of morphine and Dexedrine. As prophet of pot and acid, and leader of countless demonstrations against the Vietnam War (he was arrested with Benjamin Spock and tear-gassed in Lincoln Park), Ginsberg was a natural instigator of the Flower Power movement, with 100,000 students defying the communist authorities to crown him in Prague on May Day 1965.

He has roamed the world tirelessly since the early 1950s, ever the radical dissenter and campaigning homosexual, living among the Mayan Indians in Mexico, discovering Buddhist meditation in India, collaborating with the Beatles, Bob Dylan, Ezra Pound and Mick Jagger, arguing with Fidel Castro about gay rights and championing the Nicaraguan poet politician Ernesto Cardenal.

Becoming professor at Brooklyn College six years ago slowed him down somewhat. 'I've been sort of tied down to very short trips. I don't feel like going to Europe or anywhere for a week at a time. It's too wearying.' An attack of diabetes didn't help. 'But now I'm on a macrobiotic diet and it seems to be working. I've had a complete remission. So I don't have to take insulin any more. I can even get a hard-on.'

He's taken a six month sabbatical to travel again. He saw Burroughs before he left. Bob Dylan and Gregory Corso, too. 'Most of us keep in touch.' Inevitably he has run into controversy. In Belgrade he found that the majority of people in the city were opposed to the Serbian government and its sustained involvement in ethnic cleansing. 'But they're getting no encouragement from outside. The Western US/UN blockade is also a cultural blockade. So they're cut off from sympathy and liaison with outside society. The cultural blockade is actually prolonging the war and any peace efforts within Serbia. It's a monstrous mistake, strengthening the fascist government.'

In the former communist bloc, Ginsberg found his poetry valued as 'a clarion call and as a sample of the possibilities of candour and openness'. Ironically, these values of freedom of expression are again under threat in the US from right-wing fundamentalists. 'It's a combination of religious demagoguery, nationalist demagoguery, sometimes anti-Semite demagoguery and anti-gay demagoguery.'

He has been an uncompromising campaigner against censorship since he overcame his own inhibitions in writing exactly what he felt. The sexual frankness of *Howl* only came about because he assumed when writing it that it could not possibly be published 'because I wouldn't want my daddy to see what was in there'. His breakthrough in American literature was to annihilate the distinction between what writers actually felt and what they were prepared to publish. Ginsberg's father, a poet himself, eventually appreciated the value of what his son was doing. 'It worked out very well finally. Years later we gave readings together.'

Ginsberg grew up in Paterson, New Jersey, near the poet William Carlos Williams. 'I knew him when I was a teenager. He was a kind of mentor and had an impact on my thinking, although I didn't see him that often. He edited *Howl* and wrote the preface, pointing out what was good and what we reckoned we could leave aside.' *Howl* was a rhythmic articulation of feeling – 'an animal cry' – rather than written to carefully observed rules and structures:

> It's part of the notion 'first thought, best thought'. Awareness is swifter than linear thought. It's not that it's irrational, it's just that the whole holistic awareness is quicker than putting it into words, so to speak, or into stanza form. Rhythm can be as valuable as actual speech. It needn't be metronomic, like nineteenth-century poetry. Classical poetry was much more variable in tone and rhythm than nineteenth-century models. One of the interesting things that Ezra Pound pointed out about Yeats was that he wrote with a tune in his head. There is a muscularity and a power in his stanzas and rhymes because he always had it tied to an actual physical melody. Most people who write lyric poetry have forgotten than the word lyric comes from the word lyre, which is a stringed instrument. It's a musical form.

Ginsberg is sceptical of attempts to label 1960s permissiveness – the euphoria of sex, drugs and rock and roll – as a contributing factor in today's drug-abuse problems and the spread of AIDS:

> Sex, drugs and rock and roll is a very limited view, a media stereotype. The 1960s was also anti-war, ecological awareness, gay liberation, women's liberation, liberation of words from censorship, the influence of Eastern thought and meditation. If you want to get upset about drugs, then you have to get upset about George Bush, the National Security Agency, the Iran/Contra scam and the use of cocaine to fund CIA operations. So you might look to the government to be disillusioned rather than to the counterculture.

But he's not without optimism. 'Rosy-cheeked Clinton is a lot more cheerful than dour, sour-puss Bush. At least Clinton didn't mind having a joint between his lips.'

My ten-year-old granddaughter Rachel called in on her way home from primary school on a summer afternoon in 2013. A nun who was one of her teachers had been ill and died a few days before. 'You know,' Rachel said, 'Sister Mary is not the only person who is dead. A poet called Seamus Heaney is dead, too. We read in class a poem he wrote, a poem called 'Mid-Term Break'.' Seamus Heaney was a couple of years younger than me but he always seemed my elder, even in his late thirties one day in October 1979 when we first met at his house on Strand Road looking out on Dublin Bay near Sandymount, where I grew up.

There was a dream in which I was interviewing Seamus Heaney about his new poems *Field Work*, a dream more in words than images. From nowhere his wife Marie, whom I somehow knew although we had yet to meet, interrupted: 'Say one thing at a time,' she told him, with slow deliberation as if to make sure I got the quote accurately. 'That is what you do best.'

Now the dream is coming true. We're in the attic of their home. Planks of wood laid across tea chests are his desk. The walls are crammed with makeshift bookshelves. There is a mattress on the floor. Through the windows trees are everywhere, creating an illusion of rural space in the Dublin suburbs. Marie brings up a tray with cups of coffee and I mention the dream. Their eyes meet and Seamus laughs. 'I think that's what the muse would say,' he says. 'It's very good instructions.'

'Tell him,' Marie says.

'Marie once said what you dreamed, in an entirely different way, but it was the same thing. She said my mind had all the manoeuvrability of a combine harvester. But she did admit that it had a certain relentless onward push. So you aren't so far off the mark.'

Heaney's four collections *Death of a Naturalist*, *Door Into the Dark*, *Wintering Out* and *North* have gained him international recognition. Robert Lowell has spoken of him as 'the best Irish poet since W.B. Yeats,' a claim that makes him uneasy. 'I feel people may put me on a pedestal as a writer and I like to live in a burrow.'

Poetry, he feels, should not be seen as some form of rarefied rite, practised by an elite remote from ordinary life. That was what daunted him as a student in Queen's University Belfast. 'I never thought of myself as a writer or destined for writing. You tend to think of poetry as a realm beyond yourself. It wasn't until I started to teach that I read contemporary Irish poetry. Reading Patrick Kavanagh was to some extent like reading your own life. It was a kind of revelation. I felt I could write something like that myself.'

His first poems were published straight away in *The Kilkenny Magazine*, *The Irish Times* and *The Belfast Telegraph*. Then three appeared together in the *New Statesman* and Faber & Faber approached him for a book. 'I was in a bedsit in Belfast, sending poems out, and this letter arrived. If I'd had a book ready I'd never have sent it to Faber because, again, I thought they were on some celestial plain. It was the best inspiration. I was shocked into life.'

Most of the finest poems in *Death of a Naturalist*, published by Faber in 1967 when he was twenty-seven, are right out of his childhood on the land in Derry. 'I wasn't conscious of a theme at the time. You're just eager to write and you head for the subject where things come alive for you.

'I always think of the image of something being hermetically sealed, and then suddenly opened, because just as I was moving into adolescence I moved from the ground I grew up on into a new place. It was awkward. I didn't know the people there so well. I was in boarding school at St Columb's, most of the year anyway. Then I went to university. And suddenly, about ten years later, this first ground that had been shut off and left was just lying there ready. I just took off the lid and the stuff came up like fumes.'

The sounds and sights of the countryside were to become the language of his poetry; like Antaeus, his strength renewed by every contact with the earth. In 'Follower' he evokes the image of the child he was, stumbling in the hobnailed wake of his father as he expertly worked a horse plough. Poetry has developed in him as a craft akin to the ploughing of his father, with digging as a metaphor for uncovering origins. The sod, rain, bog and even potatoes take on associations in *Door Into the Dark* (1969) and *Wintering Out* (1972) that enable him to apprehend what it is to be a Northerner. The birds and plants he so sensuously describes become the deposits of a tribal memory.

There had been an awakening of poetry in Northern Ireland in the 1960s, with Michael Longley, Derek Mahon, James Simmons and Seamus Deane all publishing collections. 'Through a writers' group formed by the English poet Philip Hobsbaum I made contact with a kind of literary environment. I had never met published poets before. We met every week, reading and criticizing our work. There was a sense of having discovered a voice of some kind.

'It's good for every young writer to have some kind of audience. But after a while is became a hindrance to me, because everything you wrote was vetted and a kind of committee decision was taken on it. You wondered if your own self and your own temperament were getting as free an expression

HEANEY, SEAMUS

as they should have. We were a mixture of Catholics and Protestants and in some kind of unspoken way there was the sense that maybe we were moving things forward a little.'

But inevitably he was caught up in the violence. He joined the civil rights marches, gave interviews to English newspapers and wrote articles in *The Listener*. 'The writers discovered themselves in a small way acting as spokesmen, and then they ran like hell from the responsibilities, saying that they were only writers. Which I think in the end was a good thing. But having taken up the aesthetic position and having refused to tangle with the sectarian thing, I began to feel impatient with myself.' More and more a spectator of what was happening, he gave up his lectureship at Queen's and moved to a remote cottage in Devil's Glen in Wicklow with Marie and their two young sons 'to unravel all that was in my head.'

It seemed he needed to distance himself from the experience in order to give it expression in his poetry. *Death of a Naturalist* had grown out of the country upbringing from which he had been isolated. Now with *North* he was to illuminate the Ulster he had left. His seven-year-old daughter Catherine interrupts us, looking for paper. She has been drawing pictures of the cover of *Field Work*. Does she like poetry? 'I make up poems but I don't write them,' she says.

Wicklow was a redemptive break with everything, a retreat to solitude: for four years he was to test himself, living only for his poetry. 'Part of the intensity of the experience was that I had brought my family to this wilderness. Was there any spiritual vindication for this?' He need not worry. If he were to write nothing more his reputation would be secure with the deeply human 'Glanmore Sonnets', which resolve his experience and which he has placed at the centre of *Field Work*. 'They're the heart of the thing in a way, because I wanted to put a mark on that place at that time, just for myself, to keep something of it.'

In *Field Work* he has sought to put a plain voice into his poetry, a directness typified in 'Casualty', a harrowing elegy to a friend 'blown to bits out drinking in a curfew' but full of unexpected associations as in 'The Skunk', which turns into a love poem for his wife.

He breaks some tobacco into his pipe, which he has taken to smoking in place of cigarettes. There is a pause. Working the head, as his fellow poet Richard Murphy would put it. Then he says: 'The part of the *North* book I liked best was the first section, which was more about closing your eyes and imagining, using language to entrance. The first person singular didn't get into it much.

'I liked all those bog things and mythological things and there was a terrific intensity in me when I was doing them, and they were very pacifying. But then, having gone through that, I wanted to write plain things. It was almost a direct reaction, come and say it plainly.'

Michael McLaverty had once quoted Willa Cather to him: 'Description is revelation.' This became the substance of one of the closing poems of *North*, and anticipates the approach of *Field Work*: 'Just to gaze at something rather than to argue. I think that whatever kind of poetry I can write, I'm probably better at something that's more like a gaze. But the curious thing is that in order to write plainly you have to make it more conventional. You climb up the ladder of narration along rungs of rhyme and metre.'

Obviously directness is what has attracted him to Dante, whom he began reading seriously four years ago, prompted by a version of one of the cantos in Robert Lowell's 'Near the Ocean'. This finds expression in the nightmarish 'Ugolino' at the end of *Field Work*, a long translation from the *Inferno*: 'Dante is plain. There's very little lyrical flourish. The poetry is in the energy of the stories. There's something about the way his presence is felt in the poetry, the immediacy of a life and a personality appearing through it that confirmed me in doing the opposite kind of work from the first section of *North*. I've come to the conclusion that record is more important than polemic, that that also includes a record of yourself.'

There is neat expression of this truth in 'Song', which is inspired by the Finn MacCool story about the sweetest music of all being the music of what happens. 'But,' he laughs, 'there would be a position to take up that the best music in the world is the music of what might happen.'

It's not that he isn't still drawn to language in its own right. He has always experienced a kind of nervous reaction to language in poetry, particularly the language of Hopkins and Keats. 'I love the music of words themselves.' His idea of a poem is something that has a literal fullness to it, 'with an aura and energy breaking out of it that suggests something else'. Like an old photograph? 'A good analogy,' he agrees.

Since moving to Strand Road in 1976 he has been teaching third level English literature at Carysfort Training College in Blackrock. 'I like being with people who are going to be primary teachers. They are a crucial force in the country.' He was involved in the Benson *Report on the Arts in*

Education and would like to see more time and resources given to creative work. Subjects like art that the universities can't examine are undervalued. 'Students are bowed down with timetables. They're over-instructed. Yet we're talking to them about the theory of growth of the personality of the child.' The ideal would be to teach children to think for themselves rather than to cram for university points. 'Time for repose. Wordsworth was a great poet of laziness. The best thing you can do is lie in the fields. Let nature be your teacher.'

Much of the year Heaney has been in America, teaching creative writing in Harvard. 'The students are all very highly motivated there, a kind of elite, all wanting to write their own work. Every time I went into the Harvard yard there were students bearing down on me with manuscripts, every post brought more writings. I ended up feeling like a target.'

But five weeks during the summer he got away from students, telephones and radios to a house in Long Island, where he completed a version of *Mad Sweeney*, which he had been attempting to finish since moving to Wicklow:

> The language didn't seem right, the temperature was wrong. The kind of words I was using had too much polysyllabic Latin and French to render the Irish faithfully. And they were in free verse. It did not seem to have the edge that was required. I had a notion of the noise I wanted, but I hadn't struck it. So this summer I took out all the Latin and put it into metre and rhyme. It's sharpened now, for better or for worse, and I'm ready to publish it.

He finds his manner of writing has become much more considered:

> I used to go into a kind of trance. You know, shut your eyes and concentrate back. But I've begun over the years, in the act of writing, to try to wake myself up more, to have more strategy rather than surrender to the thing. I suppose it's just a matter of getting older. The critic in me has changed. I'm more aware of what I'm doing.

We stand at the door. Dimly through the October drizzle across the flat sands, a ship glides past the Pigeon House power station, a dream image like the liner in Fellini's *Amarcord*. In *Field Work* he has used dreams for the first time, particularly in the title poem, 'but I finished it differently'.

We shake hands and as he holds mine he says: 'I think my ideal poem would not be a reported dream but it would have the effect of a dream, pain and hallucinatory at the same time.'

Joseph Heller, 1984

The last time Joseph Heller talked with me, a year before his death in 1998, he had just been savaged by Lynn Barber. She arrived early to interview him for The Observer *at his house on Long Island, and was huffed when he made her wait. Barber accused the 74-year-old author of being 'outrageously egocentric, he always brings the conversation back to himself'. Yet she was interviewing him about his autobiography; he could hardly not have talked about himself. In fact,* Now and Then *is arguably one of the more self-deprecating memoirs written by a major American literary figure. There's no whingeing about his impoverished Coney Island childhood, the son of immigrant Russian Jewish parents. He looks back on it as a time of great happiness and good luck. He devotes less than a chapter to war experiences – during which, according to others, he showed considerable bravery – although it provided the inspiration for his darkly hilarious first novel* Catch-22, *a title that has achieved iconic status in English dictionaries as a term to describe a no-win situation where you're damned if you do and damned if you don't. Heller hasn't a bad word to say for his first wife Shirley Held, although their divorce after thirty-nine years and two children was bitter and painful. There is virtually no name-dropping other than to mention how his friend Mel Brooks advised him that every Jew should have a big Gentile for a friend, advice which helped him to survive working in Norfolk Navy Yard. He makes no great claims for his novels. He wrote only six in thirty-five years: two of them,* Catch-22 *and* Something Happens *are American classics, and another,* Good As Gold, *comes close. He points out that he's a slow writer and has few ideas. Yet even a lesser novel like* Picture This *(1988), a mock history bringing together Rembrandt and Socrates in a shared story that jumps back and forth outrageously from classical Greece to New York in the 1980s via sixteenth-century Holland, is peppered with still apposite satirical one-liners (such as 'Peace on earth would mean the end of civilization as we know it' or 'Rich is the country that has plenty of poor'). I first met Heller over lunch in Le Bistro off Lexington Avenue in New York in early summer 1984. 'Pick a restaurant,' he'd told me when I called. 'I don't know Manhattan any more. I hardly ever come to New York.'*

There's nothing much to being a bombardier, except of course somehow managing to stay alive. It's like being a target in a fairground shooting gallery on Coney Island. Joseph Heller should know. This was his situation on sixty bombing missions over Europe during World War Two. 'I was the guy in the nose of the plane who had the mechanism for dropping the bombs,' he says. 'Since we always flew in V formation, I simply watched the plane in front of me and when it opened its bomb bays I opened mine.'

Like Yossarian in *Catch-22*, who came to realize that to be grounded you have to be crazy but you must be crazy to fly so if a pilot asks to be grounded, it means he is not crazy anymore and has to keep flying, Heller's only mission each time he took off from his base on the Sardinian coast was to come down alive, knowing that if the plane came under fire the bombardier was most likely to be hit. 'Not that my novels are auto-biographical,' he says.

'From now I'm thinking only of myself,' Yossarian told air force psychiatrist Major Denby. 'But Yossarian, suppose everyone felt that way?' 'Then,' said Yossarian, 'I'd certainly be a damned fool not to feel any other way, wouldn't I?'

Whatever about Yossarian, Heller has survived not only anti-aircraft fire and a failed marriage but more recently a rare neuro-viral disease called Guillain-Barré syndrome. He takes a three-by-five notecard from his wallet and writes it down for me. 'The body creates cells, which begin attacking the tissue surrounding the nerves,' he says. The paralysis that immobilized him for several months in 1982 struck at breakfast one Sunday. 'I found I couldn't swallow a piece of potato. Then I went to the car and my fingers couldn't open the door.' He'd just sent the third chapter of his fourth novel *God Knows* to a typist. 'It was four months before I was able to read what she'd typed. I couldn't even hold a page of typescript.'

The ultimate irony for a writer to whom irony is second nature was that what was happening to him duplicated the situation of the central character in *God Knows*. 'It's a biblical novel about an incapacitated King David regretting his physical decline and his sexual decline. Beautiful virgins are brought to his death bed to warm him. But, according to the *Book of Kings*, he didn't know them sexually.' Not that this was a problem that afflicted Heller. He recovered enough from his paralysis to marry Valerie Humphries, one of the nurses who helped him learn to walk again. 'Babies learn to walk all the time. But they're a lot nearer the ground. It doesn't matter how often they fall. Someone my age looks ridiculous falling. Besides, I could break a hip.'

Sitting across the table from me in Le Bistro he looks the picture of health again. His face has a glowing tan. His mop of curly white hair is like a lion's mane. Brooke Astor has persuaded him to attend a benefit dinner for New York Central Library tonight even though it means donning a tuxedo. 'I never wear them as a matter of principle.'

New York has come to mean divorce hearings for him. He's been in and out of court since separating from his wife Shirley Held in 1980 after thirty-six years of marriage. 'It's very hard to get a divorce in New York State. Both parties have to agree to it. You have to prove adultery or mental cruelty. The courts don't accept unhappiness as a cause for ending marriage.' His illness coincided with the separation. 'I don't think there's any association. Nobody knows.' Then he smiles. 'God knows.'

By now he's just about able to jog again. 'But not gracefully. I've forgotten how to run instinctively.' The trouble is that all his physical actions have to be thought out until they become habit again. 'Nothing is on automatic. It's all manual control.' He shrugs. 'I cannot think of anything I can do now I could not do better before.' None of which affected in any way his novel. 'Because like all my novels I had it in my mind before I started writing. I write everything in my mind. I know what I'm going to put down on the paper before I sit down and write it. What I eventually write will only change marginally from what I've written in my mind. I have to know everything beforehand.'

He didn't deliberately set out to write about God. 'I never begin with a subject in mind. It's always lines going through my head.' An opening line comes to him that triggers a flood of ideas so that a whole novel flashes before him within minutes. It can happen while he's brushing his teeth, or jogging in the gymnasium, or stopped at a traffic light. 'My mind is at it all the time. This is the way I do most of my work. Then it's a question of recalling, of information retrieval.'

He carries a sheaf of notecards around everywhere:

> With *Good As Gold* the ideas flowed in so fast I had to get one of those pocket-sized dictating machines. It's just daydreaming. Things don't come to me in any sequential way. If I get a thought I put it down and may get to it four years later. When it comes to actually writing the book many cannot be used. They seem like very funny ideas or very wise paradoxes when they come to mind, but they don't fit in with the character or the character of the novel itself.

That's how he began writing as a kid in Brooklyn:

> I'd a compulsion to fantasize. Other boys would do class assignments on Lincoln. I'd imagine I was the gun that shot Lincoln. I've never been very good with factual material. I wouldn't make a journalist. None of my novels could be called realistic. If they rely on facts it's only to a small degree and then my imagination takes over. I don't have much of an eye. There is very little description in my writing. I've only one nephew and I didn't notice that he had blue eyes until he was thirty-four.

Back in 1968 *Look* magazine commissioned him to go back to Europe with his family for the summer and visit the places he'd mentioned in *Catch-22*. 'Of course it was interesting to get the data I hadn't bothered to get when I was writing the novel, but I didn't know what to do with it. I couldn't make it interesting to read.' He's never been able to write to order. 'If you offered me a hundred million dollars to write an Irish novel I wouldn't be able to do it. I'm dependent on my imagination and it frightens me, because I don't know where certain thoughts come from. And I've always wondered whether I'll ever get any more. I've only ever had four ideas for novels and I've written them all.'

The first story he ever wrote was rejected by the *Daily News*. That was when he was eleven. Reading literature at New York University after the war – he was able to study there, thanks to the GI bill of rights – and as a Fulbright Scholar at Oxford, he began placing stories in *Esquire* and *Atlantic*. 'By the time I finished college I realized they were not that good. I decided not to write again until I had something to say.'

He was over thirty and working in an advertising agency when the idea for *Catch-22* came to him. 'I didn't decide to write a novel about the war. I was just lying in bed in my apartment and the opening lines popped into my mind: "It was love at first sight. The first time so-and-so – the name Yossarian came later – saw the chaplain he fell madly in love with him …"' Straight away he wrote the first chapter. He didn't write a second chapter for another year. The novel took eight years to complete. 'I took my time writing it because I had to. I discovered I could not write rapidly. If I wrote more than one page an evening I'd have to keep rewriting.'

Although *Catch-22*, in which a small group of American flyers in Italy in 1944 become a microcosm of the world as it might seem to someone dangerously sane, was eventually to sell over eight million copies – and become a cult movie success, directed by Mike Nichols –it wasn't a bestseller when it came out in 1961. 'This took the pressure off me. I could write something completely different the next time, and nobody was hurrying me.'

His second novel, *Something Happened*, took twelve years to complete. Again the idea came to him as a couple of opening sentences: 'In the office where I work there are four people of whom I am afraid. Each of these four people is afraid of five people.' These lines in fact provided the start of the second section of the novel, which eventually opened with, 'I get the willies when I see closed doors.'

He had to keep leaving *Something Happened* for other work to pay bills. '*Catch-22* didn't earn enough for me to give up everything except novels.' He taught fiction at Yale University. 'I'd give them Joyce's 'The Dead' and challenge them to find a single word that you'd need to go to a dictionary for.' He scripted the movie *Sex and the Single Girl*. 'They paid 5000 dollars a month, 1000 dollars expenses and transported the whole family to California for the summer.' He even wrote a play, *We Bombed in New Haven*. 'Not the biggest success, not the biggest failure. One of the reasons I like to write novels is that I don't have to collaborate with anyone.'

Even before publication in 1974, *Something Happened* had become a runaway bestseller. 'I knew I was going to make a minimum of $300,000–400,000 compared to the $30,000 a year I could get teaching.' With the pressure to earn an income eased, he could write more freely. 'I realized with *Good as Gold* and *God Knows* that I am not as slow as I thought.'

The waiter brings chilled Chablis and suggests tripe. Heller settles for sole. 'I'll tell you something you don't know,' he enunciates carefully. 'The cheeks are busy all the time when a person eats. Because my cheek muscles are still weak, I have to push them in and out with my fingers. Otherwise the food collects behind the teeth ...' He has no idea what his next novel will be and he won't even start thinking about it for at least another year. 'Until all the fuss of this one is out of the way, I'll enjoy it while it lasts. I like being a successful writer. Usually it takes about a year before people lose interest in me, including my publisher.'

That's when the melancholy will set in, 'the feeling of depression that follows success'. Like when all the hype subsided after *Good as Gold*. He was sitting out in the sun and words began suggesting themselves: 'I've got the best story in the Bible. Genesis, a fairy story. Moses, he's okay, but I've got better wives than Moses.' Then another sentence incongruously intruded: 'Michelangelo made statues of us both.' Straight away he knew he was going to write a first-person novel that wouldn't be chronological and that the narrator was somehow still alive. He rushed over to East Hampton public library and read everything he could find on David.

But it wouldn't worry him if he never wrote another novel. 'I don't have any burning ambition to write. If I'm in the middle of writing something and someone calls I'll drop it and go out for a meal.' That's the real reward of success. 'I'm better off than the president of the United States or the chief of any big corporation because I have two things they don't have. I never have to do work I don't want to do and I don't have to associate with people I don't like.'

Not that he's ever likely to become complacent. 'Every success has failure built into it,' he says, pressing his cheeks with his fingers to speak more clearly. Or as David says at one point in the new novel: 'Nothing fails like success. Believe me, I know.'

Michel Houellebecq, 2008

In the aftermath of Donald Trump's shock victory in the 2016 US presidential election, many commentators predicted that the extreme-right National Front leader Marine Le Pen would pull off a similar coup in the French elections. But Michel Houellebecq had already offered a more intriguing scenario in his 2015 novel Submission: *he imagined François Hollande being succeeded by a Muslim president as the other parties unite to block Marine Le Pen. Like all his novels, it's a Swiftian social satire projecting a dystopian future from the flaws of contemporary society. 'I show the disaster produced by the liberalization of values,' he claims.* Submission *was published in 2015 on the same day that terrorists gunned down staff of* Charlie Hebdo, *a Parisian satirical magazine that had just published a cover story on Houellebecq. Since then he has had police protection. But perhaps Houellebecq's best protection is that even people close to him are seldom sure where he might be: he has a fetish about anonymity.*

Nobody can find Michel Houellebecq. Already one of the most renowned living French authors – some might argue notorious – he was supposed to attend the 2008 Locarno Festival screening of his directorial debut *The Possibility of an Island*, but didn't show up. Affronted French critics sniggered and walked out, accusing him of getting cold feet and dodging the press, scared off by predictions his science-fiction parable would be 'the flop of the season'. Predictably, *Le Figaro* dismissed it in advance as 'catastrophic, ridiculous, full of cheap street philosophizing'.

Preferring to drive through the Swiss Alps rather than travel by air – his father was a mountain guide and he's always been drawn to mountains – he miscalculated the time and eventually arrived in the middle of the night, seemingly unaware of the sensation he'd caused. His mobile had been switched off. Rather than apologize, he promptly cancelled all the interviews that had been arranged, including a reshuffled press conference, but agreed to meet me at the Belvedere Hotel, which overlooks Locarno and is reached by a funicular ride.

But now Houellebecq – his name is pronounced 'Wellbeck' – seems to have disappeared again. A flustered festival official who doesn't know what he looks like asks me to see if I can spot him. It didn't occur to her that a forlorn figure in an anorak sitting alone in a corner of the foyer could be someone so famous. He brightens when he sees me, remembering an interview we did several years ago over a bottle of red wine in the Shelbourne Hotel in Dublin.

He's sanguine about the furore surrounding him. 'French critics think they know me,' he sighs. 'It's become a personal thing. I don't think they read the books anymore. I can do nothing about it.'

The Possibility of an Island foresees an apocalyptic breakdown of western society through the preaching of the charismatic leader of a sect that regards DNA cloning as a way of achieving immortality. It's a flawed film, partly because its miniscule budget ruled out state-of-the-art digital special effects. Houellebecq relies instead on the stunning impact of Lanzarote's lunar landscape and the surreal architecture of futuristic Spanish resorts to evoke a sense of the seeds of consumerism's collapse.

Even if the costumes and gadgets, as one French critic sneered, 'resemble those from a science-fiction B movie from the 1950s or an early black-and-white episode of *Doctor Who*', the genetic science is convincing. 'If you don't have a lot of money, it's absolutely necessary that the science is serious and credible,' he says.

Genetics is a recurring theme in his fiction. Biology has speeded up since Aldous Huxley imagined a genetically engineered *Brave New World*, set in the twenty-sixth century. If Houellebecq's novel *Atomised* is correct, we'll all be clones as early as 2070. What's happened is that the decoding of the genome has opened up the possibility of every cell being perfectly copied. It's no longer fanciful to conceive humanity giving way to a new species that is asexual and immortal, a species that will have outgrown individuality. '*Brave New World*, given that it was written in 1932, was incredibly prophetic,' he says. 'For us today, it's not so difficult to prophesize these things. You don't need to be necessarily well informed.'

Although the logic of the characters in *Atomised*, written from the future looking back at the death pangs of 'this vile, unhappy race, barely different from the apes' is hard to refute, Houellebecq himself is less sure. 'Most of the time I don't think of what will probably happen,' he says. 'I'm sure I don't know. It's impossible to have any certitude. A lot of historical things are not predictable. I'm very conscious of that. Nobody predicted the fall of the Berlin Wall. Most things in the human story take us by surprise.'

Atomised won the Prix Novembre when it was published in France in 1998 and has been translated into twenty-six languages. His subsequent novel *Platform*, which elaborates on the theme of packaged pleasure and sex gone wrong at the core of *Atomised*, has sold over 300,000 copies. No other French writer enjoys such international success.

He keeps away from all the fuss as much as he can, as Locarno is now discovering. He lived for several years on Bere Island off the West Cork coast with his wife Marie-Pierre and their corgi Clement. The final pages of *Atomised* were written there and are set in a biological research centre in Connemara where, between long walks on the mist-shrouded mountains, the protagonist Michel achieves the genetic breakthrough – via experiments with Dolly-like cloned cows – that changes mankind forever.

The fact that Houellebecq uses his own name for the central character in *Atomised* – and in his first novel *Whatever*, in which the central character encourages a friend to indulge in the perverted pleasures of sexual murder – does not mean that it should be taken as autobiographical.

'It's not important what name I call my characters,' he says. 'What is very important to do is to use the first person. When you call a character "I", it changes what you can do with him. I like to reproduce parts of reality, but sometimes it is not my own reality.'

He depicts the behaviour of the characters, particularly their sexual promiscuity – Bruno and Michel are casualties of the wave of permissiveness that seduced western society in the late twentieth century – with clinical detail. 'There is something always very precise in what I write,' he says, sipping white wine. 'I never forget to point out to the reader the level of alcohol that my characters have. It's why I like film. You can see from the number of bottles on the table. Writers usually think in terms of words. I think in terms of light. I imagine different lightings when I write.'

He has collaborated with the director Philippe Harel on film adaptations of *Atomised* and *Whatever*. He made a documentary for Canal+ on the subject of erotica, featuring his wife. Ideas to him are as much visual as verbal. 'Any new philosophy is in fact a new visual conception of the universe,' he points out in *Atomised*. The character Michel is inspired by the Book of Kells. 'All that exists is magnificent interweaving, vast and reciprocal.'

Houellebecq was born in 1958 on the island of Réunion in the Indian Ocean, formerly a French penal colony. 'I have no relationship with Réunion,' he says. 'I left when I was five. I have few memories. Just details. Pineapples and sugar cane fields. A few things.' Abandoned soon after birth by his hippy mother, he was brought up first in Algeria by his mother's mother and then alone in the Burgundy countryside by his father's mother, a communist whose name he adopted. 'There's very little to say,' he says. His half-sister, born four years after him, was brought up separately. 'If I had a childhood like him I would have killed myself,' his writer friend Frédéric Beigbeder has said. 'He is a zombie back from the dead and telling us what it was like.'

It's possible to read the half-brothers Michel and Bruno as versions of himself and his half-sister, but this would be to misunderstand the nature of fiction and the reimagining of reality. He has never returned to Réunion. 'I don't feel any urge to go there. I know more or less what it looks like from pictures. I think I will go back before I die.'

Unlike the French eighteenth-century rationalist Diderot, Houellebecq doesn't treat his characters merely as a vehicle for arguments. 'It's not only a dialogue of ideas between the half-brothers Bruno and Michel,' he says. 'You have feelings that they share. They have the same blood.'

Atomised, for all its ruthless logic – 'there is no power in the world that can compete with rational certainty' – is a deeply human novel, particularly in its depiction of death. All the women who matter die, the grandmothers who rear the two sons, the women who become their lovers, the mother who abandoned them in order to lead a life of hippy indulgence (a forgiving Michel says: 'All she wanted was to be young.') Houellebecq shrugs. 'There's a lot of death, a lot of ways to die. It's not an original theme.'

By now he's used to being attacked for the views expressed by his characters. The main character in *Platform* experiences a quiver of enthusiasm 'every time I heard that a Palestinian terrorist, or a Palestinian child or a pregnant Palestinian woman, had been gunned down in the Gaza Strip'. Houellebecq compounded the offence by remarking in an interview that Islam was 'the most stupid of all religions' – particularly since the word 'stupid' has even stronger connotations in French. Four French Muslim organizations brought an action charging him with inciting racial hatred. He's unsure of his defence. 'I can say I have a right to think a certain religion is stupid,' he says. 'I suppose we have this right in France. It's not clearly written into law. You can be accused of defaming or libel.'

He discovered science fiction as a precocious six-year-old when he first read H.P. Lovecraft, whose phrase 'I never participate in what surrounds me, I am in what surrounds me, I am not at home anywhere' seems to have become his personal mantra. He graduated as an agronomical engineer and became a computer administrator at the French National Assembly before achieving notoriety as a 'pop star of the single generation' with his debut novel *Whatever*, a label that has stuck with him ever since. Loathed alike by much of the French left and right for his failure to conform, he has compounded his unpopularity by choosing to live abroad.

He now has a holiday place in the south of Spain, in a small town between Almeria and Murcia. He's lived in several parts of Ireland. 'After Cork, I moved to the suburbs of Dublin but it became too crowded, and then I moved to Clare. The Shannon is nice, yes? I'm always looking for a compromise between a nice place and not too far from an airport, because I move around a lot.' He wrote *The Possibility of an Island* walking the volcanic mountains of Lanzarote, alone with his dog, much like the character in the film. 'I always go to locations when I write a novel. In this case the locations were so impressive that the idea of doing the film came of that.'

He hasn't seen his 83-year-old mother, Lucie Ceccaldi, for seventeen years, but the publication of her memoir, in which she calls him an 'evil, stupid little bastard', has upset him. 'I don't like people talking about my private life. I really don't. I'm not detached enough to ignore it. There are always people, friends and family, who read it and say, "Did you read that, isn't it awful?" It is human nature to want to know what is said about you but you have to resist, yes? But that needs a lot of personal discipline.'

Houellebecq's brief disappearance in Locarno might almost have been a rehearsal for his more spectacular failure to turn up for part of a tour promoting his novel *The Map of the Territory* in the Netherlands and

Belgium in 2011. YouTube and Twitter went viral with reports than he had been abducted. Days later he resurfaced without any explanation. A film inspired by his disappearance, *The Kidnapping of Michel Houellebecq*, written and directed by Guillaume Nicloux, with the author playing himself, went into production two years later and was premiered at the 2014 Berlin Film Festival. Reviewers were divided on whether it was a prank or a fictionalized version of what may or may not have happened. Houellebecq, who represents himself as a hostage so cantankerous that his captors end up trying to placate him, seemed content to leave everyone guessing.

The film's approach takes its cue from *The Map and the Territory*, much of which was written in Clare and deals with the life and times of a young French artist who makes his name with an exhibition of photographs of Michelin road maps but then switches to painting, achieving Damien Hirst-like mega-fame with large-scale celebrity portraits. He travels to Ireland to paint a portrait of a recluse writer, Michel Houellebecq, attracted by the fact that 'it was public knowledge that Houellebecq was a loner with strong misanthropic tendencies.' By making himself a character in his own fiction, and then having that character murdered, Houellebecq cunningly subverts attempts to brand what he writes as autobiographical while at the same time prompting a meditation on the relationship between literature, art and the reimagining of reality. 'I feel a certain distance – not too far, not too close,' he says.

Kazuo Ishiguro, 1988

One of the pleasures of being an interviewer is to encounter a writer or artist early in life before they become widely known and established. In 1987 Kazuo Ishiguro had just published his second novel, An Artist of the Floating World. *It went on to be shortlisted for the Booker Prize and win the Whitbread Prize in that same year. When we met in London, Ishiguro was working on a third novel that would make his name,* The Remains of the Day.

It's doubtful if the Queen Mother ever employed a less likely grouse beater. Whacking the heather to drive the birds towards the gun butts at her residence at Balmoral was a Japanese would-be rock star with gold-rimmed spectacles. 'It's amazing what bad shots the royal guests are,' novelist Kazuo Ishiguro recalls from the safety of a book-lined room in London's Queen Square. 'After lunch they'd drive up in their Land Rovers more than a little drunk. Being a beater could be very dangerous.'

But it was a job. He wasn't fussy about what he did as a youth. Music was everything to him. While studying at the University of Kent in Canterbury he'd spend all his time playing acoustic guitar and piano at local gigs. 'Growing up in the 1960s and 1970s, that was our culture. Novels seemed marginal to our experience. The Rolling Stones and The Beatles were the crucial influence on the way we thought and behaved.' Up to 1979, all he'd ever written was songs. 'I suppose I only drifted into writing fiction when it became clear I was getting too old to be a new Bob Dylan.'

Although he couldn't write a word in the language of his birth – 'I'm one of the very few illiterate Japanese' – he more than made up for it in English. 'I've become British by default,' he apologizes. There had been no intention of staying in England when he arrived from Japan with his family in 1960. 'It was never a clear emigration. We were only supposed to stay two years. So we were brought up in such a way that when we went back it wouldn't be such a shock. My parents tried to keep the Japanese side of our education going in the home while outside I began receiving a typical southern English education.'

As a leading oceanographer, his father was involved in research on North Sea oil. 'It's not as exciting as it might sound, nothing like Jacques Cousteau. He didn't go deep-sea diving. All his work was at the British Oceanographic Institute in the middle of the woods in Surrey. As far as I know he never went near the sea.' Every time they were about to return to Japan, his project was extended. 'Even though he's now retired, he's stayed on in Guildford and so have we.'

As a five-year-old there was no real sense of culture shock for Kazuo. 'I was too young to have acquired a clear set of values to lose. Every day was a new experience with the shock of new things to learn. At a certain point the new things turned into English things.'

But he remembers feeling outraged by the way his English friends were treated by their parents. 'They were expected to take a back seat. They were ordered around everywhere and told to go on errands and shouted at. I couldn't get over how disrespectful their parents were to them.' It wasn't at all what he'd been used to in Nagasaki. 'The Japanese almost worship children, particularly the boy-child. Adults get up for children in the tram. It's considered of utmost importance that children have the right atmosphere to play. No parent would ever dream of interrupting them.'

Even now, he can't get over the odd way the English behave with their children. 'The whole ethos of boarding school is incomprehensible to the Japanese.' All his own education was at local primary and grammar schools: he was never sent away to public school like some of his neighbours. Thus he grew up speaking Japanese as well as English and still does at home. 'But it's terribly inappropriate Japanese for someone of my age. It's a child's

Japanese. I speak like a five-year-old and because I picked up so much from my mother, I also speak like a woman.'

In Japanese there's a different form of address for every relationship. It's far more complicated than the French familiar *tu* and formal *vous*:

> There are seven or eight different words for 'I' and you have to choose the right one according to how you perceive the relationship between yourself and the person you're speaking to. Much of the meaning is in the form rather than the content of what's said. Japanese businessmen can convey whether a deal is on or off with a slight shift in the manner of address, whereas their Western counterparts come out of the meeting not knowing what happened.

With only his family to speak to, he had little chance of building up this kind of sophistication. So much so that when he meets anyone Japanese he talks in English. 'I'd be too embarrassed to speak in Japanese.' English by now has become his natural idiom. 'I can hardly write or read a word of Japanese. You need to know over a thousand cryptograms even to be able to read a newspaper and each one stands for different things depending on what it is combined with.' Writing in one culture while coming from another is part of the distinctiveness of his style: he brings to familiar words different meanings and associations, a different tone. This is a characteristic of Irish literature, too. 'It does seem that a lot of the more interesting fiction in English comes from people who do not have an Anglo-Saxon background.'

A radio play written while working with the homeless in Glasgow, where he met his Scottish wife, gained him a place on the creative writing course run by Malcolm Bradbury and Angela Carter at the University of East Anglia. 'Nothing was prescribed. The idea was that you were left alone and encouraged to find your own voice. That sort of space is crucial when you're wondering whether to take yourself seriously as a writer.' Almost immediately, Faber & Faber accepted a short story, the first he'd ever attempted, and then gave him a hefty advance on a novel he'd started for his thesis. 'I missed out on that whole trauma of writing a first novel and not knowing whether anyone would publish it.' *A Pale View of Hills*, acclaimed by *The Times* as 'a first novel of grace, subtlety and accomplishment', draws on his own experience. A Japanese widow living in England looks back on her family's struggle to rebuild their lives in post-war Nagasaki. 'I suppose I had to work through a lot of my feelings about Japan and my being distanced from it. I had to put together a Japan of memory and imagination.'

Some people have seen in his choice of Nagasaki a dimension he didn't intend. 'To a Western reader if you bring in Nagasaki you bring in the bomb. But for me Nagasaki isn't primarily the place where the bomb fell. It's the place where I used to live. It's the Japan I remember.'

It wasn't until he was eight or nine that he came to realize the significance of Nagasaki:

> There wasn't any talk at home – certainly not in front of a small child – of bitterness or tragedy. People just referred to the bomb as a marker in time. I thought every city had a bomb. I still remember the peculiar sort of pride with which I discovered in an encyclopaedia at school that only two places in the world suffered an atomic attack and Nagasaki was one of them.

Nagasaki wasn't a direct hit like Hiroshima. Only one side of the city was badly damaged:

> But in the days following the explosion everyone had to go there for the nightmare task of burning bodies. It was the height of summer and the whole place was like an oven because everything was still burning. My grandfather was one of those who had to pile corpse upon corpse and burn them before some terrible disease spread. Soon after, he died of radiation. Nobody then knew the risk.

Although *An Artist of the Floating World* is also about Japan, he has consciously avoided ever going back to Japan. 'I thought it would disturb the world I was constructing. I feel I have to write out of what I know already.'

Japan today bears little resemblance to the Japan immediately after the war that he writes about. In a sense, he's recreated a world that no longer exists and perhaps never did. Fiction doesn't reproduce reality: it creates its own. As one of his own characters points out: 'The best things are put together of a night and vanish with the morning ... what people call the floating world.'

'What is important to me is that I have a certain authority within my own fictional world and I'm not terribly bothered if it doesn't correspond exactly to any real Japan,' he says. 'I'm not writing a documentary. I'm not a journalist. My primary concern is not to teach people about Japanese society. I don't want people to go to my fiction as a sort of textbook.'

Although both his novels are set in Japan, neither is essentially about Japan. The ageing painter who feels guilt about his past in *An Artist of the Floating World* represents the universal dilemma of idealistic people confronted with the possibility that they've wasted their lives, worse still, that they may have contributed their greatest talents to something that was actually evil: 'I'm interested in how people try to cling to a sense of dignity and try to salvage something from that sort of situation. We all live with the notion that the consequences of what we do might turn out to be quite different to what we expected or would have wished. I suppose I write out of that sort of fear.' Writing doesn't come easy to him. 'It's something very deliberate and conscious. I don't feel it welling up. It always seems like work. I suspect I'm a natural musician rather than a natural writer. My culture relies on visual and audio images rather than verbal ones.'

He has been lured into film-making, scripting BBC2's *The Gourmet*, a bizarre little parable in which Charles Gray plays an aesthete with a craving to eat a ghost. He found he had less control over the worlds he creates. 'You have to improvise with what is available to you. Any number of factors may influence what ends up on the screen. Actors will turn up without having learned their lines. Other actors will not want to deliver a line a certain way. Your location just won't look the way you imagined it.'

He'll have no problems like that with his third novel, *The Remains of the Day*. 'The great thing about writing a novel is that you're on your own and you just keep going until things are perfected.' This time his setting will be the South of England in the shadow of imminent war, mirrored in the experiences of a faithful butler. 'There's not a Japanese person in sight. I want to lose the label of being a Japanese writer.'

Nearly a quarter of a century would pass before we were to meet again. 'I'm glad to see you're still in action,' he greets me in a London hotel, just before Christmas 2011. 'I still have the cutting of what you wrote about me.' Much has changed. *The Remains of the Day* won the Booker Prize and was filmed by James Ivory with Anthony Hopkins as a butler who realizes that his lifelong loyalty to his master has been misplaced. 'I tried to keep a back seat during the filming,' he says. 'I've always worried about film-makers being over-reverential about a book. I wanted them to feel they should only put something in the film if they really felt it for themselves and they weren't paying lip service to something else.'

Another of his novels, *Never Let Me Go*, which was shortlisted for the Booker but lost out to John Banville's *The Sea*, has been filmed with Keira Knightley, Carey Mulligan and Andrew Garfield as a group of twenty-something childhood friends dealing with the knowledge that their days are drastically numbered. Although taking place in rural England in the 1990s, their world is an alternative reality where humanity has learned how to clone itself and schoolchildren are bred and conditioned to accept that in their twenties their lives will be ended for the greater good. 'I wanted to create this world in which young people become old while staying young.'

He made two attempts at writing *Never Let Me Go* in the 1990s and each time abandoned it and wrote a different novel:

> I couldn't find a convincing way of creating a situation in which the way of life of the characters would seem normal to them. Then I tried again in 2001. I imagined what would have happened after World War Two if the break-through in science hadn't been in nuclear physics but in biotechnology, and then wondered where we might have got by the late 1900s. I wasn't interested particularly in the infrastructure of this world, or how it was supervised and enforced. All I had in my head was this parallel reality.

The first time we met Ishiguro had never been back to the Japan he'd been taken from as a five-year-old. 'I eventually went back a couple of years after you talked with me,' he says. 'It was remarkably similar to the way I remembered as a small child. The neighbours were the same. The corner-shop lady was the same.' He shrugs. 'I realized that for a long time a tiny pocket I remembered on the outskirts of Nagasaki was the entire country for me. I mistook it for Japan. Tokyo could have been a different planet.'

Jennifer Johnston, 1984

Hugh Leonard, who never knew his real father, used to pretend that playwright Denis Johnston was his father, 'because he was a maverick, and I felt in a sense a bit like him'. Denis achieved a worldwide reputation in the 1930s with The Old Lady Says "No!" *and* The Moon on the Yellow River *before becoming a famed BBC war correspondent. His autobiography* Nine Rivers to Jordan *was published in 1953 while I was at Blackrock College. My English teacher Wally Finn, who had met him in the Middle East as a chaplain and became his friend, used to ask him for comments on what we wrote. It encouraged me to send one of my stories to the* Evening Herald, *where it was published and earned me £3 – a fortune for a sixteen-year-old schoolboy. Many years later I found myself interviewing Johnston's novelist daughter Jennifer on a bench in St Stephen's Green.*

Jennifer Johnston clearly remembers doing *Irish Times* crosswords while waiting for her father to die. 'You couldn't just sit there and be sad,' she says. 'It seemed to us to be struggling for clues, but other people might have thought it strange.' This is the way characters behave in her fiction, too. A middle-aged woman in her 1984 novel *The Railway Station Man* even makes a joke while RUC men are trying to tell her that her husband has been killed by terrorists.

One of the things that sticks in her mind about Denis Johnston's funeral at St Patrick's Cathedral was that for the first time she thought a photograph showed her the way she saw herself. Her father had been greatly pleased when Dean Griffin inquired if he would consider being buried in the cathedral beside his friend Lennox Robinson. He had moments of lucidity towards the end. He knew what he wanted to say but couldn't always get the right words. 'I've been elected,' he exclaimed. She realized he regarded it as perhaps the greatest honour he'd ever received. 'You know Chekhov got it right as a playwright. He always had people doing the kind of incongruous things we'd all be doing, like playing cards, while tragedies were happening in the background.'

This is the same perspective she keeps bringing to bear on the Irish situation in her stories. She doesn't treat the Troubles as a big drama, but we sense the presence of violence everywhere. It's as much a part of the landscape as the sea and the wind. 'I don't write political novels. I'm trying to write about relationships, but the rest of it just keeps coming in. You can't pretend it's not there and that everything is the way it is in Wimbledon.' Living in Derry with her young family as she does now, she's not likely to lose sight of it. 'Yet it's easier in a way being there than it was when I was living in London at the beginning of the Troubles. Everything seems much more cataclysmic from afar. When you're living with it you're seeing all the people who are involved. You find that they're just people too, not monsters.'

What's upsetting is the way people are reduced to labels, this preconditional notion of what they are:

> It's much easier for people to think of the RUC as evil creatures, but they're not. They're just men. And it's easier for Protestants to hate the Provos as Provos, but they're just men and women too, like all the rest of us. That's the trouble when you look at it from a distance. You only see the labels. That's why the British never sort the whole thing out. We're just figures to them, not people who are suffering. It doesn't really worry them.

All her fiction derives from details in her own life. The woman in *The Railway Station Man* is the same age as she is. *The Old Jest* happens in Greystones, where she spent all her holidays as a child. *How Many Miles to Babylon?* draws on the Wicklow countryside she knows so well. 'Everything has to have its base, its feet on the ground.' She writes out of a sense of memory. 'Almost as if you're living in the past at the same time that you're living in the present, something I feel very strongly about myself.'

She's not convinced that she's yet got this right in any of her novels, nor in her play *Indian Summer*, which was a kind of ghost story. 'The characters all the time had the past standing at their shoulders, both the historical past and their family past. They were carrying it around with them.' Fiction is a way of bringing some order to all the chaos. 'I'm not a tidy person at all but I have this drive to tidy up life when I write, because a novel has to be brought to an end. You have to make a pattern, whereas when you're struggling through your own life you're not sure what the pattern is until it's too late.'

Not that she has complete control over her novels either. The characters tend to take on a life of their own. *The Railway Station Man* is not the novel she originally had in mind:

> I started off wanting to write about the woman's relationship with her husband and son, which is then transferred to the other young man and the Englishman. I was even going to call it *The Surrogates*, they being her surrogate husband and son. But it worked out being very much more about the woman's own attitude to life and what she wanted to do, and everything else seemed to become secondary.

She smiles apologetically. 'All my novels seem to take over in this strange sort of way. Writing fiction is a sort of organic operation. I suppose it would be terribly boring otherwise, just putting down exactly what you plot in your head.'

She didn't publish her first novel until she was thirty-eight and married with four children. 'I think I read too much as a child and thought there was really not much point in writing because it had all been done much better before.' But like her own heroine in *The Railway Station Man* who takes up painting with some success, it suddenly occurred to her that 'it's silly to sit around for your whole life and do nothing.' Finding time to write while running a home more or less dictated the way she writes. 'I can't imagine any of my novels ever being more than 190 pages. Even if I tried it wouldn't happen. That's my length.' Hers is the language of subtle associations and connections. It doesn't require long descriptive passages.

Her father took great pleasure in her late success as a novelist. When she published her first novel he presented her with the silver Tailteann medal he'd been awarded for his play *The Moon on the Yellow River*. 'It was like being elected,' she says with some satisfaction.

Molly Keane, 1988

Born into an Anglo-Irish family with roots going back to the Norman Conquest, Mary Nesta Skrine – known to readers and theatregoers first as M.J. Farrell and ultimately as Molly Keane – grew up at a distance from her parents in a privileged world of hunting and shooting that partied on even when the glory days of the empire had long faded. To the colonized Irish beyond the gates of the big house, their hauteur was resented, their eccentricity derided. Yet the two cultures of bog-Irish Catholics and horse Protestants fed off each other to enrich the English language, a creative collision of opposites. Nobody saw through the foibles of the ascendancy classes more perceptively than one of their own, the Skrine who jumped the nest, so to speak, leading a double life under a pseudonym because for a woman from her background it would have been social anathema to write under her own name. In 1950, after the early death of her husband Bobby Keane at thirty-seven, she settled in a cottage tucked into a hill overlooking the sea at Ardmore in County Waterford, bringing up her daughters Sarah and Virginia with a freedom she had been denied, and she lived there until her death in 1996, aged ninety-four.

About the only time plump little Nicandra – named after a horse by a father unable to express himself outside the vernacular of the racetrack – got near her parents was when the housemaid, Lizzie, brought up the early morning tea on a tray to their bedroom. Nicandra would sneak in behind her hoping for a kiss. 'Oh give her a lump of sugar,' her father would say impatiently. She might have been one of his least favourite animals.

'They were longing to get rid of her,' sighs Molly Keane. At eighty-four she has defied a heart attack to create yet another bitingly sharp yet compassionate portrayal of the loneliness of childhood in ascendancy Ireland. 'I do hope the poor girl doesn't seem a boringly pitiful creature,' she says. *Loving and Giving* is just as much concerned with the love and loss Nicandra experiences later as a grown up. But all the time she is playing out a role she was born into. 'Imprinted forever, there was no getting out of it.'

Molly Keane once described herself to Russell Harty ('Darling Russell, I was struck down by his death, because he really was a friend') as having been a 'rather unloved and unlovely girl'. But nothing near as pathetic as Nicandra, she insists. 'I was never a beauty. On the other hand, I was never as unhappy as that. But I've met people who were, I really have.

She has never really got away from the world of the big house. The high Victorian grate in the sitting room of her Ardmore cottage – she keeps a turf fire burning even in summer – is from her childhood home at Ballyrankin, near Bunclody in Wexford. And the red carpet comes from the stairs at Belleville in the Blackwater valley where she moved in as a young bride to be waited upon by six servants and a butler. 'It's over a hundred years old. I couldn't part with it when we had that awful sale. So I pieced it together for here.' It's much the way she pieces together her fiction with fragments from her past in the other Ireland, that island within an island.

'It was quite a separate world. There was no crossing over. That's why so many ladies of my generation never married. They grew up just after the First World War. There'd been an absolute holocaust of men they could have married. As to marrying someone who perhaps wasn't the same class, they just wouldn't have thought of it.' She imagines them ending up frustrated like Aroon in *Good Behaviour*. 'A number of friends were absolutely furious with me over that. Each thought I had them in mind as Aroon. Well, I ask you. It's ridiculous.' No character borrowed by her from life ever turns out remotely the same. She always changes them around. Like Jasper in *Time After Time*, her follow-up to *Good Behaviour*. When French critics told her what a dreadful character he was, she replied tartly, 'Jasper *c'est moi*.'

Nobody had wanted to publish *Good Behaviour* when she finished it in 1977. She had not written a novel for thirty years. 'I'd the girls to bring up.' But her friend Peggy Ashcroft persuaded her to try again when she found it in a drawer on a visit to Ardmore. It became an immediate bestseller, narrowly losing out to Salman Rushdie's *Midnight's Children* for the Booker Prize in 1981. It was later adapted for television by Hugh Leonard. Not bad for someone who made her writing debut as a seventeen-year-old with a Mills and Boon romance, *The Knight of the Cheerful Countenance*. 'Thank God it's lost. Nobody has a copy of it. It was absolute piffle. I wrote it when I was supposed to be getting TB but wasn't. Everything was called TB in those days and I was put to bed for the summer.'

She used the pseudonym M.J. Farrell, borrowed from a local pub, 'because it didn't do to have a touch of the literary about you in that kind of hunting milieu.' Mills and Boon turned down her next book. 'They thought it was rather fast.' But soon she was achieving critical recognition from the likes of Hugh Walpole and Herbert Read with *Devoted Ladies*, which dealt with the risqué theme of lesbianism. Compton Mackenzie regarded it as 'infernally good.' By the time her first play, *Spring Meeting*, directed by John Gielgud, had become a West End hit in 1938, the secret of her identity was out. 'But by then nobody despised me for being a writer.'

Her mother Agnes, too, had hidden her literary talents behind another name. As Moira O'Neill she contributed to *Blackwoods* magazine. She was author of *Songs of the Glens of Antrim*. Her poems were included in the *Oxford Book of English Verse*. 'Some of it was jolly good, some of it pure sentimental, rather like Eva Gore-Booth, but better. She could have written much more but she was terribly idle.' Not that this made her in any way sympathetic to the idea of her daughter becoming a writer. 'She read one of my books and was horribly disgusted. She never read another.'

All that mattered in the family was the hunt. That was why her father Walter had come back from Canada to live in Kildare at the turn of the century. 'My father was like many of his generation. He was the youngest of a family of twelve in Somerset. So his father bought him a ranch in Canada. Landowners were jolly rich in those days.' Recently her younger brother visited Canada to see what had become of the ranch. 'They told him father had been one of the people who opened up Canada. They remember him there as a pioneer.' Her mother, whose father was governor of Mauritius, was from Antrim. 'I don't think anyone in Antrim was properly Irish. Who was then, for God's sake? But I think I am. I was brought up with all the terrible Union Jack waving. But I mind more about Ireland than anything.'

She remembers moving to Wexford when she was six. 'I never had any education there, just a succession of terrible governesses. I can't understand why my mother couldn't see that we were learning absolutely nothing.' During the Troubles they were burned out by Sinn Feiners. 'When they burst into the house they collected all the servants with my mother and father. My father was a belligerent little fellow and went for them with a bayonet that was in the hall. "Look," they told him with genuine concern. "If you go on like that we'll have to shoot you."' As she says this, it occurs to me that my own father, who was a local commandant in that area at the time, might well have been one of the intruders, but I keep the thought to myself. Later her father would buy another house near the old house, living there for the rest of his life. 'He always said he'd rather be shot in Ireland than live in England.'

Bobby Keane was the gentleman farmer Molly met at a hunt ball. Unlike nearly everyone else, he delighted in her writing. Feeling encouraged, she wrote a succession of plays that caused James Agate to proclaim: 'I would back this impish writer to hold her own against Noel Coward.' They would foray out from Belleville for first nights, none finer than *Spring Meeting*, which marked the debut of Margaret Rutherford as one of the aunts that were to keep recurring in all Molly Keane's fiction. 'We always had aunts living with us in Wexford.'

With Bobby's death in 1946 the fun went out of writing. Her last M.J. Farrell novel was published in 1952. She stopped writing altogether after her play *Dazzling Prospects* flopped on the West End in 1961. Critics compared it scathingly with John Osborne's *Look Back in Anger*. 'I wouldn't write plays in London now,' she says. 'The audiences have become completely different, more clever but more brutal, too.'

With her children finally reared – Virginia is married to Kevin Brownlow, director of *It Happened Here* – she at last began writing again in the 1970s. 'I'd much rather cook than write. But I needed some money.' She has to discipline herself ruthlessly to write every day. 'It's like learning something by heart as a child. I write two or three hours in the morning – always in longhand, because I can't type. I can't even think about something unless I have a pen in my hand. I write slowly in reporter's notebooks, leaving the left-hand page blank in case I have a sudden idea.'

Soon after she started *Loving and Giving* she had 'this beastly trouble with my heart. I was laid up all last year. When I finally finished the novel I was afraid they'd only publish it out of kindness.'

Yet none of this shows in the writing. It zips along with an astringent eye for human weakness readers have come to love in Molly Keane. So much so that her M.J. Farrell novels, reissued by Virago, have become popular in the US fifty years after they were written.

Now completely recovered from her illness, she is busy preparing for a lunch party to which she has invited forty guests. Her friend Arabella arrives with bunches of gladioli and sweet pea. Molly begins arranging them in vases and bowls. She moves about the cottage, a little bird of a woman in a denim pinafore, her dog snapping possessively around her ankles. She plans to serve summer pudding with the wine. 'Do you think they'd enjoy it? It's a recipe from my childhood in Wexford.' Although she has surrounded herself with mementoes from a past that lives on in her fiction, she sees herself as a woman of the 1980s. 'I wouldn't go back to the big house for any money. Not even if I won the Booker. I really wouldn't. Anyway, the whole social context of armies of servants who were paid hardly anything has gone. And jolly good, too.'

Benedict Kiely, 1981

Dublin pubs in the fifties echoed with writers, only a handful of whom were ever published: talk came more easily. You'd see Paddy Kavanagh shuffling along Pembroke Road to the Waterloo ahead of Brendan Behan, who got a kick out of hectoring him. If Anthony Cronin wasn't in The Duke you'd find him in Grogan's, maybe with Flann O'Brien or John Ryan. Much of the city's journalism was conducted over pints at Mulligan's, around the corner from the Irish Press *on Burgh Quay. It got so the paper's proprietor Vivian de Valera would hide behind the door hoping to trap wayward staff sneaking back, or so said my father who became editor in 1957 with Benedict Kiely as his literary editor and Behan one of his columnists, writing in Irish, which Father didn't speak. By the time I met Kiely, much of that culture was dead or dying, but he was still in full flow, a captivating storyteller comparable to Seán Ó Faoláin, Frank O'Connor or William Trevor, on the page or off. He enjoyed another twenty-five years before his death aged eighty-seven in 2007, some months after marrying his partner of forty years, Frances Daly. Our interview on a spring day in 1981 meandered gently from morning into evening, long after the tape ran out.*

'Sure I have to flog myself into it,' says Benedict Kiely. He finds it all too easy to be lured away by conversation from the lonely discipline of writing. It's why he doesn't always answer the door of his terraced house on Morehampton Road. 'Unless the bell is given a certain ring, like in the old bona fide pubs.'

You'd hardly imagine from the unhurried way he talks that he's one of the most published of contemporary Irish authors, but then conversation has always been the stimulus for the remembered past of his fiction.

Since his writing first began appearing in the *Capuchin Annual* while he was still a schoolboy in Omagh – 'blank verse', he laughs, apologetically – he has produced eight novels, three collections of short stories, most of which originally appeared in *The New Yorker*, a biography of William Charleton, the nineteenth-century fellow Tyrone author, and several other books about Ireland. All that during a prolific career in journalism with the *Ulster Herald*, *Irish Independent* and later the *Irish Press*, in addition to lecturing in American universities and becoming a father of four by his marriage to Maureen O'Connell.

He ushers me into the high-ceilinged front room he uses as a study. Books are piled everywhere: Updike, Faulkner, Fowles, Bowen, Walter Scott and a beautifully red-bound set of thirty-seven volumes of Charles Lever – but there's a TV set, too.

'Did you watch *Deliverance* on RTÉ last night?' he asks. He knows the poet James Dickey, who wrote the story on which John Boorman based the film. He's been up the Chattanooga River where the action takes place, backwoods country:

> They're suspicious mountain people, there. They come out on the trail behind you, dragging a gun. 'Well, stranger, are yuh looking for something?' I used to suppose it was because of bootlegging or the old fear of Indians, the frontier mentality. But apparently it goes back before that. Many of them are of Scots Presbyterian stock. They've been there since the battle of Culloden.

He laughs. 'It reminds me of Brackey, where Paisley comes from, where they never open the front door.'

Daffodils from the garden are in a vase beside the TV. 'I'm not a gardener but my father was. They say it misses a generation.' They were planted by An Seabhac, the much-loved Irish language author who lived here before him. 'Many of his stories must have been written in this room.'

The house next door has less happy associations. English agents on the Michael Collins hit list were gunned down there on Bloody Sunday during the War of Independence. 'Your origins are all around you,' an American professor remarks in one of Kiely's stories. He's conscious of reminders everywhere of the divided community of his childhood. Not that Omagh was a particularly bigoted town. 'The last time Paisley had a demonstration there he had to bring in demonstrators from outside.'

Perhaps the tolerance came from being a garrison town. 'Every corner boy had seen the Taj Mahal, or said he had or even thought he had.' Kiely's father Tom, who came from Moville, County Donegal, joined the Leinster Regiment when he was eighteen and was decorated for heroism in the Boer War. His service record helped him get a job as porter in the Munster and Leinster Bank after he married Sara Alice Gormley, a barmaid he met in Drumquin in the Clogher valley, the setting for several of Kiely's stories including 'A Journey to the Seven Streams', a homage to his father.

Four Protestant boys sat with Kiely in class at the Christian Brothers and played soccer on the same team with him. 'We'd sometimes play the young army team. Pretty tough guys: if they had a sore leg they'd get the day off in hospital and they thought you felt the same way.' He walked out the sister of a man who was a second cousin of Paisley. Years later he saw him again drinking in a pub with a centre-half back on the Tyrone Gaelic football team. 'When someone introduced us, he told everyone, "Sure I know him – if that man hadn't fled Omagh I'd have a Papist brother-in-law."'

Kiely adds with his soft West Ulster voice: 'That's the way things should be in the North, if you could only get rid of the crazy minorities on both sides. Let them go up to the Greenland cap and settle it between them and leave the decent people alone. It's become crazy beyond description, like one of those children's games. You put one hand on top of another and there's no end to it all.'

All his fiction is rooted in the soil of this history, perhaps because he got away from it while he was still young. 'You need to make a distance to see it all. Joyce did, too. Not that I'd compare myself with him, but he wasn't driven into exile. He deliberately went away to see more clearly.' After school, Kiely got work as a sorting clerk in the post office. 'Jobs were shared equally between Protestants and Catholics in those days. But when I left to become a Jesuit I was replaced by a Protestant. Bigotry was beginning to be imposed by Stormont. It didn't come from the town.'

But Benedict Kiely SJ was not to be. After a year studying at Imo in Kildare – the setting for his novel *There Was an Ancient House* – a bad back landed him in Cappagh Hospital for eighteen months. 'It was an honourable exit. They'd probably have thrown me out anyway.' He had to learn to walk again. Peadar O'Curry gave him part-time work on the weekly *Standard*. He read English, History and Latin at UCD. His literary career took shape with the publication in 1946 of a first novel *Land Without Stars*, which made an analogy between Ulster during the war and the defeated Gaelic Ireland of the poet Egan O'Rahilly, 'a land without any dry weather, without a stream, without a star.' This was to become a characteristic of his writing, all the time conscious of the past of a place but making connections with the present. 'Everything in Ireland reminds me of something else,' he says.

Not that the Irish have always liked being reminded, particularly in the censor-ridden 1940s and 1950s. Three of his novels were banned, what he calls 'the national literary award for being in general tendency indecent or obscene'. Attitudes haven't changed all that much. His 1977 novella *Proxopera: A Tale of Modern Ireland* angered Irish Americans because it takes the proxy bomber as a symbol of Provo cowardice. Kiely doesn't aspire to be a political writer. He just tells stories, but the stories mirror the society he comes from and the scars it bears.

Compare his early stories with those of the 1970s and you become aware of violence insidiously corrupting the Tyrone he has made so familiar, like a cancer on a friend. *The State of Ireland*, his first comprehensive selection of short fiction, which includes *Proxopera* and seventeen stories, gets its backbone from a sense of betrayal and indignation that has been growing through his work. Its publication in the US was acclaimed as a major literary achievement. 'People ask me why I don't abuse the Orange crowd as much as the Provos. But I grew up with them and they were never more than gate-lodge keepers for the English. The others claim to be inheritors of a great tradition and I'm not going to stand for that.'

It's afternoon by now. He's still in his dressing-gown, which is tied around the waist with an old tie. He pours me a glass of Rioja. Someone once likened him to a Bavarian farmer, with his burly build and love of the country. But there's a look of the world in his high-browed face. It's no surprise to hear that he travelled in the back of a taxi under a rug with Kim Novak. 'Seamus Kelly said I never made use of my opportunity, letting Roderick Mann of *The Daily Mail* get off with her afterwards.'

He's as at home lecturing at Hollins College in Virginia or listening to hunting talk in the barber's shop in Georgia ('Leftie shot thirty possum.

What's good with possum?' 'Negroes eat 'em.' 'Don't any more. Want steak now') as rambling along the banks of the Suir. Wherever he goes he is absorbed into the village of his imagination.

His fiction was to become an extended truth. Nearly all his characters are drawn from people he has known. 'It's much easier to describe somebody you've actually seen than to try to make it up. But you add a bit here and there. It's just the description you borrow, not the person. I find it gets confusing. Looking back on your old stuff you begin to wonder what was real.' He brings notebooks with him wherever he goes. 'Whether I use them afterwards or not I don't know. But it's good to have them. If you come on something interesting and try to keep remembering it, you get all befuddled, whereas if you write it down, you know you have it. Even if it's only a code word, it brings it back to you.'

Memories take on a life of their own. 'Your memory probably goes back to your grandparents, because you've been listening to your parents listening to their parents. What a child hears becomes as much a memory as an actual experience. So your memory may go back one hundred and fifty years or more.' His mother's mother could actually look back on her own past from the threshold of her farm at Drumquin. On a clear day she could glimpse Mount Errigal. 'Oh, the poor Donegals, the poor Donegals,' she'd say.

As a boy he remembers seeing a strong Presbyterian farmer hiring a labourer from Donegal at the fair in Omagh and he'd feel the biceps the way Georgia cotton planters used to with the black boys and girls at the slave market. His grandfather's memories have become his too, the first man in RIC uniform to learn of the murder of Lord Leitrim. But with Kiely there's no telling where a conversation – or a short story – is ever going to lead.

Perhaps it comes from all the Walter Scott novels he read as a boy. 'Scott was so madly interested in landscape that he'd suddenly forget about the story and give you nine hundred lines of scenery.' So he tells me a fishing story, not forgetting for a moment Lord Leitrim.

'Poor man, apart from getting sunstroke in India and having a little bit of weakness for the ladies, he never harmed anyone.' Apparently Kiely's brother brought a nephew from America fishing off the rocks at Mullaghmore. He'd never fished before. Everyone ran for cover when he let fly with the spinners bait in the general direction of Donegal Bay. 'My brother swears that the fish must have been there with its mouth open. The line no sooner hit the water than he pulled out a big mullet. Always after that at Mullaghmore they'd bring you to that point where the miraculous draught of fishes happened.' After a pause, he adds: 'But the good has gone out of it now. Just a little out from the rock is where the Mountbatten boat was blown up. It has left a pall. A place can become tainted, I suppose.'

The Provos issued a statement regretting the death of the young boatman: they had expected an older boatman to be at the helm.

'Old boatmen are expendable,' says Kiely, bitterly. The man had been his friend. He had gone fishing with him. Mountbatten, too.

'The water never knew what was happening,' says Binchley's son in *Proxopera*. 'I doubt that,' says Binchley. 'Water may know more than we think. And grass, and old rocks.' The power of Kiely's fiction is to make the water speak. Out of his consciousness of place comes a consciousness of what we were and are becoming.

Michael Longley, 1980

Quietly and bravely, during some of the worst years of the Troubles in the North, Michael Longley and his friend Seamus Heaney travelled around Ulster giving readings together, a Protestant and a Catholic defying the sectarian divide through the power of imagination. Both the same age, and for four years co-editors of Northern Review, *they emerged in the late 1960s at the heart of a new generation of Ulster poets that included Derek Mahon and Medbh McGuckian. Heaney went on to win the Nobel Prize, Longley received several major prizes – the T.S. Eliot, the Whitbread, the Hawthornden, the Wilfred Owen and the Queen's Gold Medal for Poetry. Heaney once described Longley as 'a keeper of the artistic estate, a custodian of griefs and wonders'. Longley's poems are a celebration of the past and the present, family and community, nature and the city, what he calls 'the fundamental interconnectedness of all things'. Having come of age as a poet during the most horrific period of the Troubles, he did not hesitate to engage with events, arguing in a letter to* The Irish Times *in 1974 that 'though the poet's first duty must be to his imagination, he has other obligations – and not just as a citizen. He would be inhuman if he did not respond to the tragic events of his own community, and a poor artist if he did not seek to endorse that response imaginatively.' Longley did this in particular with 'Wreaths' in* The Echo Gate *(a Poetry Society Choice published in 1979, the same year as his mother's death)*

by itemizing the bald detail of particular atrocities, and then in 1994 in his poem
'Ceasefire' (using a free translation of Homer's Iliad, *in which old enemies Achilles*
and Priam achieve a tentative reconciliation) to allude to the culmination of the
peace process without mentioning the North. In 2014, at the age of seventy-five,
he revisited recurring themes in The Stairwell, *confiding in its title poem, 'I have*
been thinking about the music for my own funeral.' We spent a day together in
London in 1981, wandering the streets, talking about writing and politics.

It's hardly a coincidence that the most violent decade Northern Ireland
has known has also been its most creative. Poets in particular, among them
Seamus Heaney, Michael Longley, Derek Mahon, Paul Muldoon and John
Hewitt, have being making a contribution to literature far out of proportion
to the size of the province from which they come. 'I think it's because you
have two tribal cultures colliding,' says Michael Longley. 'On one level the
sparks that fly are street violence, riots and murder, but on another more
imaginative level the sparks become artistic expression.'

Too often each faction has chosen to learn exclusively from the vices
of the other, 'the stereophonic nightmare/of the Shankill and the Falls'.
But there has also been what W.R. Rogers called 'the creative wave of self-
consciousness', which occurs when the two racial patterns meet. 'One is
obliged in terms of friendship, let alone in terms of art, to attempt to define
and redefine oneself and one's attitudes. That's bound to bring a kind of
alertness that will give edge to the paintings, the plays and the poems.'

Longley is the son of English parents who moved from Clapham
Common in London to Belfast in 1927. His father, Col Richard Longley,
was a recipient of the Military Cross for bravery in the First World War.
His wife, Edna, is a Catholic academic he met at Trinity. Longley is deeply
conscious both of the Protestant tradition in which he was brought up
and of the Catholic tradition he was to discover through friendships and
involvement with Irish music in his twenties. 'The confluence and confusion
of different tones and colours is enriching,' he says.

We're talking at a hotel on High Street Kensington, neutral ground so
to speak. It is the morning after the night before: he had met friends from
Toronto after giving a reading at the Poetry Centre and stayed talking until
6 am. Now he's trying to keep awake with coffee. His stock of dark hair
and beard is tousled, his shirt unbuttoned. 'I find London two-dimensional
compared with Belfast,' he says, pouring more coffee. 'You're aware here of

a society that has been settled for years and years. To use a geological meta-phor, it's sedimentary, whereas Ulster is still volcanic and evolving. In some ways it hasn't happened yet.'

Poets in the North have sometimes been unfairly accused of keeping distant from the Troubles, averting their eyes from the hatred and violence, towards safer and more ethereal themes. But to say that is to misunderstand the function of poetry. 'A poem is a way of expressing all one's confusions, and of saying more than one thing at the same time,' he says. 'It doesn't matter what your political feelings might be, if you actively wrote a poem which voiced them in a straightforward way, you'd just be writing propa-ganda. There are rights and wrongs on both sides in the North. It's not like Hitler's Germany.' He adds:

> I know what I would like to happen politically, but I know other people with diametrically opposed views and I cannot say that they are altogether wrong. There has been on the part of Northern Ireland poets, and indeed Irish writers too, a proper hesitance to hitch a ride on yesterday's headlines. Nobody considered the Troubles as subject matter in the beginning. It all had to filter down into the subconscious and then emerge. In a way, everyone who lives in the North is a conscript, but all the poets are non-combatants. There's nobody I know writing poetry who lives in the front line in the Falls, the Shankill or Ardoyne. Most of us have comfortable middle-class job, which means one approaches the suffering of fellow citizens with deference. One of the important words I'd apply to the poetry that has come out of the North about the Troubles is that it is well-mannered. It's important, too, that poems about the Troubles should be surrounded by poems about other things, because life goes on in Belfast and people do ordinary things.

This concern for a truth to be found within the interplay of seemingly unrelated things defines Longley's poetry. His allusions range from Sulpicia and Tibullus (he read classics at Trinity College) to Walter Mitty, Florence Nightingale, Rip Van Winkle and Fats Waller. In *The Echo Gate*, he writes of Oliver Plunkett, etymology, country lore, love and his father: '*I thought you blew a kiss before you died, / But the bony fingers that waved to and fro / Were asking for a Woodbine, the last request / Of many soldiers in your company.*' But mixed with these poems lurk some the most searingly direct images of the North's nightmare. 'Wreaths' is a simple setting down of the daily litany of horror, each of its three parts focusing on the detail of a particular atrocity. It's Longley's way of achieving the impact of a newspaper photo.

LONGLEY, MICHAEL

'Conor Cruise O'Brien once referred to the politics of the latest atrocity and I agree with him that this is inadequate for politics,' he says.

> But I believe in the poetry of the latest atrocity. It is a poet's duty to bear witness rather than to try to set some atrocity in an historical perspective. That would be an impertinence. The thing to do is to record the fact that somebody was shot or somebody was tortured. That is why my poems were written – to record my shock.

Longley has a slow deliberate way of talking, showing care with his choice of words, never leaving a sentence hanging in the air:

> I think of words as physical objects that are made by the tongue and the lips and the teeth. They are born in the mouth and their proper resting place is the ear. They are more important that way than symbols on a page. When I'm writing I always say it out loud. It's got to be tested in the air. And I'll intuitively stop writing when it sounds and feels right.

Unexpected connections are the core of his poetry, a bringing together of opposites that comes from living in a divided society. A description, for instance, of the linen industry can become a celebration of love. 'When two disparate things illuminate one another, that's the point where I take off, that's my ignition point,' he says.

Poetry comes from some deep disturbance. A poem comes up out of the subconscious like a pearl being formed around some irritant. It exists because of life's difficulties and confusions. I don't find that I write so much when I'm happy and contented. I write when I'm under some kind of psychic pressure. Poetry is a way of becoming healthy, a way of working things out of one's system that might otherwise fester. I'm quite sure there'll be no poetry in heaven.

He feels an affinity with the scientist in trying to discover patterns and shapes and order in the world outside his head. 'Except that scientists have to prove their theories, but you can't prove a poem.' He works 'like a good scientist', never knowing what he's going to write about when he starts a poem. 'The poem itself is the exploration. There is absolutely no way I can sit down and just write it. It has to present itself. I don't know where I'm going. The verbal patterns and shapes are like a map and compass.'

He may go through long periods of not writing anything:

And then, all of a sudden, there's a spurt and any one book is made up of about four or five spurts. I have this notion that one only has so many poems to write. A bit like a woman and her ovaries, her supply of eggs. Experience comes along and fertilizes eggs occasionally, but a lot of the time they're just being washed away.

Longley came to poetry when he was about twelve, discovering 'La Belle Dame sans Merci' by Keats and Walter de la Mare's 'The Listeners'. 'And then when I was fifteen I fell madly in love and started to write verse.'

At Trinity it became an obsession. 'I remember one night when I should have been studying for exams, I wrote a poem about forty lines long. I knew it wasn't right and I worked until eight in the morning, changing it into two sonnets. That was a kind of baptism. I realized that poetry was a formal problem as well as psychological and emotional things.'

Back in Belfast he met Heaney, Mahon and James Simmons, and became part of the writers' group formed by Philip Hobsbaum. 'What he did was to give us all a sense of our own importance. I believe in a solidarity of the imagination, some kind of brotherhood of writers. It's important during that vulnerable period when a young poet is on the verge of bringing out his first book.'

By now the Hobsbaum group have all gone their different ways. But Longley finds himself getting nearly as annoyed over a bad review of Heaney or Mahon as he would be with a bad review of his own poetry. Not that critics bother him much. He shows each poem he writes to Edna, to a close friend, Michael Allen, to Heaney, Mahon and Muldoon. 'If they like it I don't really care what anyone else says.'

He was a critic once for *The Irish Times*. 'I regret it in a way. I was very good with the hatchet. I wonder if it's a good thing for a poet to write criticism. I think of a poem as a mote in your eye and if you try to focus on it, it disappears.' He has been happier in his more positive role as director of literature for the Arts Council of Northern Ireland, encouraging younger poets to emerge. 'The new generation of Paul Muldoon, Frank Ormsby, Ciaran Carson and Tom Paulin, it's an impressive list. You only have to shake a tree and six fall out.'

He concedes that his approach to poetry is quasi-religious. 'I accept old-fashioned terms like inspiration. For me when it's really happening properly there's an extraordinary feeling of being a hundred times more intelligent and more sensitive than one normally is.' But he has no time for the ivory tower of Yeats, who had special carpets put down at Coole Park so footsteps wouldn't disturb him. 'Some of my best poems come out on the sofa when I'm surrounded by children and noise. Nothing can stop them coming out. It's like a woman who's going to have a baby. She'll lie down in the street or in the aisle of a plane and just have it.'

If he has any regret it is that at RBAI he was cut off from things Irish:

> Irish wasn't on the curriculum. I was taught nothing about Irish history, Irish art or Irish music. I went through childhood without knowing a Roman Catholic. It wasn't because I avoided them but because they went to different schools. There was this terrible apartheid. That whole education policy, manipulated on one side by the Unionists and on the other by the Church in the South, has been a disaster. When you meet closed minds in the North, you've got to forgive them because that's the way they were educated and brought up. That's what's wrong with Ireland. There are too many brutal certainties. What art does is to weaken the certainties a little.

A room-service waiter brings another pot of coffee. 'I'm not making much sense,' Longley apologizes, pouring another cup. 'The tragedy for Ireland is the fact that it is in two parts, like a divorce, and the two parts have stagnated. There's so much I find unattractive in both and it's because of this stultifying divorce.'

He suggests we take a walk. We step out into the street. 'I feel Ireland is a whole,' he says. 'I don't really think of myself as Northern Irish. I think of myself as Irish, basically.'

Norman Mailer, 1997

If not to judge a book by its cover is good advice, even better advice is probably to beware of judging writers or artists by their actual lives. Back in the dark days of Irish censorship Romy Schneider provoked controversy by joining a campaign in which prominent women admitted to having had abortions. There were calls to ban her films in Ireland, a country already busy mutilating hundreds of films by major directors on the grounds that they were the work of people leading 'immoral lives'. We couldn't see Persona *because Ingmar Bergman and Liv Ulmann were in an adulterous relationship. We couldn't see* Midnight Cowboy *because John Schlesinger was a homosexual. We couldn't see Fellini's* Roma *uncut because he was a blasphemer. So when Norman Mailer died in 2007 it was depressing to see some feminists dismissing his books on the grounds that they were the work of 'a sexist homophobic reactionary'. His macho attitudes and aggressive behaviour towards some of his wives were deplorable, but to argue that as a writer he was therefore a fraud 'who pulled off a stunning confidence trick' is surely absurd. When we met in Dublin in 1997 he was frail and seemed older than his age (he was born in Trenton, New Jersey, on 18 October 1923), often self-deprecating and rueful about his life and extended family.*

On the morning Norman Mailer was getting married to his sixth wife, Norris Church, he woke up feeling very depressed. 'I got out of bed,' he explains, 'and turned to her and I said, "You know, all my life all I ever wanted was to be free and alone in Paris." To which Norris responded: "Well honey, just suppose you were free and alone in Paris, what would happen? You'd meet a girl. You know how you are, she'd soon be pregnant. And you know how you are, you'd get married. And you wouldn't be free and alone in Paris anymore."' Mailer coughs a laugh. 'And I told her: you know, you're right.'

What Norris realized was that Mailer, for all his bravado, was at heart a family man: perhaps it's why they're still together. He'd grown up in Jewish Brooklyn with fiercely immigrant parents: his mother, Fanny, was brought to America aged two in 1892 by parents fleeing anti-Semitic persecution in Lithuania: his father, Isaac, an accountant of similar Lithuanian descent, arrived in New York from Cape Town in 1919. 'I'm sure when his mother conceived him she was convinced she was carrying a genius,' Mailer's first wife, Beatrice Silverman, used to say, 'and I think she made him one, at least made him believe he was one.' Fourth wife Beverly Bentley claimed: 'His mother was the only Mrs Norman Mailer.'

Mailer has been willingly supportive of his own nine children from various marriages. He'd have them all to stay every summer in Provincetown on Cape Cod. 'They become a fulfilment of a large part of your life,' he says. 'So I have them all together – that's one thing we always did, my former wives were always good about that – and we'd go to places like Maine, trail hiking and rock climbing.' Now in 1997 at seventy-four, and no longer hearing or seeing so well – by his bed in the Shelbourne Hotel I notice *Home Remedies for Common Ailments* – he's kept up this tradition with his five grandchildren, too. 'More and more of the social life goes into dealing with the family, as years go by, which is kind of agreeable, but a little tough on one's wife. I can just go upstairs and write and then come down to dinner. She has to shop and organize everything.'

In 1980 just before he married Norris, who'd given birth to his son John Buffalo two years previously, he first married and then divorced a few days later Carol Stevens, to legitimize his child by her. 'Each wife is a culture, after all,' he says. 'You get a little slap-happy going through so many cultures. Nevertheless, it's interesting.' He seems unbothered by a sensational memoir by his second wife, Adel Morales, whom he stabbed at a drunken party in 1960. 'Well, I did stab her,' he says. 'It's the only thing that's accurate. But that stabbing, that crime, took place thirty-seven years ago. That was half my life ago.'

He admits that when at twenty-four he became famous overnight with *The Naked and the Dead* – inspired by his war service in the Pacific – he didn't know how to handle himself. Particularly after the critical failure of subsequent novels, the allegorical left-versus-right *Barbary Shore* and his sexually explicit satire on the Hollywood blacklist, *The Deer Park*, his drinking and amatory excesses became legendary. 'I squandered it,' he says, 'and of course by the time I squandered it, I wanted it again. So I learned a lot, but I learned the hard way, the stupid way.'

He'd always felt a compulsion to write ever since his mother, noticing that he was bored as a small boy, gave him a pencil and notepad and said, 'Here, write something.' But over the years, with so many wives and children to support, writing ended up becoming an economic necessity:

> I write more now than when I was younger. When I was younger I would go months without writing. But now I wouldn't know what I'd do with myself if I didn't write. I began writing because it was the first thing I was really good at. It just lit a fire in me. I've no idea how much one is born to be a writer and how much it's an accident. All I know is in my case once I started writing all through those years at Harvard studying engineering I did more writing than anything else. I must have written a million words before I sat down and wrote *The Naked and the Dead*.

The only activity that gave him anything near the same pleasure was boxing. He has written memorably about it, notably in his coverage of the famous Muhammad Ali / George Foreman showdown in Zaire in 1974. Until he was nearly sixty he used to work out every Saturday with ex-light heavyweight champion José Torres. 'By then, getting hit on the head was no fun anymore.' He prefers writing to being a prize fighter:

> When fighters are young, they love boxing. They're good at it, they're fast, they're strong, they're afraid of no one. But as they get older, they take punishment. They go in and they know they're going to urinate blood for three weeks after a fight if they catch it in the ribs. So they are doing it because it's the one thing they're really good at. But the youthful joy is gone. I still love writing when it works. But there's a feeling of O brother, what a price to pay – because there's no getting around it. It's not a healthy activity sitting on a chair all day and pouring out your insides to get a few words out on the page.

One of the pioneers of the so-called New Journalism in the 1960s with his Pulitzer Prize-winning *The Armies of the Night*, which had as its subject his experience of a pacifist march on the Pentagon (its subtitle was *History as a novel, the novel as History*) and with *Miami and the Siege of Chicago*, drawing on his impressions of the Republican and Democratic presidential conventions, his fiction has invariably been rooted in fact, with versions of himself as a character. He regards this as more true than the false objectivity of reportage. His anatomy of the covert activities of the CIA in *Harlot's Ghost* prompted *Time* magazine to note: 'For a heady period, no major public event in US life seemed quite complete until Mailer had observed himself observing it.'

The roots of contemporary violence have been a recurring preoccupation. 'It's the last frontier left to the novel,' he says:

> Sex used to be thirty or forty years ago. But now it's violence. It's hard to write about. That book *American Psycho*, although well written, didn't have any inner life. I thought it was essentially a most unpleasant book because it was performing the function of pornography, which was to get you excited without illuminating anything. Excitement plus illumination is the first approach of what might be art. Excitement without illumination is the broad road to pornography.

Mailer brilliantly achieved this perspective with *The Executioner's Song*, winner of the Pulitzer Prize in 1979, which was triggered by transcripts of interviews with convicted murderer Gary Gilmore on Death Row. 'God is a better novelist than any novelist,' he tells me. 'When you take the sort of things that are going on in the twentieth century, there's no need to go looking for stories that will outstrip the real ones. The problem is to get to the bottom of the real stories.'

Which is the motivation behind his 1997 novel *The Gospel According to the Son*, in which he assumes the autobiographical persona of a Jesus Christ who, irritated at being so often misquoted, now wants to put the record straight. It's a surprisingly gentle book, making Jesus believable as a human being, like anyone else, who just happens to be the son of God and has to deal with that. 'I think the fundamental message of Jesus – that we all have to take care of one another – has been blurred, because we wait for divine intervention. We live under the authority of God rather than the compassion of God.'

If he'd had his way, he'd have published *The Gospel According to the Son* anonymously. A writer of his time, ever ready to engage in controversial issues, his notoriety has tended to get in the way of objective appreciation of his fiction. 'I'm absolutely in the way of this book,' he says. 'People are saying, "What's all this stuff, c'mon, Norman, you're an atheist."' Putting himself inside the mind of God is no more presumptuous than an actor portraying God in a movie. 'Novelists are like actors. They take on roles when they write stories. As with an actor, you don't expect them to imagine that they are the characters they play.' So what would have happened if he'd been taken out into the desert like Jesus, and exposed to temptation? He leans forward in his chair, a short stocky man with strong boxer's hands. 'The Devil would have said, Hey, Norman, there're some broads down there.'

Confrontational as ever, he published *Why Are We at War?* in 2003 and underwent heart bypass surgery two years later before dying in 2007, aged eighty-four, his lungs finally failing him. Macho to the end, he claimed to have learned from Ernest Hemingway 'that even if one dulled one's talent in the punishment of becoming a man, it was more important to be a man than a very good writer, that probably I could not become a very good writer unless I learned first how to keep my nerve'.

Dacia Maraini, 1993

Alberto Moravia once described Dacia Maraini as 'a realist writer who loves reality for what it is, not what it should be'. You don't have to have lived with Maraini for eighteen years as he did before she walked out on him (she was twenty when they fell in love) to come to the same conclusion. All her novels are about women trying to find the strength and confidence to be what they really are rather than what they're expected to be. She strips away the cosy social conventions that condition relationships between the sexes. She co-founded, with Moravia, the Porcospino (Porcupine) theatre company in 1966 to pioneer new Italian plays. Winner of the Prix Formentor for her novel The Age of Malaise *and a finalist for the Man Booker International Prize, she featured in a 2013 documentary* I Was Born Travelling *dealing with her fabled journeys around the world with Moravia and close friends Pier Paolo Pasolini and Maria Callas.*

Flip open any page of Dacia Maraini's sensually written and savagely amusing novel *Woman at War* and you'll find a passage like this:

> *'What does your mother do?'*
> *'Nothing, she stays at home.'*
> *'You mean she makes your dinner, she makes your bed, she washes your dirty underwear, she irons your shirt, she does your shopping, she cooks for you, she washes your dishes. Doesn't she? Isn't that what you mean?'*

Her challenging of male assumptions is not contrived. The characters are being true to themselves, not to some schematic ideology. Maraini writes fiction, not propaganda. 'I don't like to be labelled a feminist writer,' she says, sipping a cup of tea in the Shelbourne Hotel in 1993. She's a small, deep-voiced woman with cropped hair and a big smile. 'The fact is that I am a woman and I write novels and I put my own experience into them. Fiction should never be used for other meanings. It has its own meaning and its own laws, which are very important. You can't use it to put over opinions.'

Not that a novel may not have ideological implications. But the implications come out of the actuality of the experience, the experience is not a vehicle for them. 'I never start out from an ideological point of view. I try simply to draw on my own experience and the experiences of people I know and feel close to.'

People can read what they like into her novels afterwards:

> If you look at them in a rational way you may find things that are ideological. I think all writing is political in a deep way like this, which has nothing to do with propaganda. The actuality of politics changes from one day to another. It's linked to slogans. So propaganda has a very short life. The actuality in writing is much more long term. A writer has to think in the long term.

To impose ideas on a novel is to take away its life. 'It becomes something else, a book of philosophy, or whatever. It is no longer a novel.'

This commitment to fiction as fiction has been unwavering since she published her first novel, *The Holiday*, in 1962, a time when the Italian avant-garde was proclaiming the death of the novel. 'They wanted to abolish plot, characters and facts. Novels were to be about fragments. Somebody even published a novel consisting entirely of blank pages.' She shrugs dismissively. 'It didn't last long, because people want novels. They need to read fiction.' Novels, she argues, are an extension of our selves. Through them we can reach into other worlds and other lives:

> They are an exchange of experiences. I've been only once to Russia but I'd read so many Russian novels and poems I felt I'd been there before. This happens with centuries as well as countries. You can travel in the past. If I read Boccaccio I'm living in the fourteenth century and sharing the experience of that time. People don't want to settle for the limitations of their own lives like a tree rooted to the ground. They want to spread out and enter into other lives. That's the allure of novels. They give us so many lives.

She wrote *The Holiday* while still a student at Naples University. 'I'd grown up with books. Writing was a natural thing to do.' Her father was the anthropologist Fosco Maraini, her mother a Sicilian princess and painter, Topazia Alliata di Salaparuta. Her grandmother wrote books 'and was once married to an Irishman called Cross from Galway ... my father still has an Irish stepsister'.

She remembers hardship as a child. 'We were in Japan when war broke out. My father was studying a dying aboriginal population in a remote part of the north. He was asked to sign a declaration approving fascism. When he refused, we were all put into a concentration camp. I was five and my sisters were two and one. We barely survived.' Back in Sicily after the war, her parents separated and her father moved to Rome, where Dacia joined him some years later when she was eighteen. 'We'd lost everything. But we weren't poor in the more usual sense because we had this great cultural richness to fall back on.'

Not the kind of upbringing that leads to an unquestioning acceptance of traditional roles and values. With plays and novels like *The Age of Discontent* and *The Silent Duchess*, which won Italy's equivalent of the Booker Prize in 1986, Maraini articulated the growing self-awareness of women in a changing Italy, but never in a strident, polemical way. Her novels are human documents, with all the laughter and tears of life: rather than illustrations of an argument, their immediate concern is private rather than political:

> If anything, they're becoming more personal and reflective. When you are young you just put things down because they are so strong. Now I'm trying to give the emotions that are around things. My writing is becoming more and more autobiographical. There is less difference between the characters and me.

This parallels the shift in modern literature towards deeper subjectivity. 'Writing and rewriting your own story like Italo Svevo.'

Women have taken to it more readily. 'Perhaps because a woman is more used to staying at home and looking after herself – writing diaries and letters was always considered a feminine thing.' Appropriately, *Woman at War* is written in the chatty form of a diary:

> I want people to be able to get into the story without any difficulty. I hate books that are too intellectual even if I recognize that a novel must have an intellectual structure. Ideally novels should operate on two levels, one more accessible, the other deeper. After all, they deal with very common human

feelings, which everybody should be able to understand. They're not just for professors.

This urge to communicate with as wide an audience as possible has led Maraini into theatre and cinema was well as novels and poetry. Her plays are performed throughout Europe. Hanna Schygulla won the Best Actress award at Cannes in 1983 in the title role of Marco Ferreri's film version of her novel *Piero's Story*. They've got together again for another film co-starring Schygulla and Ornella Muti. 'It's based on an original idea of mine rather than a novel,' she says. But she's embarrassed by the title, *The Future is Woman*. 'Marco thought of it,' she says. 'But it makes the film seem polemical, which it's not. It's not what I'm about.'

Paula Meehan, 2015

Joyce's Ulysses *all takes place in a single city during a single day. Bernard MacLaverty's candidly observed 2017 novel* Midwinter Break *follows an elderly couple who face the truth of their relationship on a weekend break in Amsterdam. Unity of time and place are one of a variety of limitations writers set themselves in creating a fiction. There are other more technical techniques that also prompt inspiration, like telling an entire novel in a single sentence (Mike McCormack's* Solar Bones*) or limiting their vocabulary to fewer than two hundred words (Georges Simenon). Until free verse became fashionable, poetry flourished with the help of exact forms – fourteen-line sonnets, seven-line haikus and many other verse formats. Paula Meehan's 2016 collection* Geomantic *is a dazzling rediscovery of the creative power of such self-imposed limitations. It comprises eighty-one poems each of nine lines, each of them of nine syllables. She got the idea from a quilt she slept under as a young girl, 'nine squares / by nine squares, blue on green spots, stripes, bows / alternate with gold on red chevrons'. Far from being inhibited by the rigidity of her chosen structure, Meehan finds within it the freedom to let her lyrical rhythms soar with evocative intimations of love, community and the essence of poetry. Although Meehan's poems have been giving me joy since she was first published by Beaver Row Press in 1984, my first real meeting with Paula didn't take place until 2015.*

When Michael D. Higgins hosted a cultural evening in the Forbidden City in Beijing on his state visit to China in December 2014, he invited Paula Meehan to read six poems from her book *Dharmajaya*, a collection inspired by *The Tibetan Book of the Dead*. Translations by Huiyi Bao, a student at University College Dublin, were inserted into the programme. Ever so obliquely, the poems were a cry from the heart of a philosophy under threat.

It's more than forty years, and nine books, since Meehan emerged from childhood in the inner-city Dublin tenements to give voice to the disenfranchised everywhere, less in anger than with compassion and an intuitive understanding that verse imbued their lives and memories with mythic dignity. 'The work of poetry makes a better fist at arriving at what is human in the world than most things,' President Higgins said in 2013 when he announced Meehan's appointment as Ireland Professor of Poetry, a three-year job rotating between Queen's University, Trinity and University College Dublin during which through workshops and readings she has sought to bring together 'the energies of the academy and the energies of the street'.

Eavan Boland has marvelled at Meehan's 'wonderful zest and warmth of tone', noting that her 'themes are daring and open up new areas for her own work as well as for contemporary Irish poetry'. To England's poet laureate Carol Ann Duffy she is 'that rare and precious thing – a vocational poet of courage and integrity'.

Now here she is in Roly's Bistro, a tiny figure with flowing white hair making her way between the tables like a feather caught in the breeze of the Dublin 4 lunchtime chattering. We sit at a window looking out on Ballsbridge. She sips sparkling water. A puppy she got at Christmas chewed her credit card this morning. 'It's as if he's wired to the moon. He takes a ball to the top of the stairs, drops it, chases it, and he'll do that all day.'

Born in 1955, she was brought up by her grandparents while her parents were looking for work in England. 'We lived on the corner of Sean McDermott Street and Gardiner Street, which is gone now. My childhood city is practically obliterated, the last coherent community in the North inner city. The people had nothing, but they had a sense of sharing. I grew up in an oral tradition. I got my language there. I'm not nostalgic for the poverty, but the attempt to ameliorate those terrible living conditions led to much displacement and breaking apart of the community.' She remembers hiding under the table and listening to things she couldn't begin to understand until she was older. Her granny would see her. 'Out, she'd say, out. And up on her lap, with the smell of kitchen and sleep, she'd rock me. She'd lull me. No one was kinder.' Her mother died at forty-two. 'And I was convinced I would too when I reached that age. But my doctor assured me I was fit as a hoot.' This year Paula will be sixty. 'I'm just delighted I survived. I still can't believe it. I keep reminding myself I'm only a whippersnapper. If I glimpse myself in a mirror, it's like, who's that?'

She lives in Baldoyle with poet and broadcaster Theo Dorgan, whose childhood in Cork in many ways parallels her own. 'I'm eldest from a family of six, he's the eldest of fifteen. He had to take responsibility from an early age. He jokes that he became Secretary of the Soviet of Orphans. There's something fearless about him. He understands people and sees something in everyone, yet at the same time knows when to remain detached.' Paula's grandfather taught her to read and write. 'Without that I don't know how I'd have survived school. Underlying everything was a sense that girls didn't need an education. We were learning the skills for young girls to go into service or factories. So being able to read and write from the start was like a weapon. It gave me independence.'

She moved to Finglas as a teenager. 'There were bands everywhere. Music was a great unifying culture. We were the first global generation. We felt connected with what was happening in the world. Thanks to Donogh O'Malley's free education scheme, we were now allowed to go to secondary school and university.'

The nuns at St Michael's Holy Faith Convent didn't know what had hit them. 'They couldn't handle girls coming in from what they would see as corporation housing. I was not compliant. So I didn't last long. We were absorbing the language of protest and reading about revolutions. I led a protest. So they threw me out. Looking back I've a lot of sympathy for them having to put up with us. It must have been a culture shock for them. But for us it was a sense that we had a right to education.'

She studied for the Inter Cert by herself and went to vocational school for the Leaving Cert, which got her into Trinity College:

I wasn't a good student. I just did the things I wanted to do. Eiléan Ní Chuilleanáin taught me entomology, the history of words and sounds. I couldn't wait to get to Greece listening to W.B. Stanford, a great classicist. I'd skip lectures for street theatre with Jim and Peter Sheridan, Neil Jordan, Garret Keogh and Suzie Kennedy. I'd scribbled poems since I was at school, inspired by music and songs. But I didn't have confidence in my writing. I was surrounded by very strong and articulate men and they were the writers. It was a very male milieu. I became a secret writer.

She dropped out for a year, hitching to Crete 'to walk in the landscape that gave rise to the ancient myths, to stand in the cave where Zeus was born'. This sense of the past in the present, the living myth embedded in landscape, fed into her memory poetry. It was enhanced when a scholarship brought her to America to study for an MA in Creative Writing with James McAuley and the Beat poet Gary Snyder. 'The North West was a vital place for poetry. It had only been settled a hundred years before. Looking back through the stories of the indigenous population gave me a new take on our own early culture, which was also full of stories and songs about hunting and fishing.'

Dublin now seemed to her 'a haunted city, haunted not just by my own childhood but through the architecture by all the people who had lived before'. Kevin Byrne, who remembered her poems from a John McGahern workshop, published her first collection *Return and No Blame* at Beaver Row Press in 1984, an eye-grabbing debut from the very first page:

> *The legion of Mary's virgins*
> *Snare the small children*
> *And arraign their innocence*
> *While a fat priest's pink finger*
> *Let drop the hammer on the nail*

Although it caught the attention of Eavan Boland, it didn't pay any bills. As the 1980s recession deepened, Paula moved to Leitrim, living on the dole. 'They registered me as unskilled labourer. When they learned I had three chickens, they docked me fifty pence. I had to argue they were domestic fowl not livestock.'

Some of her poems were published in New Irish Writing, which had just moved from *The Irish Press* to *The Sunday Tribune*. It gave her the confidence to write her long breakthrough poem 'The Statue of the Virgin at Granard Speaks', which was inspired by the death of a fifteen-year-old who came to give birth at the statue's feet:

> *They kneel before me and their prayers*
> *Fly up like sparks from a bonfire*
> *that blaze a moment, then wink out.*

Tom Murphy wrote a wonderful letter, which she read and reread until it was in shreds. 'That galvanized me. Feck it, I thought, I'm going to stand up for the word.' Six more collections followed, culminating with *Painting Rain* in which she plays with different poetic forms and rhyming to interweave contemporary voices amid sonnets in a memorable Stephen's Green sequence, 'Six Sycamores'.

Poetry can be many things to many people. Jeanette Winterson has called it 'a shot of espresso, a rope in a storm, a conversation across time'. Paula likens making a poem to a child at a window making a mark with her breath. 'It's something we've all done, and I still do.'

Brian Moore, 1985

Graham Greene used to say that Brian Moore was his favourite living novelist, possibly because they were both lapsed Catholics who wrote about crises of conscience and finding redemption in failure, but more likely it was a case of one great storyteller appreciating another. My father introduced their books to me, but this too may have been because Greene had praised his debut novel The Irish Volunteer *(1934) for telling a story about the Irish War of Independence through the eyes of a twenty-year-old revolutionary that rang true in simple human terms. Although Moore was Irish he rejected any suggestion that he therefore had an obligation to write Irish novels: like Greene his novels ranged across the world, as he did in his life. Somewhat appropriately, we did our first interview at the Canadian Embassy in Dublin.*

Alfred Hitchcock was on the phone. He wanted Brian Moore to write a screenplay. He'd read *The Feast of Lupercal*, Moore's 1957 novel about a Belfast teacher torn with doubts, and empathized with the Catholic guilt theme. 'He thought I was the right person for him,' says Moore.

By the time they'd spent six months closeted together, Moore knew he wasn't. There's little of Moore's distinctive vision in *Torn Curtain*, the resultant 1966 Paul Newman and Julie Andrews spy thriller about a defector who's really a double agent. 'Hitchcock had made fifty films and I'd made none. I didn't like to contradict him. I finished up merely helping him to make another Hitchcock film.' Not that nearly twenty years later, he has any regrets. It helped him realize that he could only write on his own, which he's done with considerable critical and popular success ever since. But Hitchcock wasn't altogether wrong. Like Graham Greene, what matters about Moore as a writer has always been his Catholicism, or rather his loss of it.

That happened while he was still a student at Queen's University Belfast. It's why he never went back to Belfast after volunteering during World War Two and serving in North Africa and Italy. 'I stayed away because my parents were religious and I was not,' he says, looking out over St Stephen's Green.

He'd always got on with his family. His father was a surgeon at Belfast's Mater Hospital who married when he was over fifty and had nine children. He's related to the politician Michael McDowell through his uncle Eoin MacNeill, who had tried to call off the 1916 Easter Rising. 'But you have to have something to react against. With me it was my strong Catholic background. I suppose I'm grateful for that.' This was to become a recurring theme in his fiction: the loss of faith. 'Parents form the grammar of our emotions more than wives or lovers or anything else. I will always be haunted by memories of my childhood.'

He didn't write his first novel *Judith Hearne* (1955, reissued in 1957 as *The Lonely Passion of Judith Hearne*) until he was twenty-eight. 'I'd always thought I would write but I was intimidated by all the good writers I read.' By then he was working on a newspaper in Canada. 'I'd fallen for a girl and chased her there from Poland and then she rejected me.' This later became the theme of his second novel, *The Luck of Ginger Coffey* (1960), which was filmed with Robert Shaw and Mary Ure. 'Everything in my life seems to be by accident. What I've tried to do as a writer is to go along with the accident and see what happens.' With *Judith Hearne* he was determined not to write an autobiographical novel. *Portrait of the Artist* had already been written. So he tried changing things around a little. 'Dealing with someone else who had lost their faith but wasn't me, a friend of my mother's, a solidarity lady.'

Imagining himself into a woman character was to become one of the strengths of his fiction, notably in *The Doctor's Wife*, *I Am Mary Dunne* and *The Temptation of Eileen Hughes*. 'It's a way of being sure that nobody accuses you of being autobiographical.' But it also works as a novelistic device.

'It may be about you, it may be Madame Bovary *c'est moi*, but it also makes you say alright, this isn't me, it's someone who wears a skirt, who wants to have her hair done, who behaves in a different way and has different preoccupations and who is a victim more than a man is.'

If there's more than a bit of Moore in his women, all his characters are also, in a sense, Irish in disguise. 'This happens even in Beckett. His characters don't exist in a limbo. If you listen to their speech pattern, it's the way Irish people talk.'

Moore lives in Malibu in California with his second wife, Jean. But he is a Canadian citizen. 'Having become one early on it never occurred to me to change. Canadians are more like us. But while they're happy to welcome me, they don't regard me as a true Canadian.' He doesn't really belong in the United States either. Nor even in Ireland. 'I chose not to stay in Ireland and having made the choice I don't regret it. Perhaps my fate is that I'll always be an outsider everywhere.'

He uses this in his fiction. Mary Dunne has a different personality for each of her three husbands and finishes up not knowing who she is. In *The Mangan Inheritance* (1979), a poet divorced from a Hollywood star becomes obsessed with his likeness to a daguerreotype of the nineteenth-century writer James Clarence Mangan. Identity is also a preoccupation in his latest novel *Black Robe* (1985). 'We're not colonizing the savages, they're colonizing us,' complains one of the characters, a French Jesuit missionary in seventeenth-century Canada. Apparently, many early settlers became semi-native. 'They were attracted by life in the open air and by the fact they could sleep with Indian girls,' says Moore. The native Amerinds, like the French, were apprehensive about losing their identity. 'We have begun to need their trade,' frets the Indian guide who brings Father Laforgue upriver from Quebec to a remote mission in Huron Country. 'It is our undoing and will be our ending.' This proved to be true. 'They were destroyed because they adopted Christianity,' says Moore.

Against this clash of culture Moore yet again explores the tensions caused by religious doubt. 'It's another *Catholics* but this time the priest doesn't lose his faith.' Only when Laforgue gives up his essentially selfish desire for sainthood and martyrdom does he in fact become a true saint: he ends up helping the natives without insisting that they believe what he is doing.

'I keep being drawn to characters with moral dilemmas, particularly people who are forced to face a period of crisis in their lives,' says Moore.

'It's not a formula for me but it's something I gravitate towards. I try to have the crisis happen within a very fixed period of time. This helps with the Greek unities of time, place and action.' He would rather that *Black Robe* not be regarded as an historical novel. 'It's more in the nature of a Conradian tale, like *Heart of Darkness*. I kept it short, too, the sort of novel you should be able to read in one sitting. The basic thing about an historical novel is that it is long. The writer has done all his research and he wants to put it all in. But I deliberately leave it all out.'

To enable us to share the priest's sensation of being among uncouth savages, Moore has the Amerinds speak with the foulest four-letter words:

> I felt it was a risk I had to take even if it limited the sales of the book. It was preferable to having them talk in the pidgin English you get in films. I wanted to make clear that they bear little relation to the Red Indians of fiction and folklore. It's a fact that they did use scatological language and scatological language is the same everywhere.

The novel is structured cinematically with the kind of abrupt cuts Moore has always favoured. 'Cinema has changed totally the reader's conception of movement in a novel. You can make cuts now exactly like a film and you don't have to explain them.'

He's just finished a controversial film version of Simone de Beauvoir's *The Blood of Others* for director Claude Chabrol:

> It shows the poor record of French intellectuals during the Occupation. They didn't really get on the side of the allies until they knew the Nazis were losing. Coco Chanel, who is still regarded as a glamorous figure, lived with a German general in the Ritz all through the war and was a notorious anti-Semite. The Germans didn't have to round up the Jews, the French did it for them.

But he hesitates to blame the French. 'We've no right to judge. We were never occupied.' He's similarly cautious about the North. 'Fiction shouldn't confront political issues directly. Otherwise you're competing with journalism. I think it presumptuous of people like me to say anything about the North. I don't know anything about it. I'm an outsider. I hesitate to say anything because I don't know anything.'

V.S. Naipaul, 2001

Nobel laureate V.S. Naipaul was a sensitive man, easily upset. He'd fallen out with friends, most notoriously the equally difficult Paul Theroux. Perhaps that's why they got on so well when they first met in Kampala in Uganda in 1966. Naipaul became a mentor to the young American as he established himself as a celebrated travel writer and novelist. The break up of their friendship came suddenly in 1996 when Naipaul put dedicated copies of Theroux's books up for auction. Soon they were trading insults and it took Ian McEwan to patch things up at Hay Literature Festival fifteen years later. Their reconciliation was consummated at the 2014 Jaipur festival in India when Theroux compared Naipaul to Charles Dickens. Naipaul, who was in a wheelchair, reportedly broke down in tears. He died on 11 August 2018.

'I have never been able to look at people kissing on the screen,' says V.S. Naipaul. 'I'm embarrassed by it. And I hate pornography in books. I can't read it.' It's September 2001. We've met at the Shelbourne Hotel in Dublin. His novel, *Half a Life*, his first for seven years, has just been published to mixed reviews. The protagonist, Willie Chandran, an Indian-born man living on a plantation in Portuguese Africa in the 1970s, more or less happily married, belatedly meets a woman who makes him feel wanted. 'For a second or two, no more,' he recalls to his sister, 'those eyes had looked at me in a way no woman had looked at me before.'

Although the affair that ensues – like that between Salim and Yvette in Naipaul's 1979 novel *A Bend in the River* – is charged with eroticism, the sex never for a moment becomes explicit on the page. 'That's where pornographic writing is so false,' says Naipaul:

> Because that's not how it is for most people. Their sexuality is something else to them. It requires another kind of writing to deal with sexual satisfaction. I think sexual dissatisfaction is probably easier to write about. Everyone's sexuality is so personal. They bring their own experience to it. That's why it's so important not to have these upsetting physical descriptions. It's better for these things to be imagined, to be contained somehow in what is written.

Born in Trinidad in 1932, the eldest son of an immigrant Hindu family, Naipaul defied the lack of a colonial literary culture to establish himself as a world-class writer, winning a clutch of major literary prizes, including the Booker in 1971 for *In a Free State*. His first comic novel, *The Mystic Masseur*, published in 1957 when he was twenty-five – but not his first book; he'd already written *Miguel Street* – marked him out as an innovator of the literature of the dispossessed.

With twenty-four books ranging from fiction to travel and history, Sir Vidia – he was knighted in 1990 – is an always honest, sometimes brutally frank, interpreter of the Third World and the schizophrenic colonial experience. Questioning and ever curious, as if sharing a personal journey of discovery – the critic V.S. Pritchett likened him to Socrates – he has given a voice to the voiceless, but not always a voice that pleases.

What is surprising about *Half a Life* is not that it is unlike other contemporary novels – a characteristic of all Naipaul's writing – but that it was written at all. Naipaul has increasingly made it plain that he regards the novel as an all but exhausted literary form. Contemporary writers, he would claim, are merely 'recycling with new material' the great nineteenth-century novels of Balzac, Dickens, Flaubert and Maupassant. Similarly, films today are a just a parody of the themes that were explored in the first fifty years of cinema. 'It's very hard to do again what's been done before,' he says. 'Perhaps there's no way of dealing with modern life.'

Like the story that opens the novel – a story told to a half-caste boy in India by his father that keeps changing as he grows up – the idea for *Half a Life* had been in Naipaul's mind for many years.

I was in India with a man. The car had broken down. The man began to talk, not looking at me. I just looked at the back of his head and he began to talk into the empty night about his past and his life. And that is where the root of the idea came to me. I typed out a page of the fantasy based on what I had heard. Single spacing on a quarto sheet of paper, and just left it among my papers. And it's been there all that time, with lots of other notes and impressions.

It's tempting to read *Half a Life* as a version of what Naipaul himself might have become if he had been born in India instead of Trinidad. Willie Chandran is drawn to England in the 1950s, as Naipaul was, a scholarship boy struggling to find himself in the bohemian post-war immigrant community. 'Willie is not able to see when he comes over. He is in a new country but he has no means of seeing it, no means of understanding people. He is bewildered. That's one of the themes of the book, a man developing the ability to look at the world and place himself in that world.'

Naipaul's family was part of a migration of indentured Indian labourers who came to work in the sugar-cane fields of Trinidad at the turn of the nineteenth century:

> They brought a lot of India with them. So when I was growing up in the 1940s, I was growing up with people who had very clear memories of India and who had many Indian things in their house. India was recreated to some extent in our community. They were carrying on what they felt themselves to be. Of course, it wasn't India. It wasn't the real thing. It was full of dilutions.

His father, Seepersad, was a journalist – a correspondent with the *Trinidad Guardian* – who wanted to be a writer. 'He was a very talented man,' says Naipaul, who depicted him in *The Mystic Masseur* and *A House For Mr Biswas*:

> It was a pity that people didn't require talent in that colonial set-up. It was an agricultural place. You're not required to be talented there. But somehow he was born with a wish to be a writer and he transmitted it to me. He suffered, and he died very badly when he was forty-seven. I suppose I became the writer he wanted to be. He gave me the ambition, and it stayed with me, although there were times, in the beginning in England, when it was very hard to hold on to it.

During those early years, Naipaul, who arrived in England on a scholarship to read English at Oxford, never to live in Trinidad again, had a nervous breakdown and attempted to gas himself. Somehow he got back on his feet. He began doing broadcasts for the BBC Overseas Service, encouraged by his first wife, self-sacrificing Patricia Hale, a fellow student. 'She would spot what was good in my writing and tell me, "That's alright, do something with that." I had to learn how to write. I had no one before me. I had to do everything in my own way.'

He'd had trouble reading as a child:

> I couldn't understand English novels. My father read little bits to me. I was much more at ease with spoken narrative, the fables of Aesop and the stories of Andersen. I liked that fairy-tale kind of writing rather than the sophisticated artificial things. Because I could understand the characters, I could understand what they were talking about.

He felt at a disadvantage not coming from a literary culture. 'I envied those writers – people who were rooted – who had a direct relationship with the people they wrote about. I couldn't have that, because the people I wrote about didn't read my books.'

That drawback became his strength. A sense of separateness kept his eye sharp. Whether in England, India, Africa or the Arab world, he has shown an ability to see truths – sometimes unpleasant – that people who belong might not, or prefer not to. The India he visited for the first time in 1962 was nothing near that of writers such as Kipling or E.M. Forster. 'Indian misery and wretchedness is beyond anything one might notice in any other country,' he says. 'We're still quite close to the wretchedness and the horror of 500 years of Islamic rule. It was a hateful period. Not a school was built. India was a wasteland. The British, out of no altruistic wish – it was just a by-product of their legalistic system – redeemed India.'

Naipaul elaborates on this perception in *India: A Wounded Civilization* – the 'wound' being Islamic extremism – and in his two books on the spread of Islamic rule, *Among the Believers: an Islamic Journey* and *Beyond Belief: Islamic Excursions among the Converted People*. Naipaul sees it 'as a hatred of the outsider, a hatred of who is not itself. It tramples on culture. It becomes a hatred of the world. It can end in the blowing up of the World Trade Center, because the main goal is paradise. You want to spend an eternity in paradise. The best way of doing that is to engage in a jihad, a holy war.'

Naipaul has attempted to find out through writing – 'literature is about life too, it is about the world' – how such people can come to have so little understanding of human worth in their selves and in other people. 'My work was to use my talents as a novelist to meet people and assess their minds and write about them. I suppose it's because I come from a very small place and very soon realized that I had to move out into the larger world. And I had to keep an eye on the world.

He lives with his second, younger, wife, the Pakistani journalist Nadira Khannum Alvi in a cottage in the Avon Valley. Wiltshire is the setting for his 1987 novel, *The Enigma of Arrival*, dealing with a writer not unlike himself who found peace wandering in the English countryside. Not that it is autobiographical. 'A writer divides himself in his fiction,' he says. 'He is all the characters he writes about. It's amazing at this late stage in my life that there are still bits of me I can split up among people.'

There remains something of an enigma about Naipaul:

> We all have secrets. There are always a couple of secrets we won't let go. I'm trying to work out what would have happened if I hadn't written. I think I would have been full of half-expressed and half-understood feelings. The writing forced me, particularly in *The Mimic Men*, to get very close to the colonial schizophrenia, the world of shame, the world of really not having a place in the world.

He can be abrupt with interviewers, particularly if they ask what they already know. Sometimes he has walked out. I didn't see that side of him. As we part, he says: 'I am moved. I'm immensely moved, actually.'

NAIPAUL, V.S.

A few weeks later he was awarded the Nobel Prize for Literature 'for having untied perceptive narrative and incorruptible scrutiny in works that compel us to see the presence of suppressed histories'. As always with Naipaul, it proved controversial. Edward Said accused him of promoting 'colonial mythologies about wogs and darkies'. Salman Rushdie claimed he was 'a fellow traveller of fascism and disgraces the Nobel award.' Perhaps the Nobel citation is closer to who he is when it says: 'He transforms rage into precision and allows events to speak with their own inherent irony.'

Edna O'Brien, 1994

Being banned in Ireland was once regarded as better than a good review. It put you up there with Philip Roth, William Faulkner, Jean-Paul Sartre, Thomas Mann, Frank O'Connor and Seán Ó Faoláin on a virtual roll-call of forbidden twentieth-century literature. What infuriated Edna O'Brien when her debut The Country Girls *fell foul of the censors in 1960 was that the decision was motivated not so much by anything she'd written but by moral disapproval over her running off with an older married man. Around the same time twelve books, including Doris Lessing's* Five, *J.D. Salinger's* The Catcher in the Rye *and Raymond Chandler's* The Big Sleep *were seized from me by customs officials on the grounds that they were indecent and obscene. Following protests, Minister for Justice Charles Haughey intervened and they were returned just as they were about to be burned at Dublin Castle – but not before my article ridiculing what had happened was syndicated to newspapers throughout the United States. It proved to be the death rattle of a system of State-sponsored literary repression that shamed Ireland. Yet acceptance of O'Brien in Ireland even when she was no longer banned was begrudging, perhaps because she preferred to remain in self-exile in London. She didn't rate a mention in Seamus Deane's* A Short History of Irish Literature. *An honorary doctorate of literature from the University of Galway in 1991 eventually broke the ice. Irish PEN presented her with a lifetime achievement award in 2001 and, then at eighty-one, she won the Frank O'Connor Cork International Short Story Award in 2011 for her collection* Saints and Sinners. *Four years later came* The Little Red Chairs, *her first novel since* The Light of Evening *in 2006. Dealing with the fallout when a Bosnian Serb war criminal, disguised as a 'holistic healer', arrives at an Irish village where a local woman falls in love with him, it was welcomed by Philip Roth as 'her masterpiece'. James Wood in* The New Yorker *found it 'astonishing … both harrowing and absurdly funny'.*

Edna O'Brien is about to confront one of her oldest fears. 'I'm going to Inisheer to learn how to swim,' she tells me on the phone from London, soon after we first met judging the 1995 Hennessy Literary Awards with Joseph O'Connor. 'If I could manage that, it would be a great relief. The fear is something people don't understand.' Perhaps it comes from growing up on a farm in East Clare, not far from Lough Derg. 'My mother's family are all buried on Holy Island,' she explains. 'They'd bring the coffins over on boats. I remember the awful sense of winter.'

A week later she's greeting me at the door of a cottage in Ballsbridge belonging to a friend. She's sheltering there from some of the media flack provoked by *Down by the River*, a novel about incest, which she admits is 'shocking and inflammatory'. So how did the swimming go?

'Inisheer is for stalwarts,' she says. 'It was the worst three days of weather. People's glasses flew off their faces as they walked along the road. And the sea shelves so steeply, not unlike Inishmore where I first tried to swim last year. Talk about the rough and rude Atlantic …' But she's not giving up. 'As they say in Victorian novels, the lesson is to be continued, but on another island.' She's wearing a long black dress that clings to her tall body. She sits on an upright chair – 'I like a high chair. I'll tell you why. I get breathless' – and fixes me with her intense green eyes. 'You can ask me anything,' she says.

Edna O'Brien has always confronted life head on. She seems to know no other way. 'Greater unhappiness and very often insanity and tragedy come from throttling and repressing and suffocating things than from airing things,' she says, her lyrical voice investing the words with feeling. She has a directness and impassioned belief in truth that can land her in controversy and trouble. She not only scandalized official Ireland in 1960 with *The Country Girls*, but also grievously angered her parents and the small rural community where she grew up. The local parish priest burned her book in the church grounds. Her offence was not just that through her engagingly naive heroines Kate and Baba, on the loose in Dublin, she had written frankly about sexual awakening, but that the characters were clearly derived from her own experiences: she was, according to one of her detractors, 'a smear on womanhood.'

Political rather than moral sensitivities were ruffled by her novel *House of Splendid Isolation*, giving rise to scurrilous speculation about her private life. 'I wrote about an IRA man and to some extent it had a resemblance or some suggestion of Dominic McGlinchey and Irish people as well as English – not all, thank God – seemed to think that I had done something criminal and disgraceful':

> I find that pretty amazing, Dostoevsky wrote about killers and he wasn't attacked for it. Nabokov wrote about a child molester. It's my privilege as a writer to go into any territory. There's only one rule. *Really* go inside. Don't fuck around with it. Go into the heart of it. Yet there were suggestions more than once, because I wrote about an IRA man and his journey, both his inner and his outer journey, that my reasons had in them some adulterous or clandestine undertones. That's the biggest load of garbage I've ever heard. It takes you two years to write a book. If you want to be chummy with someone or for that matter go to bed with someone – which is what I think they imply – there are easier ways to do it. If I'd had an affair, it would have had to have been in a Portacabin with two gardai looking on. I was very open about how I had gone to Portlaoise and seen Dominic. And I think that Dominic, God rest his soul, was a tragic figure and as much a victim of a divided Ireland. He said to me: 'Edna, you didn't grow up in Bellaghy. I did.'

Down by the River, her fifteenth novel, deals with the trauma of a 13-year-old girl, sexually abused by her father, who runs away to London for an abortion and unwittingly finds herself the pawn in an ideological *cause célèbre*. Inevitably the parallels are being drawn with the notorious X case.

'What about the Y case and the Z case?' she asks. 'I couldn't write about the X case. I'm not from the city. I don't know the flora and fauna of Dublin the way I do the country. I have very little knowledge about the X case except what you know and everyone else knows from what you read in the newspapers.'

She concedes that there is a resemblance in so far as she was aware of the uproar and the marching on the Dáil by anti-abortion groups. 'But you can't write a 96,000-word novel out of what you read in the newspapers. What you research are the technicalities. The inside has to come from you. I can see into the life of a child because in some strange way I am one eternally.'

What horrified her was the lack of compassion for the girl from Youth Defence, pro-life campaigners and other Catholic pressure groups. 'To have an abortion is a huge, enormous, agonizing step to take and to live with forever. What frightens us is the increasing realization that our lives can in certain situations become the property of others, the decision-makers. That is a very frightening thing.'

Down by the River transcends the dank details of sexual abuse through the poetic power of writing. The opening few pages are among the finest Edna O'Brien has achieved. Written in short chapters, sometimes only a couple of pages, she generates a claustrophobic sense of an insensitive adult world, inexorably closing in on an inarticulate, frightened child. She fights intolerance and bigotry with ridicule.

Down by the River is both an agonized cry from the heart and the darkest of satires, yet it never becomes a rant. There is compassion for the judges who have to decide the girl's fate. There is compassion even for the father. 'In his way he loved the child. And that's a tangle. Nothing is simple, except maybe daisies. And they're not simple, either. Nothing is simple in human relations. That is what is so extraordinary, what is so wonderful and what is so terrifying.' Incest is as old as Adam and Eve, she points out. 'It's in every scenario. Don't let's pretend it's not there. Out of the mire of the underneath of the soil comes the fruit in nature. People aren't all that different. They pretend they are with bourgeois codology. I hate that pretence.'

In the past Edna O'Brien has said harsh things about her childhood. Her father, who was a farmer in Tuamgraney, has been described by her as 'a gambler, a drinker, a man totally unequipped to be a husband or a father'. The theme of sensitive women, misunderstood and abused by unfeeling men, is central to her fiction. 'Although I like drink, I'm terrified of drunks. I really panic. They get out of control.' Her painful memories have so coloured her attitudes that she once said 'it was hard for me to imagine harmony, or even affinity, between men and women. I would need to be reborn.'

The bitterness has now eased, perhaps through writing, although she doesn't believe

> that there is a healing or exorcising through writing. If anything, if you're both lucky and unlucky to be made of that stuff, each book brings you to more turbulent matter, which becomes the next book. It's not like wiping your

hands after you wash up. It doesn't get rid of it at all. It couldn't really. All it does is to give a form and a story and a shape to something that was shapeless and amorphous within you.

For better or worse she is the writer she is because of the child that she was. 'I am thankful in between being unthankful, if you like it, for the upbringing I had, because it was very – I want to get the right word, I'm not dodging it – it was very intense.'

There was not much money; there had been, but it was gone. There was the feeling where we lived – away in the fields – of being very isolated. And I did live in a personal sense of danger and a feeling that something catastrophic would happen. Some of that would be my own temperament and over-worked imagination. But some of it was not a fantasy.

My actual mother and father are both dead and I would not pillory the dead. My mother was very shocked by *The Country Girls*, she was really appalled by it. My father, to his great credit, was much less shocked. Obviously I have inherited a lot of stuff from my parents, and some of that I wouldn't call serene or happy.

I've asked myself, to tell you the truth, could I have written *Down by the River* if either of them had been alive. And the answer is no, I don't think I could have. Not because this is my story. It's not as simple as that. But I think my parents – there has always been slaughter within families, look at Greek drama – all parents act as the judgemental arc over their children. I was afraid of both my mother and my father in two very different but equally visceral ways. You imagine that the death of parents releases you from that, but of course it doesn't. Your parents live inside you forever. You cannot kill the inner parents.

Towards the end of her life her mother had become more tolerant. 'She had a biggish house and she loved cooking and she kept people overnight, bed and breakfast, people from different parts of the world who'd have read my books, and she became more forgiving about the writing.'

But the trouble with families and small communities, whatever you write they're going to be convinced it's them. It's very hard to say, well actually there's a little extra neuron in the brain called imagination. Otherwise one would keep a diary and just fling it down. It's quite hard for people to believe that. Because if you describe a gate or a tree or a mound or a road that does have its place in reality – that could be photographed – then they say, if that's real, then the other bit is real.

She didn't have a chance to read much as a child. At the national school in Scariff we had extracts from the legends and English writers, essayists like Addison and Steele and Thackeray, and of course I read the prayer books and the Gospels, which were very beautiful. I was drawn to the language – *In the beginning was the word, and the word was with God, and the word was God* – and I made a connection for myself in my little dotty way between the sacredness of words and being a writer. I do think that literature is a spiritual experience.

Not that school was a happy experience. Once out of the Convent of Mercy, Loughrea – where she claimed 'everything was an occasion for fear, religion was force-fed the way they feed the geese of Strasburg for pâté' – she fled to Dublin and into the arms of the first man to take her halfway seriously. Never mind that author Ernest Gebler had been married and was considerably older than her. Soon they were married and living together in his Roundwood home overlooking a lake. Gebler was a father figure, 'a Professor Higgins' who encouraged her to write seriously for the first time, not just the snippets she had been in the habit of jotting down since she was eight. 'My memories of that period are bright and starry and have absolute clarity,' her first son Carlo told me, 'and like a dream resonate with feelings, although not very much happened.'

She was commissioned to write *The Country Girls*. 'I was given £50 and in order to seem like a good wife – I was a good wife, actually – I bought a sewing machine and for my two children Carlo and Sacha I bought weapons and I spent the £50 immediately, because I'm not good with money, I've no idea of money. And I sat down to write, and all I knew were the first lines:' – and then, without hesitation, she quotes – '*I awakened quickly, sat up in the bed abruptly. It's only when I'm anxious that I awaken easily. For a minute I could not remember what it was. And then I remembered, the old reason, he had not come home, my father.*'

She soon fell out with Gebler, packing Carlo and her second son Sacha into a taxi and fleeing to London. The mail-boat journey into exile was her first time out of Ireland. The shock of their departure still haunts Carlo, who was five at the time. Home suddenly became a semi-detached in the south London suburb of Morden. 'It's the first time I consciously remember feeling unhappy,' Carlo recalled. 'I wanted to be dead. For all we know, the Garden of Eden may be a true story and God really did make the world in seven days. But even if you don't believe that, I'm sure it corresponds to everyone's experience: growing up is a kind of expulsion and loss.' When I tell her this, she says: 'Yes, it was very hard. But it's always hard. Not just for me.'

Within a few weeks of arriving in London, she completed *The Country Girls* ('all the time I was writing it, I couldn't stop crying'). Its immediate success accelerated the break up of her marriage, changing as it did the subtle balance of the relationship: the pupil had outshone the teacher. Despite being a single mother, she reared the two boys while still finding time to write morning after morning, filling copybooks with her longhand. *The Lonely Girl, Girls in Their Married Bliss* and *August is a Wicked Month* (dealing with the misadventures of a separated wife who flees to the continent for sun and sex) followed *The Country Girls*, confounding predictions that she would prove a one-book wonder. Her short-story collection *The Love Object* added depth to the world of love, loss and nostalgia for Ireland she had established as her own.

She wrote plays (*A Pagan Place, Madame Bovary*), a memoir (*Mother Ireland*) and a screenplay (*Zee & Co*) for Elizabeth Taylor. Her success was not unrelated to the fact that her central theme of complex women suited the growing self-awareness of the feminist movement. *Ms.* magazine applauded her for sending back 'bulletins from a battle-front where women do not go'. Yet she never set out to be the darling of feminists. She wrote not for a cause but out of the pain of her own memories.

By the 1980s she had slowed down somewhat. There was a gap of eleven years between *Johnny I Hardly Knew You* and *The High Road* in 1988. 'The reason why one is in a permanent state of anxiety bordering on desperation is that you never know if it will happen again. A phrase you wrote yesterday is no guarantee for today.' Although she lives alone in London and wrote in *Mother Ireland* that 'I live out of Ireland because something in me worries that I might stop if I lived there' she is not an exile. She is frequently in Ireland. 'I'm here and there, I'm everywhere and nowhere,' she says. The criticism of *House of Splendid Isolation* that hurt her most was the suggestion that it was easy for her to write about the North because she didn't live there. 'My involvement in and trepidation about the North is a very real thing,' she says, her voice trembling. 'Why would I write about it as a lightweight or a freelance?'

Although she has been under attack for much of her life, often vilified, she's never got used to it. 'I don't take on themes to threaten people':

> I try in my own small way to open people's minds just a chink to things they are so against. And also to give a little voice to people who don't have a voice themselves. I'm very lucky I wasn't in the Soviet Union. I'm not going to be put in jail. So I'll have to take the cudgels. I'll leave it to God to kill me or silence me. But it would be a great weakness and caving in if in the case of *Down by the River* or *The Country Girls* or in the case of any of my books, I let these onslaughts or attacks silence me. If anything they make me go further. It's a battlefield, and each book is a new frontier.

Tom Lawlor arrives to photograph her. She puts on a light raincoat, with the collar up. She ties up her flaming red hair, baring her long neck. Tom brings her outside to stand on the grassy bank of the River Dodder: water again. He sets up his camera. 'I want to be lovely,' she says.

Pier Paolo Pasolini, 1974

Pier Paolo Pasolini came of age in Mussolini's fascist Italy and somehow survived, a major poet, novelist, philosopher and cultural provocateur who is perhaps most widely renowned for deeply felt and strikingly original films that pushed the boundaries of social tolerance. Sadly few of them, apart from The Gospel According to St Matthew, *could be seen in Ireland in his lifetime. While Irish literary censorship all but disappeared after 1965 when Justice Minister Brian Lenihan introduced legislation to allow the unbanning of books, major films continued to be mutilated and suppressed into the 1970s and beyond (as late as 1994 Abel Ferrara's* Bad Lieutenant *and Oliver Stone's* Natural Born Killers *were prohibited on the grounds that 'they were subversive of public morality'). In January 1971 we began publishing in* The Sunday Independent *a monthly blacklist – based on secret information leaked to me by various anonymous distributors – that named films that had been cut or banned or were under appeal. To shame the authorities even further, my editor Conor O'Brien sent me to Cannes Film Festival each year to report on major directors whose films the Irish public were only allowed to see with substantial cuts, if at all. After the 1974 Festival premiere of* One Thousand and One Nights, *a poetic extravaganza based on the Arabian Nights legends, Pasolini talked with me for the first and only time. The following year he was murdered on the beach at Ostia outside Rome by a gang of teenagers who repeatedly ran him over with his own car, crushing his skull.*

'I am against the neo-capitalist world, the bourgeois concept of a purely consumer way of life which has no time for the essential human values,' says Pier Paolo Pasolini.

The irony of his 1964 film *The Gospel According to St Matthew* was that it took an unbelieving Marxist to provide one of the most moving and spiritual interpretations of the origins of Christian faith. Rooting the life of Jesus in the physical reality of African landscapes and using peasant non-actors, as in a documentary, he reclaimed the story of the gospel from pious propagandists and gave its humanist message a searing immediacy.

Ten years later, Pasolini is trying to achieve something similar with *One Thousand and One Nights*, which completes a trilogy with his earlier films, *The Decameron* and *Canterbury Tales*. 'It's my most ambitious film yet,' he says. With high-boned, sunken cheeks and a thin smile beneath prominent spectacles, he speaks with penetrating intensity. 'It's an account of a young man's initiation into sex in its most simple and its most complex forms.' He has interpreted the text of the *Arabian Nights* instinctively rather than literally in order to express his attitude towards society. 'Whatever moved me most in the text, I use. My choice was based on childhood memories. It is the reflection of an aesthete.'

But are the sexual sequences in keeping with an Arab civilization that until recently insisted on all women being veiled?

'I am describing the golden age when sex was explicit, the age of tolerance, not as it is now. What I am trying to make clear, as in *The Decameron* and *Canterbury Tales*, is my major obsession that peasant culture, as distinct from that celebrated by the capitalist bourgeoisie, is a very tolerant culture, whereas the purely consumer way of life has no time for essential human values.'

His choice of locations in Iran, Africa and Nepal, which give the film its great visual power, is similarly subjective. 'I went to Eritrea and fell in love with the countryside and the faces of the people. So the first scene is there instead of in Baghdad according to the text.'

The narrative alternates from dream to reality with subtle variations in sound and music to catch the changes. 'It's a sort of musical collage,' he says. 'We use popular Arab music and live sound for the moments of realism and Mozart and Stravinsky in the dream sequences.' His next film *Salò, or the 120 Days of Sodom* will be fundamentally different. 'My subject will be ideology, its necessity and where it is going.'

Forget the class war. According to Pasolini there is no longer any real distinction between the bourgeoisie and the proletariat, the bosses and the revolutionaries, the fascists and the anti-fascists. All are united within the dehumanizing civilization of consumer goods. It's a perception that tormented him in his last months after we met: the realization that Italy had lost its soul. 'A genocide took place. The whole population was culturally destroyed.' He was appalled that nobody seemed to appreciate the enormity of what was happening. People were unthinking accomplices in their own spiritual emasculation. He sought to counter this apathy in *The Decameron*, *Canterbury Tales* and *One Thousand and One Nights* by presenting memories of what has been lost.

As a homosexual he was conscious of being particularly vulnerable to the 'penitentiary of consumerism.' He argued: 'I am like a negro in a racist society that has felt the need to indulge in a spirit of tolerance. That is to say, I am tolerated. The fact that someone is "tolerated" is the same as saying that he is "condemned".' Pasolini developed these ideas in a series of articles, published in *Corriere della Sera* and *Il Mundo* in 1975, later translated by Stuart Hood in *Lutheran Letters* and published in Ireland in 1984 by Dermot Bolger's Raven Arts Press.

Consumer society to Pasolini represented the ultimate totalitarianism 'even if its repression is not police repression'. The process of persuasion that conditions people to be good consumers is far more insidious than any authoritarian effort at persuasion. Through it the deconstruction of life brought about by the breaking down of taboos and social conventions – so-called permissiveness – led only to a new conformism. The youth spawned by such a society particularly concerned Pasolini:

> *oh unfortunate generation*
> *you'll weep but lifeless tears*
> *because perhaps you won't even know*
> *how to return to*
> *what, not having had, you couldn't even lose*

The compassion of this 1970 poem, included in his *Selected Poems* (John Calder), hardened to a more apocalyptic vision in his later journalism:

> There is no group of boys one meets in the street that might not be a group of criminals. They have a light in their eyes; their features are copies of the features of automatons with nothing personal to give them character from within. The stereotype makes them treacherous. Their silence can precede the thrust of a knife.

By a horrible irony Pasolini was himself destroyed soon after he wrote those words by the very evil he diagnosed. While in the company of a youth he picked up at a café he was waylaid and killed by a gang of youths on the night of 2 November 1975, aged fifty-seven. The last forty-eight hours of his life were reconstructed in 2014 by Abel Ferrara in *Pasolini*, with Willem Dafoe in the title role. By taking a fragment of a life it manages to suggest the whole of it, not by sensationalism but by shooting in black-and-white somewhat in the manner of one of Pasolini's own films.

Ferrara shares with Pasolini the distinction of being banned in Ireland on the grounds that his films were 'subversive of public morality'. 'Come on,' he told me when we met in 1995. 'Censorship among adults? Who's kidding whom? What's the point of it? ' His 1979 low-budget debut horror thriller *Driller Killer*, in which he plays a demented artist who goes around murdering vagrants with a portable electric drill, gave rise to the term 'video nasty'. Although screened at Dublin Film Festival, his 1992 film *Bad Lieutenant* was also banned. Harvey Keitel plays a corrupt cop who is eventually driven to seek personal redemption by the horror of a rape case involving a young nun. While Ferrara's approach is graphic and explicit, the underlying tone is oddly moral: even in the sewer of urban degradation, Catholic guilt stirs.

'Yeah, well it was written by Nicky St John, a guy who teaches catechism to nine-year-olds,' he says. 'We grew up together in the small farmland town of Peekskill in upstate New York. That's where the Catholicism came from. It's a powerful thing. It's there and it can't be denied. You believe in Jesus. That Jesus died for your sins.' He's never really lost that belief. 'It's something you have to deal with. Where are we from? Is this all there is? I don't know how you could go through life without questioning what creation is about and what the future is about. What happens after death? That's basically what it's about.'

Ferrara's films, apart from their baroque undertones, are invariably set in a New York underworld that he imbues with a disturbing mythic quality. He was born in the Bronx, son of an Irish mother and Italian father, but moved to the country when he was eleven. 'I suppose the distancing gave me some space and room in which the imagination could roam.'

He's since moved to Rome to trace his roots. 'I have Italian cinema from the era of Antonioni, Fellini, Rossi and Pasolini in my DNA,' he said in Venice after the *Pasolini* premiere. 'It's what I used to watch when I was twenty. It was a type of cinema that pursued a vision, with complete freedom on the part of the director.' Pasolini was very much committed to this world. 'He came along and changed everything, as if he were Jesus Christ.'

The success of *Pasolini* hinges on a natural empathy Willem Dafoe shares with the character and the man. Like Ferrara he too lives in Rome. His wife, who comes from there, helped improve his Italian by getting him to read Pasolini's *Lutheran Letters*. The son of blue-collar parents from Appleton, Wisconsin, the seventh of eight children ('a traditional Catholic family'), he dropped out of high school to join Milwaukee's avant-garde Theatre X , touring the US and Europe.

He brings from theatre to the screen a chameleon-like ability to seem different in every role he plays despite his distinctive sharp cheekbones, thick brows and full sensual lips. 'That's partly because I keep playing very different roles. There's no pattern to them except that I usually end up dead.'

In Oliver Stone's *Platoon* he sinks to the mud in a slow-motion genuflection as his body is riddled with gunfire from his own men. He's nailed to the cross in Martin Scorsese's *The Last Temptation of Christ*, his whole life and purpose flashing before his eyes in agonizing detail. As with *Mississippi Burning*, in which he played Gene Hackman's know-it-all civil rights partner, the sometimes vicious controversy triggered by the film prevented it being judged fairly in its own right. 'All people saw were their own prejudices.'

The challenge for Ferrara and Dafoe is to avoid this by subverting the sensationalist expectations suggested by Pasolini's somewhat lurid public image. The film opens with Pasolini in an editing room working on a sequence from *Salò* in which nubile girls are brutalized and raped by a group of local fascist dignitaries. 'To scandalize is a right, and to be scandalized is a pleasure,' he tells an interviewer disturbed by the images. 'Those who refuse to be scandalized are moralists.'

What follows is a quietly observed meditation on Pasolini's final hours, shot in the manner of a documentary. He visualizes incidents from a novel as he flies home from Sweden. His mother wakens him with a kiss on his last morning. An actress friend drops in at lunchtime. He talks with his assistant about a book she should read. He gives an interview to a reporter from *La Stampa*. 'I'm an assassin and a good man. We're all victims and we're all guilty.' He goes to a favourite restaurant with a friend and talks about a film he's writing, scenes of which we imagine through his eyes. He returns home but then goes out again, picking up a youth he takes to a café for spaghetti before driving out to the beach. A gang of youths encircle him. He's left for dead. The next morning a friend wakens his mother. Her cry of grief and loss is ours too.

Salman Rushdie, 1988

When the Iranian leader Ayatollah Khomeini issued a fatwa against Salman Rushdie in February 1989, sentencing him to death because his novel The Satanic Verses *was 'against Islam, the Prophet and the Qur'an', Rushdie went into hiding with around-the-clock police protection. For nearly ten years he lived as a non-person under the alias Joseph Anton. The name, a combination of the first names of two writers he revered, Joseph Conrad and Anton Chekhov, became the title of his 2012 memoir. 'I made the title* Joseph Anton *because it always felt very strange to be asked to give up my name,' he said. He has since found black humour in what happened by appearing as himself in the US satirical series* Curb Your Enthusiasm, *explaining to Larry David how the notoriety of being in hiding adds to your romantic appeal and helps get the best tables in restaurants. In his 2017 novel* The Golden House, *dramatizing the previous eight years of US politics, a young American filmmaker observes the political 'insurgence of a ruthlessly ambitious, narcissistic, media-savvy villain sporting makeup and coloured hair'. So far Donal Trump hasn't tweeted a riposte.*

Salman Rushdie makes no apologies for rewriting the Koran. It seems Muhammad wouldn't have known what to say without the impious advice of an Indian film star who time-travels back to seventh-century Arabia via Rushdie's 1988 novel, *The Satanic Verses*.

'There are no subjects that are sacred or off limits in fiction and that includes God,' he says, sitting amid holly and mistletoe in the Shelbourne Hotel a few weeks before Christmas 1988. 'Because if you say there are limits who sets the limits? That takes you out of a free society.'

Try telling that to Islamic fundamentalists. Under pressure from three Muslim MPs who have yet to read *The Satanic Verses*, India has banned it as 'an indecent vilification of the Holy Prophet'. To which Rushdie replies, 'It's a sad irony that in a constitutionally secular country a book can be banned to placate religious groups. India is proving itself more fundamentalist than a fundamentalist country.'

Rushdie isn't naive. He foresaw that some people might find some passages problematic. 'But a book is a very small controllable object. If you find something in it not to your taste you shut it and put it down. The idea that you should then try to prevent the entire nation of India from reading it seems to me not acceptable.'

With all his fiction, Rushdie mixes real events with the fantastic, a sort of magical realism with a foot in historical fact. 'There's no such thing as an objective writer,' he maintains. With his 1981 Booker Prize-winning *Midnight's Children* – inspired by his birth in Bombay in the year of Indian Independence – he did nothing less than use literature, rather than history, as a mirror through which to show all that had gone wrong in India since 1947. Indira Gandhi was so angered at being cast as a villain that she attempted to make Rushdie retract in court, but the case fell through with her assassination. 'You can't libel the dead,' says Rushdie.

With *Shame* in 1983, he turned a similar mirror on Pakistan, the country he had attempted to return to after graduating from Cambridge in 1966. Through the eyes of imaginary characters, we witness the real-life ousting and execution of Ali Bhutto by General Zia-ul-Haq. 'The novel has to be free to take in everything. It has always been the most hybrid of forms, a kind of chimera. It embraces a little bit of social comment, a little bit of romance, a little bit of psychology, a little bit of the fantastical, a little bit of realism.'

With *The Satanic Verses*, he takes this approach to its logical extreme: hybridization itself becomes the theme. 'It's a novel about the consequences of migration. A whole Eastern culture migrates across the world and suddenly finds itself in the middle of a novel about London.'

This comes about through the comic device of allowing two Indian passengers to fall magically to safety when a hijacked plane blows apart over the English Channel. One is a legendary star of Indian religious films, the other a fanatical Anglophile. Hallucinating, dreaming, imagining, fearing, longing, they fall through time and history, their flights of imagination casting them in ever-changing roles. 'What concerns me is the sense in which the migrant has to live with invented selves, to don masks that then grow into the skin, so that life becomes a performance.'

Rushdie grew up in Bombay – like the Anglophile character in the novel – but was sent to public school in England when he was fourteen. 'We're opposites, however,' he says:

> He becomes even more English than the English. He's someone who embraces deracination. He wants to belong. He wants to be them. It's both his comedy and his tragedy that that's what he wants and can't be. Unlike me, in the end, he goes back to Bombay. He seems to find there the possibility of love, a new life. The interest in him for me was to write about the thing I didn't do, about the other possibilities. So in that sense it's not an autobiographical character but a kind of shadow. He's the other choice, the choice I didn't make. He's more interesting to write about than to write about myself.

Rushdie became a major figure in English literature while keeping a certain distance. We first met in 1986 at his quiet terraced home in Islington shortly before the break up of his first marriage to Clarissa Luard. Although speaking with the immaculate English that comes with his Rugby School education, the Indian art on the walls and books on the shelves hint that he is very much a writer in exile.

It still irritates him that the English keep getting his name wrong. Even the *Collins Dictionary* gave the wrong phonetic pronunciation. When he pointed out that it should be Salm-*an* (with the emphasis on the second syllable) Roosh-*dy* (not Rush-*die*), they wrote back saying that they intended to stick to their own version since it was the most used. It was only by threatening to withdraw his name that he finally got it corrected:

> It indicates the extent to which you have to fight to keep your name as a migrant. It's much easier to give in and be transformed. That's one of the things migrants must constantly decide. If you go on changing is there a point where your essential nature changes? Or is there an irreducible something in the soul which remains the same?

He never had any thought of making his life in England. 'After Cambridge I went back to Pakistan with no intention to return. I had all kinds of ideas about what might be done in television, which had just opened up. But for reasons that were all to do with censorship and the restrictions of religion, everything I wanted to do was impossible.'

Rushdie is already in the wars as a committed writer on another front – this time without the guise of fiction – with the publication of *The Jaguar Smile*. This was an instant and frankly personal response to his experience of being in Nicaragua in 1985 at a moment when the Sandinista revolution (launched in 1979, the same year as his son Zafar was born: 'I've always had a weakness for synchronicity') was under greatest threat from the CIA-backed Contra 'counter-revolutionaries' who were boosted with an extra $100 million approved by the US Congress and millions more courtesy of President Reagan's 'hero', Oliver North.

As someone who came through the whole colonial conditioning process, he could hardly avoid identifying with the situation of Nicaraguans confronted by the full might of the USA. Yet he is cautious against making too much of this affinity. Nicaragua is small and empty, less than three million people in a country the size of England and Wales, while India is very big and crowded. Unlike India, Nicaragua has virtually no industry. Yet it's a lush and fertile country where, despite poverty and deprivation, nobody actually starves, 'compared with India, where people are dying on the streets of hunger'.

Rushdie's background enabled him to perceive that the essence of the Sandinista revolution was not Marxist-Leninism or communism – as the outside world commonly supposed – but revolutionary nationalism. It represented a coming together of a broad range of forces to unseat the dictator Somoza and this diversity still prevails:

> Only a couple of hundred years ago, the United States was created by such a revolution too, and that ought to make them understand that such revolutions are not ideologically monolithic. I can't remember anyone saying the word Marx or Lenin in my presence but I remember Sandinistas talking a lot about Christ. Many came to the revolution out of religious belief and not because of the dialectic of history. It was an ethical choice.

As the poet-priest Minister for Culture Ernesto Cardenal wrote, 'In Latin America a man of contemplation cannot turn his back on political struggle.'

Much of the same awareness motivates Rushdie as a writer:

To an extent one only writes the books one can write. For many very fine writers, the imagination is not fired by public events. The thing that makes it go is the little disturbances of ordinary life. And why not? Chekhov is not an inferior writer because he does not write about the historical events of his period. I would defend absolutely the right of any writer to withdraw from the public sphere. It just so happens that my own make-up temperamentally is other than that for reasons that have to do with the historical background of my own situation.

He remembers the lies about India in the schoolbooks he read as a child, stories about the savagery of Indians epitomized by the Black Hole of Calcutta, something that almost certainly never happened, or if it did was significantly unlike the event we all know:

> One of the commonplaces of people who come from colonized countries or from countries like Nicaragua, which have laboured under dictatorships. is that our pasts are fiction. Our history was made up for us by someone else and isn't true. And the moment that you have the chance you feel a desperate need to take issue with history because you know it to be false.

It's not just incidents like the Black Hole of Calcutta, but the entire thought structure with which history is approached, when it is written by the colonizers, which is a lie. 'It seems to me that that's a very important thing for many writers, whether from India or Africa or, I am sure, from Ireland – to begin to excavate the suppressed history.' He recognizes that the past cannot be recaptured. 'When the past is suppressed it is suppressed forever. Documents are destroyed, memories fade, people die. All you can achieve is a partial reconstruction, and it is important to recognize this imperfection, otherwise you run the risk of inventing a new lie to replace the lie you have knocked down.'

Which is why he turned to fiction rather than history: by not pretending to be true, he might somehow get nearer to the truth. So much so that people keep writing to him to go to Beirut, or some other trouble spot, to write another *Midnight's Children* or *Shame*. 'But I've no intention of creating a sort of fictional atlas. I would hope at some point of my life to write books that have nothing to do with public events. I'd quite like to write a love story.' Becoming a writer in a culture that was not his own has inevitably brought to question his relationship with the English language. 'One cannot simply take unaltered the language of the colonizer. One has to remake the language.'

To him this has been one of the great gifts of Irish writers in the English language: their ability to make it un-English. 'The English language is no longer written as it used to be, substantially because of Joyce. Indeed, reading *Ulysses* as a university student almost made me give up writing because it seemed there was nothing left to be done.'

Words are not a neutral means of communication: they come loaded with distorting connotations. He cites the way the word 'communist' is applied to a country like Nicaragua 'not as an explanation, but as a blanket condemnation':

> It doesn't mean that Nicaragua is a country that uses the economic methods recommended by Marx. It means Nicaragua is a bad place. It has been a characteristic of American administrations since Nixon that words begin to lose their meaning. Democracy is a word I understand to mean the right to self-determination, the right to vote and the right to personal freedom. But that's not what the Americans understand by democracy in Latin America. Any writer has to oppose Reagan's regime, if only on linguistic grounds.

Tom Stoppard, 1987
---

*It was perhaps inevitable that having so elegantly balanced intellect with feelings throughout his career as a playwright (*Travesties *not only takes place inside some-body's head but moreover 'inside the head of an amnesiac') Tom Stoppard should in his late seventies, after a gap of nearly ten years without a play, finally confront the paradox head on, so to speak. In his 2015 puzzle play* The Hard Problem *a brilliant young psychology graduate, who believes in God as well as science, is prepared for a job interview by a lover and college adviser who believes in nothing. Critics were divided, but Stoppard's greatness and appeal has always been in his willingness to take on challenges that test his ingenuity without losing an audience.*

Tom Stoppard has arranged our meeting by radio phone from his car while picking up one of his sons from rugby practice. Home turns out to be a rambling Victorian mansion, crammed with books, right in the heart of Buckinghamshire, where he lives with his four children and second wife Miriam Stoppard, a TV celebrity in her own right. 'I buy an awful lot of books that don't get read,' he says. 'But my intentions are good. I think of myself as buying them for my children. I'll be fifty this year, so I think I'm at the point where I realize I'm not actually going to read most of them. Up to now the idea was that I'm saving them for some unspecified leisure.'

You could mistake him for Mick Jagger, with his lanky build and thick-lipped mouth and flashing white teeth – the comparison has always pleased him. He is wearing white trousers tucked into white boots and a cashmere cardigan under a three-quarter-length greatcoat. Although this is 1987, it is like stepping back into Carnaby Street in the sixties. It is important not to forget Stoppard is a product of that era.

Because he was born Tomáš Straussler in Zlín, Czechoslovakia, it's tempting to see him as being not quite the thoroughly English playwright his West End successes suggest. This is not a view he encourages. 'I've no memories of being Czech,' he insists. 'I never spoke Czech. Coming from there is just a coincidence. It's a documentary fact and nothing else.' Just before the Germans invaded Czechoslovakia, Tom's father – the family was partly of Jewish descent – was transferred to Singapore by the Bata Shoe Company. 'I was still a baby. Indeed, I remember hardly anything of Singapore, either.'

Within a couple of years, the family had been evacuated to India to escape the advancing Japanese. His father stayed behind in Singapore. 'It was women and children first. My father died in enemy hands, and that's it.' His mother married a major in the British army, who brought the family back to England and gave her two sons his name. 'All my childhood nostalgia is about India, not Czechoslovakia. I feel more Anglo-Indian than Czech.' Nobody asked if he'd like to change his name. 'When you are young you just accept things. I was called Stoppard and that was that. I simply put on English clothes and carried on.'

The clothes never suited him. In a sense, he had to reinvent himself, like a character in one of his plays. But the guttural Central European 'r' still lingers in his speech. Whatever he might say, it's hard to deny that the mixture of cultures – as so often happens – has given freshness to his writing. 'You have to be foreign to write English with that kind of hypnotized brilliance,' a critic once observed of him.

Even Stoppard's long-time friend Kenneth Tynan, who launched his breakthrough play *Rosencrantz and Guildenstern Are Dead* at the National Theatre in 1967 (following its Edinburgh Fringe success) always regarded him as something of a displaced person. 'A bounced Czech,' Stoppard admitted to Tynan. The pun now makes him wince. 'I suppose I probably did say that to Ken one day, but not really thinking it was worth recording.'

All sorts of profound significances have been attributed to *Rosencrantz and Guildenstern Are Dead* and to the predicament of two Elizabethan courtiers from Shakespeare's *Hamlet*, trapped inside somebody else's world, occasionally trying to make sense of what is happening and eventually going to their deaths for reasons that they never understand. They have been likened to Vladimir and Estragon in *Waiting for Godot*: a metaphor for the human condition:

> All I was doing was something very simple, which was writing a comedy about a situation that attracted me. When you are doing that you're just keeping your eye on the ball, which is in full view all the time, and the ball is the surface reality, the ostensible events of the play. But the course of a story like that resonates in various ways, and the thing to do about that is let it resonate for itself and not start trying to interpret it for the audience.

He has never rejected what other people read into *Rosencrantz and Guildenstern Are Dead*. 'I should like to have carved on my door: No Interpretation Denied and None Admitted.'

He has a horror of being pinned down and labelled. Truth for him does not come neatly packaged. Thinking in headlines or slogans – as he showed with sardonic incisiveness in 1978's *Night and Day* – is best left to newspapers. He should know. As a cub reporter on the Bristol *Western Daily Press*, his ambition was to become a big-name reporter on Fleet Street. 'I didn't have any tremendous urge to write. The attraction of journalism for me wasn't really to do with writing at all – it was to do with a style of life.'

But theatre proved even more attractive. New playwrights like John Osborne were revolutionizing staid English drama. He got to review Peter O'Toole's soaring performances in *Hamlet* and *Look Back in Anger* at the Bristol Old Vic, which was then becoming one of the best repertory companies in Britain. 'Many people of my age who in a vague sort of way thought they were going to write their way out of journalism turned to theatre because so much attention was being focused on it.'

For a while he became theatre reviewer on the short-lived *Scene* in London. The BBC broadcast two fifteen-minute radio plays, *The Dissolution of Dominic Boot* and '*M' is for Moon Among Other Things*. He had a story published in *Faber Introductions*. Anthony Blond commissioned his first and only novel, *Lord Malquist and Mr Moon*. Already he was displaying the verbal brilliance that was soon to catch the imagination of West End and Broadway and hold it ever since.

If art for Paul Klee was taking a line for a walk, for Stoppard it's playing with words. The word isn't so much the vehicle for a play as the play itself.

Each time, he plunges his characters into a melange of puns, innuendoes, misunderstandings and surreal juxtapositions in which the only logic is that of language. It is entirely in keeping with his sense of irony that his 1972 play *Jumpers* is a spoof on logical positivists, the philosophers who insist that the only meaning is that which can be empirically verified and that truth is essentially a matter of words.

Rather than draw on reality for plots and characters, he lifts them from other plays. 'I like to take a stereotype and betray it,' he once explained. 'I never try to invent characters. All my best characters are clichés.'

He has recycled *Hamlet, The Importance of Being Earnest* and even Agatha Christie's *The Mousetrap*. 'But I can't do that anymore,' he says with regret. 'I'd be pushing my luck.' Theatre for him can never be more than a qualified reality. 'Authenticity is always a lie,' he says, but then puts the statement itself in doubt by turning it into a question. 'Isn't it?' Almost everything that is said or happens in his plays almost immediately contradicts itself. Like Beckett, his humour lies in the truth of irrationality. As his character Malquist wonders, 'How can one be committed to anything, since all absolutes discredit one another?'

Even when he writes about real people – bringing Joyce, Lenin and the Dadaist Tristan Tzara together in Zurich in *Travesties* (1974), or having Lech Walesa and General Jaruzelski play cards in *Squaring the Circle* (1984) – he treats them partly as fictions. 'I've never written full-frontally about historical characters. In *Travesties* it was a kind of necessary escape clause for myself that the action should take place inside somebody's head, moreover inside the head of an amnesiac.'

With *Squaring the Circle*, he used the device of a narrator with acknowledged fallibility who keeps being interrupted and contradicted by the other characters. 'Because I didn't have an idea of what Walesa or Jaruzelski were like, or how they would speak, I felt awkward putting words in their mouths.'

He is just as uncertain when it comes to speaking for himself:

> I'm very bashful about talking. It embarrasses me to start being an expert on my own plays. I always resist that when it is expected of me. My public statements have all been wrung from me by invigilators. Somehow the evasive reply tends to take on the status of a principle and then gets overtaken by subsequent ones. Unfortunately the newspaper morgue preserves these dead quotes, some of which were delivered not entirely sincerely. Interviewers will never get real justice until there is a typeface called irony.

Try pinning him down on anything and he will wriggle free. Like his characters he has a compulsion to be contrary. 'If you are angered or disgusted by a particular injustice or immorality you can hardly do worse than write a play about it,' he once said. But in 1977, outraged by the treatment of the Charter 77 dissidents in Czechoslovakia, he accepted a Prisoner Conscience of the Year commission to write the teleplay *Professional Foul*, which centred on the moral dilemma of a philosopher on a lecture visit to Prague who shirks getting involved in a human rights issue. Where *Jumpers* had dealt with the issue of totalitarianism with light humour, this was more serious in tone:

> There was no sudden change, of course. I'm rather cautious about going along with the general notion that until a certain moment in my life I wrote frivolous comedies and then something occurred to me and from then on I wrote serious theatre. It's not an event I remember. I think that everything in one's life that appears to be some expression of principle is really an expression of temperament.

The fact is that his oft-professed rejection of theatre as a medium for social commitment ('I should have the courage of my lack of convictions') has always been something of a cover. What he is against is polemical theatre. Moral concern should arise out of the nature and mechanics of the play itself rather than be imposed on it. Trying to solve the problem of writing a play for André Previn that involved having a full orchestra on stage led to him situating *Every Good Boy Deserves Favour* in a Russian psychiatric prison where a lunatic, who imagines himself to be the conductor of an orchestra, shares a cell with a dissident who has been committed for his beliefs. The metaphor of a discordant note in a well-orchestrated society turned the play into a powerful plea for individual liberty.

Ideas do not come easily to him:

> I take a long time to come to the writing point. I sort of worry about a subject for ages. I don't have much to write about. The cupboard is always bare after I write a play. I've only one play at a time. One goes into a kind of cycle where for four years one has absolutely nothing. What sometimes happens is that two or three different ideas gang up and suggest the possibility that they are all in the same play. That's really the first moment when one thinks one has something to write.

The actual writing does not take all that long once this happens. 'When I start I try to work at it all the time for three or four months.' He regards himself as a 'writer for hire'. Since *Rosencrantz and Guildenstern* he has followed a parallel career in films. 'There's something comical about the way I've fallen into them,' he says. 'It's largely been a matter of chance.'

We pick up on this again eleven years later when *Shakespeare in Love* sweeps the 1998 Oscars. The film toys with the possibility that the young Shakespeare (played by Joseph Fiennes) wrote *Romeo and Juliet* as a coded reference to his own hopeless love affair with an unattainable aristocrat, Viola de Lesseps (Gwyneth Paltrow), who disguises herself as a man to audition for his play.

'It's fairly familiar ground for me,' says Stoppard, 'except that *Shakespeare in Love* wasn't my project; there was a previous script by Marc Norman. I resisted it at first for the same reason that they thought I would jump at it. I ended up changing everything. I just wrote it again completely.'

He's talking during a break in rehearsals for a new Gate Theatre production of his 1993 play *Arcadia*, which is set in a large country house in Derbyshire between 1809 and the present as historians try to solve a riddle about a possible scandal involving Lord Byron. Stoppard ingeniously tinkers with time and history and the disruptive influence of sex, 'the attraction which Newton left out'. He wrote *Arcadia* soon after we first met. 'There's a lot of detail about maps, landscape, gardening and relativity that I was quite well read up on. I'm now trying to remember desperately what I knew then. You see, my knowledge doesn't go deep. I have what I need at the time I need it and move on – and a lot of it slips away.'

His first Hollywood film, *Empire of the Sun* (1987), which he adapted for Steven Spielberg from J.G. Ballard's autobiographical novel about the Japanese occupation of China, touched on his own childhood experiences. 'The great thing about Spielberg is that you can write anything you like and not worry about whether it's feasible. If Steven likes it, it will happen.'

As with Harold Pinter, he's drawn as a screenwriter to writers and directors he admires. Whether with Graham Greene's *The Human Factor* (1975), E.L. Doctorow's *Billy Bathgate* (1991) or John le Carré's *The Russia House* (1990), it is invariably a matter of 'wanting to work with certain people rather than a certain film'.

None of his films ever turn out as he hopes. 'With *The Russia House*, the bits I liked hardly made it into the film. The studio wanted it to be a love story. They were marketing Sean Connery and Michelle Pfeiffer falling in love. They weren't marketing secret-service politics. But one accepts that films are made like that.' He pauses for a moment. 'My first feeling about the films I've been involved in has always been essentially a disappointment, which progressively I get over. But in my heart there's a movie that is never there on the screen.'

Paul Theroux, 1997

Few writers carry a grudge as entertainingly as Paul Theroux, particularly if the target of his bile is a one-time friend or even his own family and siblings. V.S. Naipaul came under fire in Sir Vidia's Shadow *(1998), but eventually they made it up. Having made his former wife and also his siblings the thinly veiled subjects of his 1996 autobiographical novel* My Other Life, *he refocused his fury again on his family in* Mother Land *(2017), in particular on his mother, prompting Stephen King in* The New York Times *to dismiss it as 'an exercise in self-regarding arrogance and self-pity'. While painters have always been free to put their wives and mistresses on canvas, it's somehow considered a betrayal when writers too explicitly bare their feelings about those they love or once loved. What nobody can deny is that whatever Theroux writes, his urge to always tell the truth as he sees it, however hurtful, invariably makes for a compelling read. He's also great company, as was apparent when we met in London in 1997.*

Paul Theroux is sitting in the mezzanine bar of the Royal Garden Hotel in Kensington in 1997, a few weeks before the handover of Hong Kong to China by the British. He has just published *Kowloon Tong*, a savagely comic novel sending up the imminent event through the blinkered eyes of Betty Mullard and her forty-year-old bachelor son Bunt, short for Baby

Bunting. They and the family's textile company Imperial Stitching, which makes the badges for the breast pockets of English club blazers, go about their complacent everyday lives refusing to believe that things won't be as they've always known them.

Theroux, who in a lifetime of travelling and writing has shown a curiosity about otherness worthy of a latter-day Marco Polo or Lafcadio Hearn, was in Hong Kong in 1984 soon after Margaret Thatcher signed the joint declaration agreeing to hand the colony back to China. 'British expats kept asking me what the Chinese were like,' he says. 'They'd never been to China all the time they'd lived in Hong Kong, even though it's less than an hour away. They could see it every day, but they hadn't gone. China, and the Orient, was a complete mystery to them.'

He remembers telling them what he thought the Chinese would do when they came back to Hong Kong. 'They're going to kick your ass,' he said. 'Do you think they're *not* going to kick your ass?' He sees no reason now to change his view:

> What is happening is that this place is being handed over to a Chinese dictatorship. A country with a free press, and where people are free to make films and write books and even have demonstrations, is going to be subject to Chinese laws. It's a pretty terrible fate.
>
> The British are just walking away. It was only after Chris Patten got there as governor that they got a bee in their bonnet about freedom. But by then it was too late. There are so many things they could have done. They could have put it on the path to democracy. They could have resisted the Chinese. They could have held elections. But it was British policy to sell Hong Kong down the river. It's like a nightmare. People can hardly believe it. Is this really happening?
>
> We Americans could have done something too, but didn't. Because we're afraid of the Chinese, that they will destroy our economy if we're rude to them. So there you are. It shows how business doesn't care, it has no interest in human rights.

Kowloon Tong is a satire that seethes with menace and suspense, yet is capable of compassion and tenderness towards the only truly innocent character, the meek, doomed Mei-Ping. Its savage illumination of the contradictions and hypocrisy of English colonialism, and the political expediency and money-grabbing behind it, has made Theroux, not for the first time, the target of personal attacks. British critics claim that his depiction of the New Chinese – combining totalitarianism with laissez-faire economics and personified by the sinister Mr Hung with his unspeakable sexual appetites – verges on racism.

Fifty-six-year-old Theroux, whose second wife Sheila Donnelly is, ironically, Chinese, is neither surprised nor repentant:

> I don't know how anyone could call me racist. I'm certainly not. But the characters in the book do think in racist terms. I think the British generally are very funny about what they've done in Hong Kong. They have such an appalling record there. Hong Kong was a trophy in the opium wars, and the British were the drug dealers. Opium was the basis for Hong Kong, and then real estate, business and the rest of it. The British passed laws forbidding the Chinese from living in certain areas. It was a sort of apartheid, a mini South Africa. Rather than attack me, they could look into their history and their hearts and say, what does that represent?

Although Theroux lived in London for nearly twenty years with his first wife Anne Castle, a producer in the BBC World Service, he was always conscious of being a foreigner. Particularly when he had the audacity to write *The Kingdom by the Sea*, a warts-and-all travel book about a journey around Britain:

> I came in for a lot of flak. I was trying to write something that hadn't been written. To treat Britain as a foreign country, in the same way as British writers do when they write about places like Ethiopia or Albania. But a lot of people felt I shouldn't be saying these things. I've found looking at Britain as it really is, or as Hong Kong really is, is a very upsetting thing for a lot of English people. A lot of English find it too terrible to contemplate.

If Theroux never really belonged in England, he doesn't seem altogether to belong in America, either. 'I grew up in Medford, a very mixed Irish-Italian Catholic suburb just outside Boston. I was sort of the odd man out, having a French-Canadian name. Most of my friends were Irish or Italian. My father was in the leather business, basically a shoe salesman. There were seven in the family, so we had to work pretty hard.'

His father died two years ago, 'a wonderful, wonderful man'. His mother is still alive. 'She's eighty-six, lives alone, cooks for herself and drives a car. I don't think that you'd want to be on the same road as her.' He remembers it as 'a kind of happy family' – he would later immortalize it in *My Secret History* – but he left home in 1963 'and stayed away pretty much after that, there was so much turmoil. I wanted to get away from my own town, my school, my family. I wanted to live my own life. I didn't want people breathing down my neck.'

Escaping the Vietnam draft by joining the Peace Corps as a teacher in Malawi only to be thrown out for supporting a political rival of Prime Minister Hastings Banda, he got to work along with V.S. Naipaul as a teacher in a bush school in Uganda, then married and became a father – his sons Louis and Marcel are both writers – and wrote Somerset Maugham-type novels about bungling Westerners in Africa (*Girls at Play*, *Fong and the Indians*, *Jungle Lovers*).

His move six years later to Singapore as a university lecturer prompted *Saint Jack*, a wickedly picaresque novel, later filmed by Peter Bogdanovich, about a pimp who is both saint and sinner. 'I wasn't exactly poverty-stricken. But I didn't have a spare cent, which was good because it meant I had to take buses. It forced me to see the place, to notice differences. I got interested in British colonialism and the nature of being an expat. I learned a love of having no privileges and no advantages.'

When he came to London in 1971 he was still poor, but soon established himself as a much sought-after travel writer with amusingly original accounts of extended train journeys across Asia to Japan (*The Great Railway Bazaar*) and the Americas (*The Old Patagonian Express*). 'It was a way of paying my way. But I don't make great claims for travel books. I've gone to a lot of obvious places only because I'd never been there. It might seem childish, but I do get a sense of discovery no matter where I'm going, any little place.'

The urge to pull up roots and start again in a distant place – a stimulus in his writing as much as his life – found its most vivid expression in *The Mosquito Coast* (1981), a parable about civilization versus the barbarian later filmed by Peter Weir with Harrison Ford as the maverick American intent on creating an ice-making plant in the middle of the Honduras jungle.

Theroux has increasingly used himself, his family and his friends as his subject matter, mischievously blurring the distinction between fact and fiction. The protagonist in *My Other Life*, which he describes as 'the story of a life I could have lived had things been different', is a writer called Paul Theroux whose marriage is breaking up. Theroux's older brother Alexander was so outraged that he denounced him in *Boston* magazine as 'the all-time know-it-all', while his estranged wife wrote to *The New Yorker* complaining about the 'very unpleasant character with my name who said and did things I have never said or done'. Theroux lived longer in London than anywhere else, but left in 1989 after his divorce. 'It was hard to live in a place with so many memories. I didn't want to leave but I had to leave. It was just too depressing. My life had totally changed.'

He moved to Hawaii, where he is yet again an outsider. 'All the people from the mainland are outsiders. There's a name for people who aren't ethnic. It's *haole*, which means another aura. So I'm a *haole*. It's like being a Martian. But I've come to like Hawaii to the point where I'll write a novel set there. It's virtually virgin territory for fiction.'

That's what keeps him going wherever he finds himself, the urge 'to write so honestly about a place that it becomes a document of how that place was'. *Saint Jack* isn't just a colourful story but a record of how Singapore was in the early 1970s before it changed for good. Like James Joyce in *Ulysses*, he deliberately uses the names of actual streets

> because I heard there was a Chinese naming *committee* set up to rename them. They say nothing will change for fifty years in Hong Kong, but actually everything is already changing. I had to write my novel about it while it meant something. I've always been attracted to the historical importance of fiction.

His pessimism about Hong Kong may eventually prove wrong. In 2012 thousands of students effectively mobilized to halt an impending 'patriotic education' campaign and many more took to the streets in pro-democracy protests to mark the seventeenth anniversary of the former British colony's return to mainland control. Despite multiple arrests, Hong Kong remained in 2014 defiantly distinct from the rest of China.

Not that Theroux is likely to return. Hawaii is in the middle of the Pacific, halfway between Los Angeles and Tokyo, a five- or six-hour flight either way: continue west and you'll be east, or east and you'll be west. If he belongs anywhere, it could be there. Or, to quote the final lines of his 2001 novel *Hotel Honolulu*: 'People elsewhere said how distant I was, and off the map, but no – they were far away, still groping onward. I was at last where I wanted to be. I had proved what I had always suspected, that even the crookedest journey is the way home.'

D.M. Thomas, 1991

Like William Golding with Lord of the Flies, *D.M. Thomas achieved iconic status with a single novel,* The White Hotel. *Although he has written sixteen other novels, seven volumes of poetry, four translations, one play and two non-fiction books (one of them a 550-page biography of Alexander Solzhenitsyn acclaimed by A.N. Wilson as the most impressive he ever read), it is his combination of the extremes of pleasure and pain in* The White Hotel, *in which he imagines himself into the erotic fantasies of a doomed young opera singer analysed by Freud in Vienna, that made him famous. Narrowly beaten by Salman Rushdie's* Midnight's Children *for the 1981 Booker Prize, it has over the past four decades attracted the interest of film-makers such as David Lynch, Bernardo Bertolucci, Hector Babenco, Dennis Potter, Emir Kusturica, Pedro Almodóvar and David Cronenberg, as well as a parade of leading stars, among them Meryl Streep, Isabella Rossellini, Juliette Binoche, Nicole Kidman, Anthony Hopkins, Dustin Hoffman and Ralph Fiennes. Thomas likes to joke that the imagined film that never happened is wonderful. Finally, in August 2018, the BBC took on* The White Hotel *as a Radio 4 drama series based on Dennis Potter's screenplay, directed by Jon Amiel who also directed* The Singing Detective *with Anne-Marie Duff as Lisa. We met in 1991, when Thomas was finishing* Flying in to Love, *a novel about Kennedy's assassination prompted by Oliver Stone's* JFK.

Blurring the distinction between the real and the unreal is a popular ploy in postmodern fiction, but with D.M. Thomas the confusion spilled over into real life. 'It got so that if one of my characters was going to be in a plane crash and I had to make a flight to America the next month, I'd be afraid that I'd crash if I made the character crash.' He became so superstitious that he deliberately changed around the chronology of his 1988 warts-and-all autobiography *Memories and Hallucination.* 'I felt that if I ended it with my present age, I'd be bound to die. By mixing the time around maybe I'd last a few more years.'

Psychoanalysis had been a recurring theme in his novels. *The White Hotel* is the imagined case history of a patient of Freud who later dies in the Holocaust. Lisa Erdmann's nightmares turn out to be less a repression of her past than an apprehension of her future. 'I'd always thought psychoanalysis was for other people. But now I found myself having to go to an analyst. She suggested that I'd been writing about it for so many years in order to stave off the necessity for it.'

The White Hotel was inspired by a dream he'd had of a train journey that then came true. Life in that case anticipated fiction, fiction was now anticipating life. 'I was getting the two totally confused. I fell into an appalling depression. All this when I was fifty-one, the same age as Lisa was when she died in the Babi Yar massacre. She was a projection of my unconscious.'

Writing a memoir became a form of exorcism. 'If I could only start writing something that I didn't have to invent, perhaps it would get me going again.' Which it did. He no longer goes to an analyst. 'That's all past.' But dreams still feed his fiction. The night he finished the first draft of his novel on the assassination of John F, Kennedy, *Flying in to Love*, he dreamt he was talking with his dead father:

> It was the first time we talked in a dream. I said something to the effect that he hadn't died alone, that there had been people around him who loved him. When I woke up I remembered that one of the White House secretaries had said of Kennedy that he would sometimes call her up when he was alone in the White House to come and sleep with him. But it wasn't really for sex. He just didn't like falling asleep alone. Falling asleep and dying are the same. Even though my father was an ordinary Cornish plasterer, I realized that in my unconscious I'd associated him with Kennedy.

The novel, ranging from Dallas right up to the Gulf War, is based on the fact that Kennedy stopped during the motorcade to shake hands with some nuns. 'I imagine one of them in later years desperate to find out what happened. But she also confuses Kennedy with her feelings for her own father. It becomes an obsession.'

With Thomas a novel has to be open to all kinds of experience and events, no matter how disturbing or personal. 'It's a very impure form. That's its glory.' This might go against the grain of contemporary English fiction, but then Thomas has never regarded himself as an English writer. He looks and sounds more like a Welshman: with his curly hair and near cherubic face you could mistake him for a spruced-up Dylan Thomas:

> Growing up in Cornwall made me conscious of being part of a minority culture within England. America was closer to me as a boy than London. It was where the *National Geographic Magazine* came from every month. Our house was called Beverly Hills because my father had worked in Beverly Hills, helping to build Rudolf Valentino's villa, before the Depression drove him back home. I learned baseball from American GIs based nearby during the war. My hero was Patton instead of Montgomery. For Cornish people there was this great open sea and the sense of other countries where you had relatives, who visited you and told you the facts of life, the way my uncle did.

The family migrated to Melbourne for two years ('just when I was reaching puberty') to join his sister, now married to the Australian soldier who had dated her during the war. 'In those two years I had most of the firsts in my life, my first experiences of music, and poetry and sexual desire.' Returning to England for National Service, he was taught Russian in preparation for interrogating prisoners in a possible World War Three. 'Another of those chance events that were absolutely fundamental to my life. It reinforced my idea of being separate in my own country. It was as though fate was making up for living in a fairly isolated community by giving me lots of foreign experiences.'

At Oxford Thomas wrote his first poems, encouraged by John Bayley, and began a lifelong involvement in Russian literature, which earned him recognition as a leading translator of Pushkin and Anna Akhmatova:

> I thought of myself as a poet for twenty years until my mother died. Then at the age of forty I began a novel because with my mother's death poems had become too painful an emotional experience. I needed to fictionalize to escape. I wanted a form that would allow me open out, talking about history, creating characters. I felt a need to make friends because I was losing friends. I made them on the page.

Penguin originally turned down *The White Hotel* on the grounds that it wasn't commercial. Yet despite its complex and innovative postmodern form, combining verse and prose and including documentary material, it became an immediate bestseller in the US, praised by John Updike and acclaimed by *Time* as a cross between Shakespeare and Sophocles. The film rights were snapped up, with Bertolucci as director. When he dropped out, David Lynch became involved. Thomas's screenplay was deemed too literary. Dennis Potter was brought in to write another in which Lise became a trapeze artist.

Meanwhile Thomas completed a series of five Russian Cold War improvisational novels, *Ararat*, *Swallow*, *Sphinx*, *Summit* and *Lying Together*. 'Originally it was going to be just one novel. But you write what it is in you to write. You have to go with your obsessions.' Thomas's use of documentary material about the Holocaust in *The White Hotel* and the Armenian pogroms in *Ararat* have been criticized as a form of plagiarism. 'One author felt a proprietorial right over sentences about rape and murder of Armenian women. That's real capitalism for you, valuing your sentences so much as information that you don't want anyone else to talk about it.'

Feminists have objected to his persistence in making women his central characters and presuming to imagine a woman's sexual fantasies. It's even turned into an oblique form of censorship. In *Lying Together* one of his Russian characters is accused of rape on a visit to England but it turns out that the woman has lied about it. 'An agent told me, "You can't have this, women don't lie about rape."' As it happened, this connected with the experience of his elder son, who was accused of rape by a girlfriend. 'There was a trial in the Old Bailey, one of the most horrifying experiences of my life. But he was rightly found not guilty. Some women do lie, not necessarily for evil reasons.'

He worries that neo-puritanism is beginning to inhibit novelists. Canadian feminist Nicole Grossard even told him that 'there are some things that cannot be said in fiction anymore'. It's not in Thomas's nature to hold back anything. 'I don't think I could be a writer without thinking I could deal with my century, which has been a time of great horror. I'm not really interested in writing a purely domestic fiction.'

Perhaps this is because he has no real experience of conventional domestic life. Although married to his schoolgirl sweetheart from Cornwall, he maintained a second household in Hereford for a number of years, openly dividing his time between them:

THOMAS, D.M.

I've always had a difficulty letting the past go. Whether it was my own child-hood and family background, or whether it was women. It would have been much more conventional to have just divorced early on, perhaps two or three times. People would then have thought what an interesting life. But if you don't get divorced and try to keep a home going for your children, then you've done something pretty awful.

Barry Unsworth, 1992

Barry Unsworth, regarded by The New York Times *as 'one of the foremost historical novelists in English', looked to the past to hold the present to account. His slave-trade masterpiece* Sacred Hunger *was an allegory challenging Thatcherite avarice. 'You couldn't really live through the eighties without feeling how crass and distasteful some of the economic doctrines were,' he told the London* Independent. *Paradoxically, the darkness of his fiction was created while living in the brightness of Mediterranean sunshine. He died in 2012 in Perugia, Italy, his home for many years.*

'Writing ability was the only ability I ever had,' says Barry Unsworth shortly after his novel *The Sacred Hunger* was declared joint winner with Michael Ondaatje's *The English Patient* of the 1992 Booker Prize. It's an ability that enabled him to become the first man in his family not to go down the mine. At school in the small pit village of Wingate in Durham his essays were regularly stuck up on the wall with a gold star. 'I remember thinking that was a way of attracting attention: to get your work on the wall. I think that's what I have being trying to do ever since.'

It's why the Booker Prize probably matters that little bit more to him than to most other writers. 'It's getting the work up on the wall with that gold star.' Not winning when he was shortlisted with *Pascali's Island* in 1983 was a disappointment that still hurts. Failing to get nominated in 1985 with *Stone Virgin* hurt even more. 'So this time I've been keeping the possibility at a distance.'

The 635-page *Sacred Hunger* is both an epic adventure yarn about the slave trade and a metaphor for the corrupting power of greed. Not just the greed of the eighteenth-century Liverpool entrepreneurs who made their fortune shipping blacks from Africa to America like merchandise, but a greed that still prevails in British society in the 1990s. 'I wanted to draw parallels and analogies with the world we know,' he says:

> I'm interested in the past only as a territory for these encounters. I attribute to the antagonists certain conceptions and attitudes that belong to our time. I don't think that a twentieth-century person writing about the eighteenth century can avoid these anachronisms of the spirit. It's the nature of the exercise.

With his neat tweed jacket, trim sandpaper beard and calm reasoning voice, 62-year-old Unsworth hardly looks like a writer who has lived much of his life in exotic places like the Aegean, Constantinople, Venice and Africa, the setting for much of his fiction. 'I married in 1959 and went to Greece with my wife on a sort of honeymoon, then stayed because we rather liked it and didn't have any particular reason for not staying.' What fascinated him about Asia Minor was 'the evidence of the past that surrounds you all the time. Layers and layers of culture are just turned up casually by people ploughing in the fields.' The interplay of history through time has become a recurring theme of his fiction.

With three daughters to educate, he eventually returned to Cambridge in the 1970s. He won the Heinemann Fiction Prize in 1973 with *Mooncranker*, set in a Hellenic spa in Anatolia. *Pascali's Island* and *The Rag of the Vulture* dealt with the aftermath of the collapse of the Ottoman Empire. *Stone Virgin* found in attempts to restore a statue an analogy for the fall from eminence of Venice. 'I'm always writing about places where I'm somewhere else,' he says.

Nothing he had seen anywhere quite prepared him for the shock of going to Liverpool University as a writer in residence in 1985. 'It was like going to another world, coming from the well-fed south east. You get out at this devasted city that looks like it's been in a war and lost. I'd never seen such urban decay.' *Sacred Hunger* ironically evokes the spirit of Liverpool in its earlier heyday, thriving on the misery of the slave trade:

People think that the slave trade was something that happened remotely. Yet in eighteenth-century Liverpool, at a time when the English prided themselves on being in the forefront in terms of civil liberty and the liberty of the subject, the slave trade, which denied all these things, was flourishing. On the steps of the Liverpool Exchange slaves were bought and sold.

Advertisements appeared in Liverpool newspapers with rewards for runaway slaves. No one raised a voice against it for a long, long time. It was vital to British interests. So it went on. It's the entrepreneurial spirit, which we're supposed to admire. It wasn't a remote enterprise, it was something that was deeply rooted in British life. And it hasn't really stopped. It might take other forms and go by other names. But the slave traders are still with us in one way or another.

Unsworth took three years to write *Sacred Hunger*, holed up in a wooden lakeside house near Helsinki. 'There was nothing else to do. I never learned Finnish. It was an ivory tower existence.' This summer he moved with his second wife to Umbria, near Perugia in Italy. 'Although my wife is Finnish born, by some accident of constitution she can't take the cold.' He's never been back to the north of England where he grew up, nor has he written about it. 'Both my parents died when I was young. I was uprooted from the industrial north. I've always felt a little guilty about not going back. I'm an expatriate within Britain. I suppose I don't go back because I think I'll be disappointed. It's usually a mistake to go back anywhere you've been happy.'

Mario Vargas Llosa, 1985

You don't expect a writer to be the epitome of sartorial style. Male writers gener-ally prefer to dress casually and melt into the crowd, watching rather than being watched. Tom Wolfe is a rare exception, Mario Vargas Llosa is even more so. Everything about his grooming was immaculate when we first met in 1985. His tailored suit was obviously not off the rack from Marks & Spencer. He wore a silk tie and his hair looked as if he'd just stepped out of an expensive salon. As a student in Lima he'd been drawn to Marxism but soon fell out of admiration for Fidel Castro, eventually finding neo-liberalism more to his taste. He was awarded the Nobel Prize for Literature in 2010 'for his cartography of structures of power and his trenchant images of the individual's resistance, revolt and defeat'. Since separating from his second wife in 2015, he has become around Madrid a much-photographed social celebrity in the company of his glamourous new partner, Isabel Preysler. He took to the hustings in 2017 in Barcelona at a mass rally against Catalan independence, organized by the ruling right-wing Madrid government. We first met in 1985 soon after he turned down an invitation to become prime minister of Peru after his country's return to democratic rule.

'The idea of a writer becoming a prime minister is not such an extraordi-nary idea,' Mario Vargas Llosa tells me. 'Even in England you had Disraeli.'

He pauses for a moment, then shrugs. 'Mind you, he wasn't a very good writer.' Throughout his life he has been outspoken in championing freedom of expression in Latin America, to the irritation of the left as much as the right: he fell out with Cuba in 1971 in protest over the imprisonment of the poet Heberto Padilla by the Castro regime. 'In Latin America it's very difficult for a writer to avoid political involvement,' he says as we sit in the cafeteria of the Institute of Contemporary Art in London:

> We live in a continent where every day essential issues are put in question. You have a moral obligation to intervene and say what you think. Because being a writer – with so many people not even able to read or write – you are a privileged person. What you say has repercussions, at least among literate people.
>
> Literature is not just entertainment but something that can really help people to awaken curiosity and to stimulate imagination, fantasies, desires and appetites. That is what art does. It pushes people to ask questions.

So why didn't he accept President Belaúnde's request to form a government in Peru in 1985?

> There was a parliamentary crisis and Belaúnde thought that maybe someone independent could help calm a little the very highly charged political atmosphere. But it is very dangerous for a writer to take that kind of job, because you immediately lose your independence. You can't be a writer and a prime minister at the same time. The sacrifice might be justified if you were properly convinced that by accepting you could give real help to the country. But I hadn't that impression.
>
> Politics can be destructive for a writer. I preferred to keep my independence and continue writing. I want to be a writer and not a politician. But not a writer totally isolated in his personal world and cut off from what is happening in the streets. I need to have at least one foot in the street.

Being also a journalist for much of his career enables him to do this. 'It's the way in which I relate to actuality. If I hadn't done all those journalistic jobs I wouldn't have written the way I do. It's opened my eyes to so many kinds of problems I didn't know even existed.'

His parents divorced before he was born – he didn't meet his father until he was ten – and he was brought up by his mother's family in middle-class Peru and Bolivia, totally segregated by social, geographical and regional distinctions. 'Journalism was a way to break through these barriers and to circulate on different social levels, giving me a wider vision of the country and the people and their problems.'

VARGAS LLOSA, MARIO

In 1985 he reported extensively from Nicaragua for *The New York Times*, arguing convincingly that an American invasion was 'no solution if you are trying to preserve democratic options.' Mixing freely with Sandinistas and their most vociferous opponents, he found that five and a half years after the overthrow of the dictator Somoza, Nicaragua was still substantially a non-aligned pluralist mixed economy, despite being under stringent state control. The challenge as he saw it was to establish social justice without sacrificing individual liberty.

'It's a shame you write good novels, but have such bad political ideas,' Nicaragua's poet interior minister Tomás Borge told him. 'Without freedom all social reforms are bound to fail sooner or later,' Vargas Llosa replied. He came away convinced that in Nicaragua, at least, Latin American culture had a chance of swallowing up the impatient Marxism of the Sandinistas and turning it into something else.

That's where he differs with Günter Grass who argued that while violent revolution could not be a solution in Germany, it was the only solution in Latin America. 'If it is valid for Latin America, why not for Germany?' Vargas Llosa says. He resents the tendency of Western intellectuals – even a close friend like Grass – to see Latin America as a proving ground or a last chance for Western theories and solutions that are no longer considered appropriate for supposedly more advanced societies:

> That's always been our problem, the idea that there is a total solution for social, economic and political problems either through Marxism or through religion. We don't accept mediocre solutions. We want great deeds. We want heroes. We want radical transformation that solves all problems and brings happiness to the world. If we don't overcome this romanticism and accept that the only real solutions are mediocre and partial, we really are doomed.

Which is the theme of his 1985 novel, *The War of the End of the World*, an apocalyptic, multi-layered epic inspired by a real episode in Brazilian history at the end of the nineteenth century when a mysterious Christ-like prophet led a ragbag army of impoverished peasants and misfits in rebellion against the new republic established in the name of progress and social justice:

> The peasants confused the republic with the Antichrist. They thought they were going to be destroyed by new ideas they couldn't understand. They felt that progress was a menace to the way they lived and acted. The progressive

elements couldn't understand why they were being rejected by the very people they were trying to help. So they produced a theory of conspiracy by monarchists and foreign powers to explain it. This confusion contributed more than anything else to the tragedy of 40,000 deaths.

The novel is a metaphor for intolerance: the blindness not only of the peasants but of liberal Brazilians. 'Nobody tried to understand what was really happening. Everyone projected onto it their own preconceptions and theories and exploited it to prove their arguments. It became a story of inventions, so many inventions that they all clashed with each other.' Before I can ask, he anticipates my question. 'Yes,' he says, 'the parallels are still there today.'

He tried to read everything ever written about the rebellion, particularly journalist Euclides da Cunha's remarkable eyewitness accounts:

> But not with the idea of being loyal to the material. I use it as a point of departure to fantasize and invent. Fiction is something to take from lived experience and add to. The added element is what differentiates literature from history or journalism or sociology. It is the transformation of reality through language. Fiction is true in a metaphorical or symbolic way, which is not the way in which history is true.

All Vargas Llosa's novels are triggered in this way by experience, more often his own direct experience. Sometimes he doesn't even bother to change his name. Like the young Mario in *Aunt Julia and the Scriptwriter*, he too married his own aunt. 'I married my political aunt, what you'd call an in-law. It's not quite the same thing.' He was nineteen, she was twenty-nine. After they divorced, he married his cousin, as did his fictional namesake. 'I use personal experience as raw material. But I never respect it. I change it.'

When he started *Aunt Julia* he wanted to tell only the story of an imagined writer of soap operas for a second-rate radio station in Lima in the 1950s. 'But after working on it I was afraid that it would become too artificial. I introduced myself as a character to give the novel more roots in reality. My idea was to mix something totally artificial and invented with a document, a living testimony.' But it didn't work out quite as he intended. 'I was pushed by the story to invent, to deform the facts. An imaginary element is always present, even in the autobiographical episodes.'

Ironically, *Aunt Julia and the Scriptwriter* was made into a TV series in Colombia. 'It's like a reoccupation of reality by the characters.' The idea appeals to him. He dislikes the snobbish distinction between high and low art. 'Everything is part of culture,' he says.

He's as happy covering the World Cup for the Peruvian media as addressing an academic seminar on Sartre and Camus. On his weekly television arts programme, *The Tower of Babel* – a Peruvian *South Bank Show* – he is apt to juxtapose a Borges interview with a boxing feature. 'I want to show people that you can look at anything from a cultural point of view. Imagination and fantasy give a cultural dimension to every daily activity.' He prefers to regard *The War of the End of the World* simply as an adventure yarn. 'The first things I wrote as a child were continuations of adventure stories I'd read and was sad to have finished.'

He was equally influenced by weightier writers like William Faulkner, whom he read in English with the help of a dictionary: the strength of Vargas Llosa's writing is its synthesis of the popular and the literary. 'I discovered from Faulkner the possibilities of structure and form, particularly the importance of time and how you can play with time to create atmosphere, mystery and ambiguity.'

Vargas Llosa stood for election as president of Peru in 1992, heading the first count with 34 per cent of the votes before losing to the subsequently disgraced Alberto Fujimori. He later moved to Spain, becoming a Spanish citizen while still retaining his Peruvian passport. Living in exile for much of the 1960s and 1970s enabled him ultimately to discover his own country and appreciate its distinctiveness. 'Until I came to Europe I don't think I read much Latin American writing. Latin America was a very vague concept for me. I found Latin America in Europe.'

He began to see it as it was rather than as Europe had imagined it. 'Latin America's tragedy is that people keep trying to make it conform to their preconceptions and theories.' We know all about that in Ireland, I tell him. 'Yes,' he says, with a smile: he takes a close interest in Irish history and culture. 'It's the reason why Ireland has such a rich literature.' In 2011 he wrote *The Dream of the Celt*, a novel inspired by the Roger Casement tragedy. 'This kind of Irish problem pushes the literary imagination,' he says.

Andrei Voznesensky, 1995

The gas masks were kept in cardboard boxes in the cloakroom. Nobody explained what they were. When parents weren't looking, we'd put them on and pretend we were soldiers, but they were too big to strap over our faces and we soon forgot about them. After the war, they were thrown away. Then came the Cold War, which didn't mean much until one Sunday morning in 1950 when, while camping as scouts in Enniskerry, we woke up to find the village plastered with 'War In Korea' news posters. Civil Defence leaflets started dropping through letterboxes advising what to do if there was a nuclear attack, which for a few tense days nearly happened in 1963 during the Cuban missile crisis. That same year a charismatic young Russian poet Andrei Voznesensky took on the might of the Soviet Union not with missiles but with words.

Nikita Khrushchev began to go red in the face. Writers denounced for flouting Party opinion and playing the game of Western ideologists had been called before a closed session of the Soviet Presidium in the Kremlin to recant, in classic purge style. Standing on a rostrum below him was Andrei Voznesensky, a frail thirty-year-old poet whose mesmerizing readings regularly packed out halls with audiences of up to 14,000 people. His book *Triangular Pear*, in which he likened artists in the Soviet Union to

American blacks (*'We are Negroes, we are poets, within us spin the planets'*) had recently sold 100,000 copies.

'I simply wish to say that for me now the main thing is to work, work, work,' Voznesensky was saying. 'What my attitude is to my country, to communism, what I myself am, this work will show.'

Khrushchev jumped to his feet, pounding the table with his fist, while Brezhnev, sitting beside him, looked on stony-faced. 'How dare you come here without a tie – you, you beatnik!' he yelled.

Voznesensky, eating salmon and drinking neat vodka in Aideen's Restaurant in Galway early in April 1995, recalls: 'From that day I have never worn a tie.' He glances with disdain at my copy of his *Selected Poems*, translated in 1966 by Herbert Marshall, and writes on its title page, *'Please don't read this terrible book of mine (not of mine at all)'.* It seems he has fallen out with Marshall over the introduction and translation notes.

Voznesensky (whose name is pronounced Vohz-ne-SEN-ski) acquired rock-star status with his reading tours in the US in the late 1960s, eluding KGB minders, hanging out with the Beat poets Allen Ginsberg and Gregory Corso, articulating dissent in a hip contemporary idiom *('We are not born to survive, alas, but to step on the gas').* For a while, when the heat got too hot back in Russia – he was castigated for 'having one foot in Gorky Street and the other on Broadway' – he prudently withdrew to the country with his wife Zoya Boguslavskaya and baby son.

He wears an open-necked shirt with a silk scarf tucked inside. A slight, un-pushy man, he speaks softly, with a squinting smile. He first visited Ireland in 1981 to read poems with Seamus Heaney at the launch of a new issue of Richard Kearney's *The Crane Bag*. He has managed to survive in Communist Russia by creating poems that defy the prosaic scrutiny of bureaucratic minds. He communicates through a mosaic of metaphor and allusion, avoiding direct attack, his tone invariably ironic, his preoccupations personal.

'All my life I have fought against censorship and totalitarian governments. Now there is no censorship in Russia. You can write and print what you want. But there is censorship of commerce. Our literary magazines are dying because publishing is very expensive. Communist censorship might kill one of your poems, or a book. But commerce is killing literature.'

His poems are regularly splashed across the glossy colour pages of the hugely popular *Komsomolskaya Pravda*, once a communist youth magazine but now the scourge of politicians, its opportunist mix of satire and sex – it devoted a lavish display to Madonna's nude photographs – pushing its circulation over two million.

'It's not because they like me, although in fact they do,' he says, 'it's because they know poetry sells. People are disillusioned with politics. They're turning again to poetry because it is cheap and they have no money. They have nothing to eat. They have no coffins for the dead. They put the bodies in plastic bags. Poetry is their only enjoyment. It's like a service of mercy.' A Voznesensky poem on the war in Chechnya, inspired by young poets he knew who were soldiers, was given front-page treatment by *Komsomolskaya Pravda*. 'I don't write poetry as news reports,' he says, 'but people are dying.'

His latest collection, *Videos and Fortune-Telling by the Book*, has been causing a stir of a different kind in Moscow. Combining surreal verse with graphics – 'not only sounding poetry, but visual poetry, because now it is a visual century' – it comes complete with a pair of golden Turkish dice that the reader is invited to use to determine page and line numbers in order to predict the future. Voznesensky intended it as a game, a jokey metaphor for the unexpected juxtapositions and surprise associations that give poetry its frisson. 'I'm not so stupid as to say I am a prophet,' he says.

But the game took on a disturbing twist. On 1 March, Vladislav Listyev, a leading television personality prominent in the campaign to open up the Russian media to democracy, was shot down at the door of his apartment. Voznesensky had been on the phone with him discussing a programme they were planning. 'He'd only just got the book. I'll never know now whether he read a line about himself in one of the poems. He'd made his name originally with a game show in which the competitors are given clues to rows of crossword-like boxes. So in my poem I gave his name as a clue, and the solution is the word 'SHOTS'. He remembers Boris Pasternak warning him as a young poet. 'He told me, "Please never write about your death, because it can happen."'

While Voznesensky is not superstitious, he has a wary regard for the irrationality of life. 'It's a mystery,' he says:

> No one knows what it means. And poetry is the same. People try to understand my poetry. They applaud it. But even I don't understand it. For me when I write something, it is as if someone is dictating to me. I'm an old man now. I have practised how to write poems for a long time. It is some kind of code that I still can't crack. Who knows where it comes from? God, maybe. I don't know.

He remembers being in Pasternak's dacha with the great poet Anna Akhmatova, and Sviatoslav Richter, then a young pianist. 'Oh, you are lucky to be a musician,' Akhmatova told Richter. 'We are poets. We need inspiration. Sometimes I have inspiration for two months or a year, and when I am finished, I am empty. But you, when you are a musician, you begin from a technical thing, and after, you go to inspiration.' Richter replied, 'No. I cannot play without inspiration.'

Says Voznesensky, 'I didn't understand then, but now I do. And it is the reason why I am still in Russia. I can't help my people. But I can be among them. And it is because I have a strange inspiration when I am there. It is terrible to see the suffering. But there is energy too, a stimulus.'

Voznesensky's poetic inspiration is as likely to take the form of a graphic image or sculpture as actual words on a page. Before he became a poet, he painted: he even studied to be an architect. 'Yet poetry was flowing in me like a river under the ice.' Moscow's Pushkin Museum staged an exhibition of his work, dominated by a thirty-foot high, reinforced concrete egg cup in which sits an Easter egg painted as a map of the world. The shell is broken where Russia should be. 'Russia is just a black hole.' The sculpture has since been smashed by fascist vandals. 'It must have taken about forty of them to knock it down,' he says. 'But I will build another.'

Another piece, a suspended blue butterfly in light aluminium, formed by the letter 'N' in tribute to Nabokov, was created for his close friend Jackie Kennedy. 'She wanted to hang it on the balcony of her New York flat. I borrowed it for the show, and now she is dead. I don't want to give it back. I am keeping it for her.'

Voznesensky became a friend of Bobby Kennedy in 1967. 'Because I was his guest, I was able to travel about America alone.' A couple of months before Kennedy was assassinated, they watched a playback of his television debate with Ronald Reagan, then governor of California. 'Andrei, which of us came across the best?' Kennedy asked. 'Don't be a coquette,' Voznesensky replied, 'there is no comparison.' 'You are a sucker for intellectuals,' Kennedy told him. 'For the majority of Americans, maybe Reagan is the better.' Voznesensky recalls: 'I didn't know America, then. I only knew American intellectuals. Bobby was right. They're not America.'

He was back in New York for Jackie's funeral. 'When Teddy made the speech, he made jokes and everyone was laughing. For me, coming from a Russian Orthodox Church, it was strange. But they told me it was an Irish thing, no?'

During World War Two, Voznesensky was taken to Siberia for safety. 'It was a time of great hunger. We came with nothing. We changed clothes for potatoes. We melted my mother's rings. We didn't know whether my father was alive or dead. Then one day he turned up. All he had was a small bag, with Goya's war prints.' Later this would provide the inspiration for Voznesensky's first great poem, 'I – am Goya!' The poem draws on an association between Goya's horrific images and Russia's suffering, more the atrocities of Stalin's gulags than World War Two.

As a teenager his mother, a teacher, had surrounded him with books by writers such as Blok, Dostoevsky and Pasternak. When he was fourteen he sent some of his poems to Pasternak, who responded and initiated a friendship that lasted until the Nobel Prize-winner – one of the greatest poets of the century, but better known in the West for his novel *Doctor Zhivago* – died in 1960:

> To meet him was a miracle. I would be nothing without him. Politically he changed my life too, because I was naive. I believed Khrushchev meant what he said when he promised to open things up after Stalin. Pasternak was the purest person in the world, a very moral, idealistic man. And yet all the newspapers said he was a spy, he was the enemy, he was the desecrator of Russia. I could see this was not true.

Being so close to such a great poet could be distracting:

It was very difficult to stay myself, not to copy his style. It became dangerous for me. He'd show me his new poems and I'd show him mine. The greatest day for me was when he said: 'Andrei, I'm selecting my new collection and trying to cut out all the bad taste from my youth. But if I'd written these poems of yours, I'd want to include them.'

I became so happy. But after I got home, I realized it was terrible. Because it meant that my poems were not really mine. I stopped writing for nearly a year. And when I wrote again it was in another style. I brought 'I – am Goya!' to him. He said: 'Yes, this is no longer Pasternak. This is Voznesensky, a poet in his own right.'

Derek Walcott, 1994

Coming from the small Caribbean island of St Lucia, Derek Walcott's life has been a succession of departures and homecomings. He travelled back and forth to Boston University, where he was for many years professor of poetry, but also all over Europe emulating the fishermen Achille and Philoctete in his masterwork, Omeros. *'We are never where we are but somewhere else,' he reflects in his 2012 collection,* White Egrets. *We first met in Dun Laoghaire in 1988 and then again in Galway in 1994. He died, aged eighty-seven, on 17 March 2017.*

Derek Walcott trained as a painter as a young man, taking his inspiration from Cézanne. Winning the Nobel Prize for Literature in 1992 finally earned him the time and the space to become the artist he once dreamed of being. 'Painting is mostly what I am trying to do now,' he says, sitting on a bench in Eyre Square.

'I'm doing it as seriously as I can. I've bought a piece of land in St Lucia. I have a cottage and a studio there. Where I am is quite cut off in the sense that there are no immediate neighbours. The view dead ahead is the sea, the open sea.'

St Lucia, a small volcanic island in the West Indies with fewer people than Cork city, is where he was born and grew up. Much of his sixty-four years has been spent away from it, as a professor of English at Boston University. 'But now I need teach only one semester, in the fall, which is lovely. And the rest of the year I have to myself and my family. So I'm going to be in the Caribbean a lot, painting.'

His three children are grown up and working, but he is not quite as financially free as the $800,000 Nobel Prize might imply. 'The week before I got it, the Swedish kroner dropped. And the US revenue people then took at least half the money. But yeah, I did well.'

St Lucia is the setting for his novel-length poem *Omeros*, a retelling of Homer's epic through the experiences of a couple of West Indian fishermen. The island's verdant beauty is a recurring refrain in his lyric verse, a beauty he fears is under threat from ill-conceived tourism development, something already satirized in his play, *Viva Detroit*. 'St Lucia has to be careful in the same way Ireland has to be careful,' he says:

> Luckily it has innumerable little bays and very steep mountains, unlike Barbados and Antigua, which are flat. So its tourism is very concentrated, perhaps too concentrated, in certain parts of the island. There's still a lot of wild land, a lot of wild beauty. Its topography can protect it for a while. But when people are determined to develop, they go through mountains, they go under seas.

He has to catch a connecting flight to St Lucia tomorrow, having just got in from Boston. 'I've clogged ears from travelling, plus a cold. My hearing is a little woozy.' But this doesn't deter him from going outside into the Galway streets to be photographed. 'Wet your lips a little,' the photographer suggests. 'Have some beautiful Irish girls pass before me and there'll be no need,' he says.

He's been in Ireland before in 1988, drawn by what he heard about it from the Irish Christian Brothers who taught him as a schoolboy, particularly Brother Liam, he told me on that visit, 'who taught us Irish songs. When I first came to Ireland, it was as if I had been already here.' Up to then he'd been educated by 'narrow-minded French priests who were just exported peasants. It was a medieval colonial Catholicism, absolutely dogmatic. It was like fresh air when the Brothers came. There was intellectual freedom. They were open for debate. You could argue with them. At that level, literature does change things. All my attitudes to Ireland come through Yeats, Synge, Joyce and O'Casey.'

He realizes that back in Ireland the Brothers do not have quite the same reputation for enlightenment. 'I think when they came to the Caribbean, certainly to St Lucia, they found parallels between the Irish condition and the colonial condition, and they understood that pretty fast. So they identified with individuality and self-expression. They didn't do anything anti-British, but they weren't bigoted or restricted in how they taught.'

There are Irish ghosts on nearly every Caribbean island, the legacy of mass deportations going back to 1655 when 2000 Irish children under fourteen were arbitrarily taken from their parents by order of the English Council of State and shipped to Jamaica. The following year 1200 men were similarly deported. Not all those who came from Ireland were loaded like cattle. Through the sixteenth and seventeenth centuries there was extensive trade with the West Indies, and as late as 1838 Irish settlers were still arriving at Jamaica. Then the missionaries arrived, setting up schools on many of the islands. As Michael D. Higgins discovered when he filmed a documentary in Montserrat, many of the older people spoke with distinctive Irish accents and had surnames such as Sullivan, Barry and Sweeney.

It comes as no surprise to find Glendalough, the Sugar Loaf, Howth and the Liffey surfacing in Walcott's Caribbean Iliad, *Omeros*. The energy in Walcott's verse comes from its ability to infuse the classical English lyric form – Wordsworth, Hardy, Yeats and Lowell are his mentors – with the sounds and rhythms of the Caribbean. With no real local literary tradition, he drew on other traditions to create his own. 'The way whales do plankton or a paintbrush the palette,' says fellow Nobel Prize-winning poet Joseph Brodsky.

Walcott found his voice in the enriching mixture of cultures that echo St Lucia's confused history. 'As a child I spoke French Creole as well as English.' He sees nothing surprising in the way he has become the kind of writer he is. 'These things are no great mysteries. I grew up in a circle of people who loved things.'

His father, who was of African descent – Walcott has two black grand-fathers, and two white grandmothers – used to run amateur theatricals and wrote verse, as well as being a good draughtsman. 'I didn't know him, he died very young, just thirty-one. But the relic of it all was there in what my mother would talk about.'

She was a teacher, but loved theatre. 'She'd recite Portia's speech. She had friends who acted and played music. It was pre-television, a generation of people singing and playing for their friends. The terrific love of the thing that is not professional, like the singer in the loft in Thomas Hardy.'

You could imagine Walcott as one of the guests at the musical evening in *The Dead*. Like James Joyce, he delights in the amateurishness of people providing their own entertainment. 'It may be the real way art survives. Not necessarily in the people practising it who become great but in people who love it. My father came from that kind of society. I just felt it was natural to do what he had done. It was the only thing to do in a sense.'

In this spirit of enthusiasm, his mother gave him the money to publish his first poems when he was eighteen. 'There was no publishing house in the Caribbean and I needed to see what poems looked like in print. So I put the book out and a couple of more after that.'

He'd started The Arts Guild Theatre Company with his twin brother Roderick, who was writing plays about St Lucia folklore. 'I suppose I do look like him, yeah – in gesture and voice, definitely. He's in Canada now. We rarely write to each other and very rarely call on the phone. We don't need to. It's there when we meet.'

While American literature went through all the modish stylistic and thematic upheavals of the 1950s and 1960s – free verse, confessional, Beat, whatever – Walcott remained aloof and overlooked, 'outside the American experience', happy to keep to his own declamatory lyrical line. Now his voice prevails. 'Neither a traditionalist nor a modernist … he is the man by whom the English language lives,' says Brodsky.

St Lucia renamed a square after Walcott when he won the Nobel Prize, as Trinidad did for local cricket hero Brian Lara to commemorate his 375-run record test innings. 'A lot of things are happening in my life that didn't happen before, yeah,' he says. 'But it makes demands too. I have a lot of invitations to receive honorary degrees in universities. People insist a lot on you coming. Without wanting to sound arrogant, you can't do everything.'

He's taking his theatre company to Boston with two of his early plays, *Dream On Monkey Mountain* and *The Joker of Seville*. He has also revisited some of his other plays. 'There are one or two I'd like to redo entirely. There's a book of essays I'm supposed to collect. That's been postponed over and over again. I want to get it together.'

But what he thinks about mostly is painting:

> I can write anywhere, but when I travel I miss the physical thing of painting. Before I came here, I was doing a painting and I thought if I don't finish that little plant in the corner when I leave I'm going to be dying to come back to it. And it's happening. I'm just dying to do that little corner of the picture.

Being a Caribbean writer and drawing on a chaotic mixture of cultures has been enriching, but can also be a burden. 'We are all strangers here,' he wrote in a 1970 essay. 'Our bodies think in one language and move in another.'

Fay Weldon, 1990

Having followed up on her deliciously scandalous and wittily titled autobiography Auto da Fay *in 2013 with a thirty-fourth novel,* The New Countess, *Fay Weldon celebrated 'entering my ninth decade' by posting an entry on her website:* 'Fay Weldon – novelist and writer 1931–20?? (It is interesting to speculate as to how and when and why the two question marks above will eventually be filled in. Believe me, I do speculate quite a lot).' *Yet far from signing off as a writer, another novel,* Before the War, *followed in 2016, making good-natured fun of writers and publishers by assuming the persona of Sherwin Sexton, a novelist who gets his first book into print by marrying a publisher's ugly daughter.*

The fatwa against Salman Rushdie in 1989 wasn't just a threat to his life: it made all writers feel threatened. Speaking out in support of Rushdie took courage. Fay Weldon, for one, didn't hesitate. 'Freedom of religion includes the freedom not to believe,' she says:

> It is the most important freedom of all. You have to pass through doubt and come out the other side. You can't protect people from doubt and you shouldn't try. Because then you retreat into what plagued the human race for centuries, the idea that you have to believe this or that. If Rushdie chooses to believe that Mohammad was a human being, then he must be allowed to say so.

She is sitting at a bare wooden table in the conservatory of her house in Kentish Town in North London almost a year to the day since Rushdie sat with me in the Shelbourne. She's just back from the dentist. 'I didn't feel anything,' she says reassuringly. 'He just gave me a Valium injection. It was all rather nice, a dreamy feeling.'

Although it must be an effort to keep talking with her jaw still a bit numb, she goes ahead anyway: her career has been geared to meeting deadlines and fulfilling obligations,

> things that have to get done by a certain time. Writing is what I do when I'm not doing anything else. Like a school essay left to the last moment, but you timed it so you always did get it done. You develop an instinct. But there's still always a lingering anxiety at the back of your mind about things you promised to do and haven't done.

She's up at seven most mornings, a habit from when she began having babies. 'Children sleep longer than you, so by getting up two hours earlier you had that much more time to write.' Although the eldest of her four sons is now thirty-three and the youngest thirteen, it's too late for her to ease up. Nor would she want to. She rather likes the idea of operating as a business:

> I'm always asked how do I manage to have a family and be a writer at the same time. All you can reply is why don't you ask the question of a man: how

is it possible to be a husband and a father and write novels as well? It's the same question. But it's somehow assumed that husband-hood is not the same all-consuming thing.

Precisely the sort of sexual stereotyping she satirizes in her fiction. She gained the admiration of feminists with a succession of novels that poked fun at the ridiculous presumptions of male society, having originally caused upset in 1967 with her first novel *The Fat Woman's Joke*, the heroine of which was a monumental woman whose world was a constant round of eating, drinking and thinking about food.

The *Daily Mail* welcomed her as 'the most intelligent and hard-hitting feminist writer'. Marilyn French raved about Weldon's 1978 Booker Prize-nominated novel *Praxis*, a sort of *The World According To Garp* with the sexes reversed, as 'the history of womanhood compressed to its essentials'. Erica Jong spoke of *The Life and Loves of a She-Devil* (1983), later filmed with Meryl Streep in the role of a wife who outrageously gets her own back on her husband and his mistress, as 'a devilishly clever parable about the nature of love and the nature of power'. If her witty debunking of male precon-ceptions no longer causes the same raising of eyebrows it's partly due to her very success in turning humour into a popular weapon of female dissent.

Not that she ever set out to be a feminist writer. 'I'm a writer who is also a feminist, and the writer comes first.' But she can't get away from being a feminist. 'You've got to put up with it if you're a woman who writes, because it's the truth. I'd never disown it. It would be like denying your Jewishness in an anti-Semitic society, or trying to pass for white if you're black.'

For much of her early life she hadn't even realized that she was living in a male-dominated world. 'It's just that growing up in a household of women, I assumed the whole world was female.' Although born in England, she was taken to New Zealand in 1936 when she was four and reared by her grandmother, her mother and her sister after her parents divorced. 'My mother was in Christchurch, my father in Auckland. We were the first of the shuttle children.'

Much of her childhood was spent just reading. 'All the books anyone had thought worth shipping over from Europe. So I read all the bestsellers of 1920 or the novels of 1890, working through the shelves. I suppose I've come to write books I want to read.'

Her mother was a writer, her uncle and grandfather too. Many of the family were musicians. 'I thought the only way to earn a living was to write.

It seemed a perfectly natural thing to do. But I wasn't in a hurry, because it smacked too much of hard work.'

After the war she was brought back to England to go to school:

> We spent the first night docked at Tilbury after a long, horrific journey in an unconverted troop carrier, a hell ship, really. Then we stayed in a house of friends that was the only one standing on the street. I had no memory of England but was too canny to have imagined it as anything other than it was – dirty, hungry, wet, bleak, miserable, whereas New Zealand had been neat, clean, orderly, oppressive and very respectable.

The sense of not belonging didn't leave her with any particular hang-up about identity:

> I didn't feel anything, really. Out in New Zealand I wasn't one of them. When I was back in England I wasn't one of them either. I've always been kind of perched on the surface of society. It's very easy to blame everything in your life on a bog of roots, as if roots will help you to know what you're doing and why. But your roots are your family really, and that's all they are.

In England she still had no awareness of being a woman in a man's world 'because I went to an all-girls school. My mother, sister and grandmother were at home. So it was no different. Nothing had changed.' It was only at university in the 1950s, reading economics and psychology at St Andrew's, that she began to notice a difference:

> All the teachers were male, most of the students, too. Girls were supposed to take arts and history. The professor just ignored us. He'd address the class as 'you gentlemen'. He pretended we weren't there. And we didn't mind. That's how things were then. You accepted that your life would be in the home. It was only later on in retrospect that I felt indignant.

If she was a late starter as a novelist – she didn't publish *The Fat Woman's Joke* until she was thirty-four – it was because with a young family she had to write first for a living. After St Andrew's she found work at the Foreign Office writing propaganda, and then became an agony aunt for the *Daily Mail* and the *Daily Mirror*, 'but giving out advice on hire purchase, never on personal problems'. As a successful copywriter she coined the slogan (which she'd rather forget now) '*Go to work on an egg*'.

She shrugs:

> I didn't start protesting until I was married and working and trying to keep house. A neighbour got into an emotional tangle out of which there was no

escape because of assumptions people had about male and female relationships, assumptions that were simply not true. Had she realized this, or had there been anyone to explain it to her, she mightn't have killed herself.

Which prompts me to quote *Praxis*: 'If only women would realize that their miseries are political, not personal.' She shrugs again. 'All those things were unexpressed in the 1960s. I thought it was worth the effort to write about them.'

Working in TV advertising made her aware of how the public were sold normality. She wanted to take it apart. Married to jazz musician and antiques dealer Ron Weldon, and with her first two children (she dismisses a brief earlier marriage as 'an aberration which I refuse to acknowledge') she was by then finally earning enough to hire someone to help in the house. She could pay for the laundry instead of doing it herself, and by using taxis found the time to write *The Fat Woman's Joke* as a play for Granada TV.

So much had to be cut out that she then redid the play as a novel, developing an acerbic style of short takes she learned from copywriting. 'People have become accustomed to thinking that way, taking things in bits and pieces from TV and the tabloids.'

Although much has changed since *The Fat Woman's Joke* and the euphoria of the late 1960s when everything seemed possible, much hasn't:

> The convention that the woman stayed at home looking after babies had got strangled in its own myth. It was so obviously not true, especially as women got better educated and had more freedom. That whole idea that it was an acceptable occupation for a grown woman just to cook, dust, wash, sew and produce another generation that was exactly the same, especially the girls. That all you were was a machine that didn't have a life of its own. But the trouble is that today you realize that there are no solutions to any of these things, just forms of compromise and sets of experiments. What has happened is that women do all this and go out to work as well.

Perhaps the only real change is that more men are now prepared to put themselves in the same plight, 'to halve the burden with women, to face the paradoxes that parenthood is'.

She has been adroit at juggling the necessities of being a mother and a wife with the demands of writing. *Praxis* was completed while she was in hospital for her fourth baby. 'I felt well with all the oestrogen.' Her reaction to that pregnancy provided the theme for *Puffball*, 'the sanctity of motherhood, not a particularly progressive or popular theme'. Experience has taught her to be sceptical about parents' power to mould their children. 'There's not much you can do about children. They grow up the way they are born. A child of twenty-five seems exactly like the child of five days. They go through all sorts of patches in between but then they revert to that temperament. You may as well have as good a time with them as you can instead of worrying.'

Paradoxically, she now finds herself in a totally opposite situation to her own dominantly female upbringing, 'married with a husband and four sons while the outside world is becoming much less male. Fathers are no longer afraid to take a child walking or to do so-called women's things.'

Her sons were well spaced, now aged thirty-three, twenty-six, nineteen and thirteen. She laughs. 'I couldn't have managed more than one at a time. The thought of a car full of quarrelling children filled me with dread.' She laughs a lot. 'But you need children to discover your nature. Without them there is nothing to dent your self-esteem.'

We get on so well that she agrees to join Neil Jordan the following year as a judge for the annual Hennessy Literary Awards that celebrate the best stories and poems published in the New Irish Writing page, which I edit. It's no bother to her when Neil gets last-minute funding for *The Crying Game* – later to win him a Best Original Screenplay Oscar – and is in such a rush filming at Shepperton studios in London that we have to do the judging early on a Sunday morning at the Athenaeum in Piccadilly. As a working mother she's well used to changing plans at the last moment.

Tom Wolfe, 1988

As pioneer of 'the new journalism' and chronicler of 'radical chic' and 'the me generation', Tom Wolfe personified everything that was 'cool' about New York in the 1960s and 1970s, setting the stage for the enormous success of his debut novel The Bonfire of the Vanities *in 1987, an audacious satire focusing on a collision between the adjoining but rigidly separate worlds of Wall Street's capitalist greed and Bronx poverty. Although he has written several more novels, Wolfe never again matched that critical highpoint. By the time of his death, aged eighty-eight, he seems somewhat a prisoner of his time, a triumph of style over substance ironically made irrelevant in the age of instant Twitter reportage and opinionated bloggers. 'The universe of blogs is a universe of rumours,' he sighs. When we met in London in 1988, it was all so different.*

Let's start off with the way Tom Wolfe looks, or rather with the look he has so assiduously cultivated ever since zooming into literary notoriety in the sixties as a gadfly observer of what he dubbed 'radical chic'.

The disarming smile of the innovator of the 'new journalism', who revolutionized popular perceptions of America by reporting fact with the techniques of fiction, is seemingly unchanging in every photograph. A cool and debonair manner goes with the contrived effect of the off-white, lightweight,

Southern-style suit, the soft pastel-hued tie, the stiff white collar over a striped shirt and the silk handkerchief peeking above the slit of the lapel pocket in three exquisitely neat folds. There's not even the suggestion of ever being caught off-guard by the camera or of involuntarily giving away anything he does not choose to reveal.

Early morning spring sunshine filtering across the heavy pile carpet through the high windows of a Regency suite in the Connaught Hotel in Mayfair exaggerates his paleness and the thinness of the grey hair swept over one side of his high balding forehead. This cult figure of 'the briefly new' has now turned around to bite the hand that fed him. In his block-busting 670-page first novel *The Bonfire of the Vanities*, in which a yuppie Wall Street bond salesman (and self-styled 'Master of the Universe') Sherman McCoy, accustomed to earning millions of dollars merely by lifting the telephone, receives a painful and ruinous comeuppance as a result of taking a wrong turn while collecting his mistress from Kennedy Airport.

Finding himself in a Bronx as alien to him as the Third World, although only across the bridge from his $2.6 million Park Avenue apartment, he panics and knocks down a black youth, an honors student at the local community school. The youth's drug-pushing companion remembers enough of the licence number of the $48,000 black Mercedes to lead to Sherman's arraignment in a case that becomes a gutter press *cause célèbre*. Grasping ethnic politicos and a district attorney eager for favourable TV exposure manipulate his humiliation and disgrace for their own nefarious ends.

The Bonfire of the Vanities is a cautionary tale with horrendous implications for a New York social set that blithely imagines affluence can forever insulate it from the realities of the other New York of squalor and racial resentment that surrounds them.

'If you choose to live in a large city in the late twentieth century you're only fooling yourself if you don't think this affects your private and personal life in a profound way,' says Wolfe. That he, of all people, should now choose to parody the way New York takes perfectly decent people and so inflates their vanity that they do unethical things has annoyed some critics who, while conceding the sheer racy brilliance and compelling readability of *The Bonfire of the Vanities*, complain that the characters are one-dimensional stereotypes without the psychological depth required in contemporary fiction. Wolfe takes this literary sniping as a compliment:

The same thing was constantly thrown at Dickens, the accusation that he was concentrating too much on the surface aspect of life. But that in fact is the social context in which we live. I wanted it to be in the foreground all the time in the way that it was with Balzac and Zola in order to hammer home the fact that living in a city today has a grip on your private existence.

The superficiality of his characters is deliberate. They make sense only in relation to New York. If the novel has a central character it is New York itself. 'The notion that the only proper literary subject is the inner self and that there's something really unseemly about attaching our lives to all these vulgar influences of society at large is a literary convention I want to overturn.'

Wolfe sees himself as a product of New York as much as anyone else. Coming there at the time he did in the sixties – from Richmond, Virginia, where his father edited *The Southern Planter* farming journal – made him the writer he is:

> It was a marvellous time to start writing, because a tremendous change took place. Standards, that had been in place for centuries, had been swept away. Faiths were falling apart. It was all part of the boom that had started in the forties and which we're not out of yet. It created a lot of fat in the economy so that all sorts of people who in the past never had money to express themselves were able to start doing so in the most spectacular way.

This was the first generation of adults who hadn't any memory of the Great Depression. 'They began to believe that the boom was going to be permanent and they began to live that way. Suddenly they found the confidence to throw away the safeguards and restraints.'

One of the most obvious indications that something fundamental was changing was the way young people could create groups and styles of their own:

> You began to see it in the approach to dress. A boy graduating from the best prep school and Ivy League college now dresses just like the boy who plays drums in a rock band. Indeed the boy from the Ivy League wants to play in a rock band. So they all look the same. Young men and young women don't have any immediate clues as to who they're dealing with. No one knows who he or she is marrying any more. Yet we're surprised so many marriages break up.

It seems that in New York if you want to show you're really a person of substance, as far as cars are concerned, you have to drive a Mercedes, a BMW or a Buick. 'It's only a German luxury automobile that creates the proper crunch as you drive over the white pebbles of the driveway of your summer home.' It's got so that boys in the housing projects in the Bronx now wear Mercedes Benz hood ornaments around their necks. 'In former times they'd have worn crucifixes. Mammon has replaced God.' People who used to be considered working class now drive Cadillacs. 'The Cadillac is now seen in New York as the car of people who don't have a bachelor's degree.' So what does Wolfe drive? 'A 1977 Cadillac. But that's part of my contrary approach to style.'

Even before he got to New York Wolfe sensed that this social upheaval was the news that really mattered in America: this was what journalists should be reporting. 'I've been criticized for my attention to dress. But the changes in the way people live in the long view of history will seem much more important than the war in Vietnam or the space programme.'

It's why when he applied to *The Washington Post* in 1959 it was as a general assignment reporter on the city desk. '"Well, later on, would you like to cover the White House, Congress, the defence department, international affairs?" No, I want to cover local news. "Right, you're hired."'

After Castro came to power he was nevertheless sent to Havana as a Latin American correspondent 'because they looked in my record and saw I'd done four years of Spanish at school.' Although he won an award for his coverage, after six months he requested to be reassigned to local news. 'They thought I was mad, the poor guy with no ambition whatever. But what was going on in Washington DC was much wilder than anything Castro could come up with.'

Eventually in 1962 he got the same job on *The New York Herald Tribune*. By then he was thirty-two. 'New York had always been the city of Golden Spires that I was going to head for. But I took a long time to get there.'

Almost immediately there was a newspaper strike. *Esquire* gave him a magazine assignment in California reporting on the craze for customized cars that kids were making by pulling apart old cars to create a new vehicle. 'After I'd run up a bill of $3000 at the Beverly Wilshire I had a complete case of writer's block. I couldn't write a thing. So I had to go back to New York and do the humiliating thing of writing up my notes and giving them to a competent writer.'

He did it in the form of a memorandum to the managing editor. '*Dear Byron, the first place I saw a customized car was so forth …*' Next day *Esquire* phoned to say they were striking off the 'Dear Byron' and running the piece as it stood. 'What had happened was I'd done what a lot of us do in writing a letter to a friend. You relax, you let your own personality come into the words, you just loosen up.'

With *The Kandy-Kolored Tangerine-Flake Streamline Baby*, the 'I' journalism of exclamation marks, catchphrases, capital letters, underlinings and headlong intimacy took off:

> I became interested in journalism as literature. I began to borrow techniques from the short story and novel. There came to be a kind of contest between myself and others like Gay Talese, Jimmy Breslin and Hunter S. Thompson to see just how far you could go with using the approach of fiction to write non-fiction.

Whether his targets were the absurdities of smart art (*The Painted Word*), smart rugs (*The Electric Kool-Aid Acid Test*), smart sets (*Radical Chic & Mau-Mauing the Flak Catchers*) or smart architecture (*From Bauhaus to Our House*), he showed an unerring knack for capturing the frisson of the moment with breathless immediacy, although by 1979 with *The Right Stuff* he seemed prepared to sublimate his writing ego to highlight better the experiences of astronauts whose lives were messed up by the follies of the space programme.

The logic of his career in journalism always pointed to the leap into total fiction he has now taken with *The Bonfire of the Vanities*:

> I thought I'd have a feeling of complete freedom because in a novel you can make up anything you like. You're not tied to fact. But instead I began to feel terribly constricted by all the things about the novel I'd learned at Yale, things I hadn't even thought about for years like the Henry James principles of point of view and Virginia Woolf's theory of psychological people. I stiffened up terribly.

All this was apparent in the first version of the novel that appeared in serial form – like the novels of his idol Dickens did – in *Rolling Stone* magazine and had a writer as the central character. 'It fell flat because I'd simply looked into my own life as a writer and I turned out to be an uninteresting figure. Writers don't do much except sit catatonic in front of a machine most of the time. With a writer I was depriving myself of bringing in another larger part of New York.' So quite fortuitously he came up with a Wall Street novel that was launched the week before the October stock market crash, further bolstering his reputation for being first with the latest trend, whereas in fact he shared the conventional wisdom that the markets would go on swelling faster than he could keep up with.

He's lived in New York for twenty-five years, yet there's a sense in which he's still an outsider. 'But then so is everyone else. I don't want to underplay my southern background. I still keep in touch with a lot of people in Richmond. But practically everyone in journalism and the business of expression in New York is from somewhere else. It's a city of outsiders.' He smiles his disarming smile. A limousine is waiting to drive him to the city for a television programme about the stock exchange. The official Tom Wolfe slips back into place. Freeze the photograph.